RAILROAD HISTORY

ON

AMERICAN POSTAGE STAMPS

Written by Anthony J. Bianculli

The Astragal Press
Mendham, NJ

5 Cold Hill Road, Suite 12
PO Box 239
Mendham, NJ 07945-0239
©2004 by Anthony J. Bianculli

Cover Design by: Donald Kahn
Manufactured in the United States of America

International Standard Book Number 1-931626-20-0
Library of Congress Control Number 2004113564

ACKNOWLEDGMENTS

This book was a pleasure to write because I was interested in the subject matter and because that subject matter lent itself to its exposition in short essays, most no longer than one page. This meant that I was never confined to one story for any length of time. Moving quickly from topic to topic provided variety and fresh vistas in short order (and makes for a more interesting read). However, this book would not have been possible without the assistance of many people. They made my task much easier still.

My heartfelt thanks are extended to Helen Morris, Director of the Mary Jacobs Memorial Library in Rocky Hill, New Jersey, who spent much time researching reviews and notes of books and plays and obtaining biographical information about lesser known individuals who are pictured on United States postage stamps.

Bobbie Woloshin at the Mary Jacobs Library secured books and other materials from libraries far and wide, resources that augmented those available locally. The entire staff at the Mary Jacobs Library were friendly and helpful and contributed in many ways to the production of this book.

Anne Calhoun, Librarian/Archivist at the B&O Railroad Museum in Baltimore offered important information about the B&O's use of early electric automobiles and about Stonewall Jackson's role in the Civil War incident that is described in the book.

Source material about Johns Hopkins is quite meager therefore the help provided by James Stimpert, Archivist at the Milton Eisenhower Library at Johns Hopkins University, was invaluable. He provided some of the source material that I used in that vignette and he also directed me to other sources.

Jean D. Schlademan, an Analyst in the Stamp Development section of the United States Postal Service in Washington, DC provided essential information about the ferryboat described in the vignette on railroad navies.

Speaking of the United States Postal Service, I must also cite the rapid and friendly responses from Angela A. Smith and Richard W. Parlier, Jr. at Washington in answer to my queries concerning licensing and manuscript approval. They, and Julie E. Sekmistrz at Equity Management, Inc. at Troy, Michigan, were especially helpful in guiding me through the licensing and approval procedure.

Some of the stamps that are shown are jointly copyrighted with the United States Postal Service. The agents of the joint owners: Dennis O'Shea of the Johns Hopkins University; Georges Borchardt of Georges Borchardt, Inc, the literary agency that represents the Tennessee Williams estate; Julie A. Laird of Lionel L.L.C.; and, Alvin Deutsch of McLaughlin & Stern, L. L. P. who represent the Mercer Foundation, were sympathetic and quick to respond to my requests for permission to include images of their properties in the book.

The Mystic Stamp Company of Camden, New York supplied many of the the stamps that are illustrated in this volume. Dorothy Fannin of that company provided information concerning limitations on their reproduction.

As in the past, Thomas T. Taber, III, was generous in sharing his knowledge of railroads with me. His information service, which he volunteers freely, is invaluable to all railroad historians.

Much basic information about the stamps described in this book was provided by the Casey Jones Unit of the American Topical Association. Especially helpful was their publication, *World Railways Philatelic*.

The book was much improved by the talents of my editor, Kathryn Bednarz, who not only corrected my grammar and punctuation errors but also made valuable contributions that made the presentations clearer and easier and more enjoyable to read. The staff at Astragal Press who worked closely with me, Marty Pollak, Missy Staples, and Dody Walker, were always ready to lend a helping hand. I offer my appreciative thanks to them.

Finally, I would like to thank my wife for her patience and for-bearance while I spent many hours before my computer during the preparation of this volume.

RAILROAD HISTORY ON AMERICAN POSTAGE STAMPS

CONTENTS

(The year of historical occurrence, approximated in some instances, precedes each entry)

INTRODUCTION

The first American postage stamps went on sale on July 1, 1847 and they, like almost all of the stamps that were issued in the nineteenth century, depicted famous American leaders. The first stamps that departed from that practice were the pictorials that were issued in 1869. In that group of pictorials was the first American stamp with a railroad subject, namely, a locomotive. Following the issuance of the twelve 1869 pictorials (which included the heads of Franklin, Washington, and Lincoln on three of them), the Post Office reverted back to their original practice of limiting stamp subjects to historical Americans.

There were only two other exceptions to the famous Americans motif before 1900. The first was the Columbian Exposition commemoratives issue of 1893 and the other was the Trans-Mississippi series of 1898. The former recognized the world exposition at Chicago and illustrated various incidents relating to Christopher Columbus and his discovery of America. Although railroading was a dominant theme at the Columbian Exposition, no stamps of this issue included any railroad subjects. Again, even though railroads played an important, even critical, part in the development of the West, the only reference to them in the latter issue was the inclusion of the $2 Eads railroad bridge stamp.

Regarding this book, several caveats are in order. First, only elementary technical details of the stamps with railroad subjects are included because this book is intended to trace some of the history of the American railroad as depicted on United States postage stamps. Thus, it makes no pretense of furnishing detailed philatelic information. For instance, variations of the same stamp are not covered individually. One that comes to mind, Scott number 2712, the 29 cent stamp showing a cast iron pull toy locomotive, was also issued as one in a block of four, and the same design was released with different colors.

Second, some of the stamps are only incidentally related to railroad history but, for completeness, they have been included. For example, a stamp commemorating the various meetings of the New York Yankees and Brooklyn Dodgers baseball teams in "Subway World Series'" was issued in 1998. The railroad significance of this stamp lies in the depiction of a New York City subway token which provides an excuse to discuss underground railways.

In a few instances, stamps have been included in this book that have no prima facie connection to railroading. However, there are railroad affiliations. For instance, Lincoln stamps are included because of his long association with the Illinois Central railroad and with the promotion of land grants for that road. A "Stonewall" Jackson stamp is used to tell the story of one of his exploits involving railroads. Again, some vignettes have been based on stamps with an even more tenuous relationship to railroading. These include a stamp with a likeness of Mark Twain, whose short story "Cannibalism in the Cars" provides a good lead-in to snowstorms and the means to combat them. Another shows a scene of the first oil well drilled in western Pennsylvania. Although Edwin Drake, who sank the well, was an ex-railroad man, the significance involved the first extraction of oil in large quantities, a situation that seriously affected railroads. A post script has been added that describes other individuals whose writings of, or association with, railroads comprised only a small portion of their output or interests. In each case, a few brief lines are recorded.

Next, necessarily, there are many gaps in the continuity of this railroad history because the choice of events is dictated and limited by the subject matter covered on the various stamps. Even if this were not so, the history of railroading is so vast, so varied, and so complex that it would require many books to treat it thoroughly.

The book is arranged in the order in which the historical events of railroad significance occurred, not by stamp issue date. However, the chronological location of some of the stamps is arbitrary, having been chosen as a good place in the narrative to begin the discussion of that particular topic. An example is the stamp showing a Railway Post Office (RPO) car of the 1920s. It is referenced in the discussion of all stamps depicting railroad postal subjects, a topic that is chronologically covered much earlier than the 1920s.

In many instances, I was faced with multiple choices regarding the stamp that I selected to illustrate a particular vignette. For example, there are more than thirty stamps depicting Abraham Lincoln. For one vignette, I chose a stamp that showed a beardless Lincoln because, during his railroad associations, this is how he appeared. In other cases, my choice was arbitrary or influenced by a particular liking for the image presented. This is in the nature of an explanation, not an apology, and the reader may take exception to my preferences. Other choices would have served equally well.

The stamps depicting the branch of railroading involved with urban mass transit are covered in a separate section towards the end of the book. This was done, not because the subject is unimportant, but rather, because interspersing the various vignettes among the regular railroad subjects would confuse the flow of both topics.

As of this writing, railroad history on United States postage stamps ends at the 1960s. Yet, significant railroad developments have occurred since that time. One can only hope that the postal service will continue to issue stamps with railroad themes and that many important, overlooked railroad subjects will be covered in the future.

Whyte System of Locomotive Classification

A brief description of the Whyte system of locomotive classification is essential to understanding some of the text that follows. Although it had not been devised until 1900, the Whyte system is generally applied to the description of all steam locomotives. Prior to 1900, locomotive classes were identified by name or by the total number of wheels. Whyte divided a locomotive's wheels according to whether they were leading, driving, or trailing wheels. The predominant type of engine in the 19th century was the 4-4-0 type, known as an "American" type. This machine had a four-wheel leading truck at the forward end, four drivers, and no trailing truck at the rear of the engine. "Ten-wheelers," 4-6-0, and "Mogul," 2-6-0, types came into use in the later 1800s. Towards the end of that century, the need for larger and heavier fireboxes necessitated trailing trucks to carry them. The 4-4-2 "Atlantic" type locomotive was one of these.

The twentieth century saw ever larger and heavier locomotives such as 4-6-2 "Pacific" types and 4-6-4 "Hudsons." Even larger were the articulated machines, locomotives with two or more sets of drivers that were independently powered. The latter group included the largest steam locomotives ever made, the 4-8-8-4 "Big Boys" of the Union Pacific Railroad, engines that weighed 599 tons with a fully loaded tender.

Electric and diesel locomotives are classified under a different system.

RAILROAD INFANCY

(1825-1850)

America's First Railroad

The Battle of Bunker Hill (actually Breed's Hill) occurred in 1775 but some thirty years later it was decided to commemorate the action with a monument on the site of the engagement. In 1823, the Bunker Hill Monument Association was formed and began to solicit funds. A site was procured and a competition for the monument's design was announced. The winner, Solomon Willard, proposed an obelisk and Gridley Bryant, a local contractor and builder, was engaged to build the memorial (Scott #1056).

Scott #1056

Bryant purchased a quarry site in West Quincy, twelve miles away, from whence granite would be brought to Charleston, where the monument was to be erected. Most of the trip could be accomplished by water but the stone had to be transported from the quarry to a wharf on the Neponset River, about three miles away. Bryant's solution was to build a railroad to do this and he petitioned the Massachusetts legislature to have "The Granite Railway Company" incorporated. Authorization was granted on March 4, 1826 and ground was broken for the railroad on April 1st.

The railroad, employing strap iron track affixed to oak stringers, began operation on October 7, 1826. The stringers rested on stone ties, placed eight feet apart. The first car, drawn by horses, had large (six and one half feet in diameter) wheels and could carry six ton stone loads on a platform that hung below the axles. The platform was lowered to the ground and loaded, then the car was run over the load. Chains were used to suspend the platform, which was raised above the rails by a geared windlass on the car.

The road owned four cars and, although it has been mentioned as "the first American railroad," it was preceded by several "rail tracks" in other places that were used to carry ice, stone, and other materials. One of these earlier rail tracks was also built in Boston in 1800 to move dirt excavated from the artist John S. Copley's homesite on Beacon Hill to marshes located below. Another, also on Beacon Hill, was constructed by Silas Whitney in 1807. There is a record of a rail track built at a quarry in Pennsylvania in 1809 and another was used to transport ice cut from the Delaware River. Still others were built at scattered locations.

None of the rail tracks were nearly as long as the Granite Railway nor did they survive for any appreciable time. The Granite Railway, on the other hand, prospered because of the demand for Quincy granite and was operated by horse-power for forty years. In 1870, the Old Colony Railroad acquired the Granite Railway and rebuilt it. Later, when the New Haven Railroad became its owner, it became known as the Granite or West Quincy Branch.

To this day, there are those who dispute the Granite Railway's claim to be the first railroad in the United States. One of the arguments advanced to contradict the claim is that the Granite road never operated a passenger service, thus was not a common carrier. Yet, it has been written that a visitor riding on a quarry train a few years after its opening was killed in an accident, the first American railroad passenger fatality.

One of the trustees of the Bunker Hill Association was Daniel Webster (Scott #725). He delivered the main address at the ceremony which was conducted when the cornerstone of the monument was laid by the Marquis de Lafayette (Scott #1097) fifty years after the battle had been fought. Another twenty years were to pass before the capstone was put in place.

Ubiquitous Little "Jimmies"

Small coal cars, wheeled by hand or pulled by mules, had been used in collieries for many years and some of the earliest freight cars designed specifically for carrying coal from mine to consumer in this country were used even before the advent of public railways. Coal "jimmies," very similar in appearance to the car shown on Scott #2259, were running on the single track Mauch Chunk and Summit Hill Railroad (owned by the

2

Lehigh Coal and Navigation Company) as early as 1827 and two years later on the "Gravity Road" of the Delaware and Hudson Canal Company. These railways were built to carry coal from the mine head to canal ports where it was carried further by boat. Both of them relied on gravity to bring the little cars down the mountain slopes but differed in the means to scale the summit. Until 1845, the Mauch Chunk used mules to haul cars upgrade while the Gravity Road relied upon stationary steam engines to tow the cars up a series of inclined planes. The latter road is described at length in the following vignette, *"Stourbridge Lion Locomotive, 1829."*

Scott #2259   ©1988 USPS

The coal jimmy was a small but strong four wheeled car that weighed about one ton and had a capacity of about one and one-half tons of coal. Mauch Chunk jimmies had hinged ends that allowed the car to be tilted for dumping the load. They had brake arms located on one side and located about halfway along the car. When a train of jimmies was assembled, it was the usual practice to arrange the cars so that all of the brake levers were on the same side of the train. In this manner, they could be connected by a long rope so that a crewman could activate all of the brakes at once.

Within a few years, most of the ore or coal-carrying roads, especially those short roads in the mining regions of Pennsylvania, used jimmies that were almost identical to the Mauch Chunk design. For instance, the Schuylkill Navigation Company had over thirty-four hundred coal cars plying the tracks of the railroads that fed its river trade. These cars were distinguished by their bright yellow paint scheme which set them apart from the black cars owned by the railroads. Although the ubiquitous little jimmy survived and proliferated throughout the 19th century, by 1878, the poor ratio of load carrying capacity to dead weight exhibited by early jimmies had not improved at all. Meanwhile, a number of railroads had moved to other more effective designs.

One of the earliest and most unusual alternate coal car design was adopted by the Baltimore and Ohio Railroad. By the 1850s, the B&O built a substantial traffic in coal from mines in Maryland and, in 1847,

3

developed "pot hoppers" to carry the commodity—cars with iron bodies mounted on wooden frames. The original design (of which only one was built) had four wheels and a single round hopper, shaped like a huge flour sifter. This was immediately followed by an improved version with two cylindrical hopper compartments, and quickly thereafter the number of compartments increased to three. The compartments intersected and were tapered at the bottom to form hoppers. Each hopper had its own discharge door. The trucks of these cars did not swivel but curves could be negotiated because lateral play was permitted by some movement of the side beam of the truck.

The Baltimore and Ohio had an inventory of over 1,100 pot hoppers cars by 1865 (this number had increased from 250 before the Civil War began) and kept using them until the turn of the century. Speaking of the Civil War, and enlarging upon the Stonewall Jackson narrative later in this book, Jackson destroyed not only locomotives in his raid on Martinsburg, Virginia but many coal cars also. One reporter described the scene two weeks after the raid, "the scattered coal cars...(were)...in long lines, with the coal still burning...looking down we could see the inside— a mass of red hot coals."

Jimmies and pot hoppers aside, most other railroads moved toward more conventional car designs for carrying coal. Some used gondola cars, those with low sides and flat floors. Although gondola cars required manual unloading, these were adopted instead of hopper cars because the latter required specialized unloading facilities...elevated tracks at coal yards or wharves. A road with limited coal traffic could not justify the capital expenditure for such facilities. Furthermore, gondolas were more versatile rolling stock; they could also be used for other types and classes of cargo. Eventually, some gondolas were fitted with trapdoor-like "drop bottoms" or hoppers.

Ultimately, railroads turned to conventional hopper cars to carry coal and other mineral commodities. Some had interior sloping floors at the ends of the car only while in others all sides were sloped, pyramid fashion, to form a hopper at the bottom. Hopper cars progressed to larger, stronger, more effective designs made of steel and are still used extensively for the shipment of bulk commodities. The addition of permanent covers on hopper cars, a relatively recent innovation, has increased their utility considerably.

Before leaving the subject of coal cars, a wild and impractical design should be mentioned. It consisted of two large cylinders which were several feet in diameter and straddled the track. These hollow drums served in place of wheels and were flanged to stay on the track. The intent was to carry bulk commodities within the cylinders. Invented by Mr. Myers in 1854, it would, according to the inventor, immobilize coal against the circumference of the drum when a speed of ten miles per hour was attained while an inner partition would stabilize the commodity at lower speeds. Myers "Railroad Car Revolver" was tested on the Reading and the Frankfort and Lexington Railroads yet, despite Myers's pronouncement declaring the trials a success, the car passed into oblivion. The concept was reactivated again in the 1860s by a Mr. Prosser for a car to carry grain but, again, even though it completed a 200 mile round trip without a problem, the Prosser car disappeared from the rails.

Stourbridge Lion Locomotive, 1829

Almost throughout their parallel histories, canals and railroads were fierce competitors. Yet, ironically, it was a canal operator, the Delaware and Hudson Canal Company (D&HCC), that was responsible for importing the first true locomotive to turn a wheel on a rail in the United States. (The earlier, experimental demonstration locomotive constructed and run by John Stevens in Hoboken, New Jersey in 1825 did not run on rails. Stevens' machine had unflanged wheels that ran on broad boards bounded by side "fences.")

Scott #2362   ©1987 USPS

The Delaware and Hudson Canal was built to carry coal from the interior of Pennsylvania to tidewater on the Hudson River from where it could be easily and cheaply transported to New York City. The canal extended from Rondout, its terminal near Kingston, New York to Honesdale,

Pennsylvania. Although it was desired to extend the canal from Honesdale to the Carbondale region where the mines were located, this plan was deemed to be impractical. The Moosic mountain range lay between the two areas and too many locks would have been required to scale the heights. An alternative, a 17 mile long railroad, was proposed and approved. This was a bold move because railroad experience in the United States was almost nil.

John Jervis was the Chief Engineer of the D&HCC and he assumed charge of the construction of the Delaware and Hudson Gravity Railroad, which involved five inclined planes on the west side of the mountains and three descending planes on the east. Stationary engines were to haul the loaded coal cars up the inclined planes and then gravity would be employed to lower the cars on the descending planes. Despite the woefully inadequate braking systems of the times, this was not as dangerous as it might seem at first glance. During the descent, the coal-laden cars would be paired with cars filled with water that were making the return trip to the mines. Thus, the descending cars would be balanced by ascending cars on the same plane. The problem was that the descending planes were separated by three nearly level stretches of track. Jervis estimated that the cost for a sufficient number of horses to move the required shipments over these "levels" would be over $71 per day. Steam locomotives, on the other hand, would cost about $41 a day.

Since there were no experienced railroaders available and certainly no locomotive manufacturers in this country, Jervis sent Horatio Allen, a young canal engineer who worked for the D&HCC, to England in 1828 to study railroads there and to contract for four locomotives to be sent to America. (Despite his lack of specific railroad background, Jervis provided Allen with very detailed advice and technical instructions to carry out his assignment.) During Allen's absence, Jervis began construction of the railroad. Surrounded by unlimited forests, Jervis decided to build the level stretches on trestles rather than earthen embankments. This fateful decision was later to affect the applicability of the locomotive secured by Allen.

Meanwhile, in England, Allen ordered one engine (*Pride of Newcastle*) from the Stephenson Works and three (*Delaware, Hudson, and Stourbridge Lion*) from Foster, Rastrick & Company. (Some authorities state that the Stephenson engine was named *America*, but others believe that the name *America* was used only to indicate that that locomotive was sent to the United States.) *The Pride of Newcastle* arrived in New York on January 15, 1829 and the *Lion* on May 13, 1829. Arrangements were made to ship the two machines up the Hudson to Rondout, the canal's port on the Hudson River from where they were to be transshipped to Honesdale via canal boat. A mystery surrounds the three engines, *Pride of Newcastle*, *Delaware*, and *Hudson*. They disappeared completely. There is no record of their arrival at Honesdale yet, years later, a locomotive part attributed to the *Stourbridge Lion* (Scott #2362) was discovered to have come from *Pride of Newcastle*.

During construction of the *Lion*, which was then unnamed, a painting of a lion was executed on the front end of the boiler and this image, along with the location of the shops in Stourbridge, England, gave the machine its name. Although Allen had specified that the locomotive's weight should not exceed 3 tons, the engine, as received, weighed over 7 tons. Its wheels were made of oak and capped by iron tires. Its two vertical cylinders drove overhead "walking beams." Connecting rods attached to the walking beams drove the wheels. Its cost, delivered in New York City, was $2,915.

Final assembly of the machine was made at the West Point Foundry in New York City and it was sent to Honesdale. Preparations for testing were finally completed and on August 8, 1829 (two months before the Rainhill trials in England), the boiler of the *Lion* was fired up and Allen climbed aboard to drive it. In Allen's own words, written at a much later time:

> "When the time came, and the steam was of the right pressure, and all was ready, I took my position on the platform of the Locomotive alone, and with my hand on the throttle valve handle, said, 'If there is any danger in this ride it is not necessary that the life and limbs of more than one be subjected to danger.'
>
> The Locomotive, having no train behind it, answered at once to the movement of the hand...soon the straight line was run over, the curve was reached and passed before there was time to think as to its not being passed safely...Soon I was out of sight in the three miles ride alone in the woods of Pennsylvania. I had never

run a Locomotive nor any other engine before and I have never run one since."

The engine worked well but the trackwork was inadequate to support the *Lion* safely (a second run on September 9th confirmed that fact). It had been designed to sustain 1.25 tons per wheel; the *Lion* provided a load of 1.75 tons per wheel. (One report of the trial, supposedly an eyewitness statement provided to the *Pottsville Miner's Journal,*stated that the machine could not navigate the first curve in the road and was derailed. This does not agree with all other accounts, including Allen's own.) Since the canal engineers were not disposed to rebuild the elevated railway to make it stronger, the *Lion* was put into storage at Honesdale and remained there for twenty years. During that time, pieces were scavenged by local blacksmiths and machinists. Around 1849, its boiler was taken to Carbondale, Pennsylvania where it was used as a stationary boiler at a D&H company facility. In 1889, remaining parts of the locomotive were donated to the Smithsonian Institution.

Novelty Locomotive, 1829

The Ericsson stamp, which was first issued on May 29, 1926, depicts the statue that was erected in Washington, D.C. to the memory of the Swedish-born inventor. The monument (Scott #628), executed by James Earl Fraser and unveiled by King Gustav VI of Sweden in 1926 is, like Ericsson's contribution to railroad history, rather obscure, standing beside the Potomac River in West Potomac Park. It shows a pensive Ericsson seated beneath the Yggdrasil, the tree of life of Norse mythology. Standing above Ericsson beneath the tree are statues titled, Vision, Labor, and Adventure. The points of the mariner's compass are inscribed around the fifty foot square base of the statue.

Scott #628

Although John Ericsson (1803-1889) was best known for the construction of the armored warship *Monitor* during the Civil War (Scott #2975a), his most important and far-reaching scientific contribution was the perfection of the screw propeller which replaced paddle wheels on steam ships. Less well-known were his contributions toward railroading history yet he was among the very first practitioners of the railroad art. Ericsson had displayed an interest and talent in engineering at a very early age and in his early twenties developed the "flame engine." This machine was intended to work like a steam engine except that hot air, not steam, was the working fluid. Since England was more receptive than his native Sweden to innovation, Ericsson submitted a paper on his engine to the Institution of Civil Engineers in London. On borrowed money, Ericsson followed to promote his engine personally. Unfortunately, when he demonstrated the machine to the Institution's evaluation committee, it failed due to the intense heat generated by the coal fuel. The bright side of this incident is that Ericsson was compelled to seek employment in order to remain in England.

The man experienced, in his words, "great, good fortune" to find a position with John Braithwaite, a manufacturer of steam engines and air pumps. Thus, when the firm of Braithwaite and Ericsson (the latter had quickly become a partner in the firm) was advised of a competition organized in 1829 by the Liverpool and Manchester Railway to select a locomotive for their road, it prepared an entry. The competition was known as the Rainhill trials; the name was derived from the location of the trials on the Rainhill level of the road between two inclined planes. Strict specifications were published and of the several contenders, only Ericsson's *Novelty* and Stephenson's *Rocket*, were finalists. (A third entry, *Sans Pareil*, built by Timothy Hackworth, sprang a leak during the contest. Oatmeal was added to the boiler water to plug the leak, a standard practice at the time. The oatmeal passed to the feed pump which became choked with porridge and disabled the machine.)

The *Novelty*, an elegant, light locomotive with a vertical boiler, was built in seven weeks and it was capable of a substantially greater speed than required. Its failing was in the boiler design. The furnace was fired through a funnel-like opening in the top which led to a horizontal firebox behind and below the boiler. A serpentine flue carried the products of combustion to a tall chimney at the rear of the locomotive. A bellows provided an artificial draft. Although *Novelty* achieved a maximum speed of 28 miles per hour (without load) and, like its competitor, hauled a 20 ton train at 10 miles per hour, its boiler collapsed and it was withdrawn from further testing.

One author contended that the judges were biased in favor of Stephenson and, to insure *Rocket's* success, changed the rules of the competition before the final tests between the two remaining contenders were conducted. This account, which is unsubstantiated by other reliable sources, charged that the changes were communicated beforehand only to Stephenson and, as a consequence, he was able to make adjustments to his machine to meet the revised requirements. In truth, Ericsson interpreted the conditions of the trial differently from Stephenson, who recognized the need for great hauling power rather than speed. *Rocket* completed the entire schedule of tests without any failure and also exhibited a much higher tractive effort than *Novelty*.

Despite their failure to win the Rainhill competition, Braithwaite and Ericsson continued to produce locomotives for the pioneer English railways. In 1839, Ericsson visited the United States where he became a citizen and remained until his death in 1889.

Early Railroad Surveys

The General Survey Act, legislation that authorized surveys of canals and roads by government engineers, was passed by the Congress of the United States in 1824 during James Monroe's (Scott #1038) administration. John Quincy Adams (Scott #811), who became president in 1825, interpreted this law broadly to include railroad surveys as well. This was an important decision

Scott #811

because there were few trained engineers in the United States...for the first twenty-five years of the nineteenth century, the only school in the country teaching engineering was the military academy at West Point. Thus, it is not surprising that, soon thereafter, the Baltimore and Ohio (B&O) and the Camden and Amboy (C&A) Railroads took advantage of the Survey Act and employed military-trained surveyors (Colonel Stephen Long, Dr. William Howard, and Captain William McNeill on the B&O; Major John Wilson on the C&A). Colonel Long had been involved with surveys of western areas (the region that we now call the "midwest") a number of years previously. He mentioned seeing emigrants migrating westward in family groups on their "rude arks" along the Ohio River, west of Pennsylvania, in 1819, before the first railroads were built.

In Long's 1829 book, *The Railroad Manual*, he wrote, that a railroad should be built so that "the route between any two points is direct, level, and coincident or nearly so, with the natural surface of the ground." However, he did concede, in a paper published in the *Journal of the Franklin Institute* in the following year, that some "horizontal flexures," i.e., curves, were admissible. It was well that he espoused this position because it developed that the B&O, of necessity, had many, very sharp curves. His primary maxim was also violated by the mountainous nature of the land that the B&O passed through. At one point, Parr's Ridge, Long resorted to the use of an inclined plane to carry the railroad up and over the mountain. Despite the obstacles, Long managed to bring the B&O through the Alleghenies although its twists and turns and high grades continued to plague the road into the 20th century. It took the B&O about eight years to build from Baltimore to Harpers Ferry, a distance of eighty-one miles. Admittedly, over a year of this time was lost as a result of an injunction placed by the Chesapeake and Ohio Canal Company, which prevented the railroad from building beyond Point of Rocks, Maryland, sixty-nine miles from Baltimore.

The Camden and Amboy, by comparison, was built through very level country, on the Atlantic coastal plain. Construction began in December 1830 and by December 1832, two years later, track had been installed from Bordentown to South Amboy, a distance of 26 1/2 miles. The 16 mile section between Bordentown and Camden was completed in 1834. Thanks to the favorable terrain (much of the road followed the Delaware River) the route was remarkably straight and most of the few curves had radii in excess of 1800 feet. Between Camden and Bordentown the steepest grade was 20 feet per mile while, over the remaining track, more severe grades were experienced at only three points and the worst of these was 45 feet per mile. At the north end of the line, a passenger had to embark on a ship and sail around Staten Island to reach New York City.

After the Philadelphia and Trenton Railroad was built in Pennsylvania, it became apparent that it would seek approval to continue its trackage towards New York City. To forestall this competition, the C&A bought the Philadelphia and Trenton and built additional trackage from Bordentown to Trenton and from Trenton to New Brunswick. When these connections were made, it was possible to travel from Philadelphia to Jersey City, on the west shore of the Hudson River opposite New York City, wholly by rail. (The C&A operated over rails leased from the New Jersey Railroad and Transportation Company between New Brunswick and Jersey City.) At that time, 1839, Nicholas Wood praised "the great highway between the cities of Philadelphia and New York." This highway—the railroad—became the favored alternative to the old stage coach line that began service in 1794 and took about a day and a half for the trip, depending upon the weather.

In May of 1871, the Camden and Amboy was leased to the Pennsylvania Railroad for 999 years.

B&O Railroad, the First Common Carrier

This stamp was issued to commemorate the 125th anniversary of the chartering of the Baltimore and Ohio Railroad (B&O). It shows the horse-drawn car *Pioneer*, the *Tom Thumb*, the road's first steam locomotive, and a modern type F3 diesel engine, all superimposed on the company's charter (Scott #1006).

Scott #1006

The Erie Canal was built in the period 1817-1825 to provide a water route from the Great Lakes to the Hudson River and thence to markets in New York City. It was the most significant factor in the penetration and exploitation of the midwestern farm lands and mineral resources and toward increasing the importance and status of New York as a center of trade. Influential Baltimore merchants realized that a transportation means to the west must be developed from their city if it was to remain an important commercial hub. Two projects were begun that were to have momentous impact on Baltimore. On the same day (July 4, 1828) that the first stone of the B&O was laid by Charles Carroll, President John Quincy Adams began the digging of the Chesapeake and Ohio Canal. The goal of both of these enterprises was to reach the Potomac River at Cumberland, Maryland. Obviously, the first of them to attain that goal—

at the entrance to the National Road—would enjoy a competitive advantage over the other.

Initial plans for the B&O called for horse-drawn coaches even though John Rogers and Benjamin Latrobe had, in 1827, published a pamphlet advocating steam motive power on the road. The directors were reluctant to commit to that radical development; instead, they approved trials of a wind-driven "sailing car" and a car propelled by a horse (or mule) on a treadmill. Neither was successful and, in fact, the latter was said to have collided with a cow and "dumped a lot of editors into the ditch." Consequently, "the press of that region was unanimous in pronouncing the experiment a practical failure." The horse-drawn car, *Pioneer*, made its first trip on the road on December 22, 1829.

Now, Peter Cooper came upon the scene. Cooper was a Baltimore iron mill owner who realized the potential of the B&O to further Baltimore's prominence. Consequently, he was an unflagging champion of the railroad. Having been a witness to Horatio Allen's history-making ride on the Delaware and Hudson Railroad, he felt that horse power should be replaced by steam power. To prove the point, he built an experimental steam locomotive that would be suitable for use on the many tight curves along the route. Assisted by Ross Winans and James Millholland, he constructed the *Tom Thumb* (shown at the center of the stamp).

This "teakettle on wheels" had a vertical boiler and its pipes, which carried steam to the single double-acting cylinder, were made from iron musket barrels. Gearing between the cylinder and the four small wheels increased the speed of the machine. The tiny engine was fueled with "stone coal," the early term for anthracite, and a belt-driven fan provided an artificial draft. The capability of the *Tom Thumb* was demonstrated on a 13 mile trip carrying the company's directors. The outbound trip was accomplished in one hour and twelve minutes but the return was accomplished fifteen minutes more quickly. At a later time, *Tom Thumb* was matched in a race against a horse-drawn car owned by the Stockton and Stokes stagecoach operators. The contest was held on a double-tracked portion of the road between Baltimore and Ellicott Mills. The locomotive was unquestionably more than adequate for the task but its blower belt worked off its pulley; the belt could not be replaced easily while moving and the race was lost. In this instance, the little engine that could, couldn't.

13

Designed as a demonstration machine, *Tom Thumb's* performance proved the practicality of steam locomotives. The directors conducted America's version of the Rainhill trials and selected a small engine, the *York*, to work on the road. The B&O then contracted with Phineas Davis, *York's* builder, for further locomotives and *York* was followed by *Atlantic* and a fleet of "grasshopper" type machines, so-called because the arrangement of the connecting rods and linkages resembled a grasshopper's hinged legs, poised for jumping.

The Baltimore and Ohio won its race with the canal and entered Cumberland in 1842; it was to take eight more years before the Chesapeake and Ohio Canal arrived there. At one point, the line climbed Parr's Ridge by means of inclined planes, where the trains were hailed up by means of a stationary engine and endless ropes. By 1852, the road had reached the upper Ohio River. It reached the Mississippi River across from St. Louis in 1857. It is noteworthy that the B&O's construction was generally of high quality and many of its early bridges were massive stone structures that are still in use carrying modern, heavy trains.

During the Civil War, the railroad was the object of frequent raids and destruction of its property because much of it was located in the battle zones. Only through the tireless efforts of its personnel was it able to maintain effective operations. After the war, it expanded and became a major trunk line. In the twentieth century, it was known for its safe and attentive passenger service, where it was an innovative leader. Volumes have been written about "The Mother of Railroads," as the B&O was termed by author Lucius Beebe. However, like many railroads, it had a checkered economic history and, ultimately, declining revenues led to its acquisition by the Chesapeake and Ohio Railway in 1962.

It is significant that a diesel locomotive was included on the stamp because, despite enjoying a substantial coal trade, the B&O was anxious to apply the new technology. In fact, it expressed that eagerness by prevailing upon the builder to build them a road locomotive before the demonstration machines were available. The type F3, which is depicted, was built by the Electro-Motive Division (EMD) of General Motors Corporation and introduced in 1945. Wartime prohibitions prevented locomotive design changes so the F3 was the first new type from EMD to incorporate all of the improvements conceived during World War II. Production of this type, 1,111 in all, continued until 1949.

Best Friend of Charleston Locomotive

If one considers the *Tom Thumb* as a demonstration machine only, then the distinction of being the first railroad in the United States over which a train of cars was hauled by a steam locomotive on a **regular** basis is held by the South Carolina Canal and Railroad Company. (The South Carolina Railroad was also known as the Charleston and Hamburg Railroad.)

Horatio Allen, one of the few men with any railroad experience in the country, was hired as Chief Engineer of the fledgling South Carolina Railroad (SCRR). It was he who convinced the directors of the road to employ steam power. He,

> "...rested the decision of the question on the position that, what the performance of a horse was and would be, every one knew; but the man was not living who would undertake to say what the locomotive was yet to do..."

Edward Miller (who, like Allen had been sent to England to become conversant with railroads) was commissioned to design a locomotive that

Scott #2363   ©1987 USPS

could attain a speed of ten miles per hour while pulling three times its own weight. Charles Detmold drew up the working drawings and the West Point Foundry of New York City was chosen to build the machine. David Matthew, who had assembled the *Stourbridge Lion* when it came to America, supervised construction of the *Best Friend*. On January 15, 1831, the locomotive *Best Friend of Charleston* (Scott #2363) made its first officially scheduled trip.

The engine, which cost $4,000., had a vertical boiler with a firebox, surrounded by water, at its bottom. Emissions from the fire passed into a jacket around the boiler and out through the chimney opening at the top. The locomotive was mounted on four wheels that were inside-connected, i. e., the power train—cylinders, connecting rods, and cranks—was entirely inside the frame. *Best Friend* weighed between nine and ten thousand pounds and developed a tractive force of four hundred pounds. It exceeded the directors' specifications and was capable of transporting 40 or 50 passengers at 15 to 20 miles per hour.

About six months after its inaugural trip, the fireman of the *Best Friend*, annoyed by the noise of hissing steam, tied the safety valve down. The ensuing boiler explosion killed the fireman and destroyed the locomotive. However, like the mythical bird that could be reborn after being burned to death, the engine was rebuilt as an outside-connected machine. Fittingly, the rebuilt locomotive was named *Phoenix*.

The circumstances surrounding the chartering of the South Carolina Canal and Railroad Company were very similar to those which applied to the Baltimore and Ohio Railroad. The city of Savannah, Georgia, located at the mouth of the Savannah River, which reached into the interior cotton-growing region, enjoyed strong cotton factoring and shipping businesses. To tap some of this business, a railroad, extending from Charleston to Hamburg, 136 miles away at the western end of the state, was proposed. In addition, communication would be established with the inland city of Augusta, Georgia, across the Savannah River from Hamburg.

Part of the SCRR was originally built on elevated tracks supported on pine pilings, a method that promised inexpensive and speedy construction, particularly over marshy areas. A second benefit was that fencing was unnecessary and farm animals could pass below the tracks. Unfortunately, the elevated structure tended to settle unevenly and the pine members deteriorated quickly in the humid Carolina climate. Allen quickly rebuilt those sections in a conventional manner.

The SCRR, along with many other lines, was consolidated into the Southern Railway system by J. P. Morgan and his associates in 1894.

John Bull Locomotive

The first American railroad charter was granted in 1815 to Colonel John Stevens "to erect a rail road from the River Delaware near Trenton to the River Raritan at or near New Brunswick." As with many visionaries, Stevens was ahead of his time because the concept of railroads was totally non-existent in the public consciousness. Canals were the darlings of the investment community at that time. They were popular, proven, relatively safe, understandable systems with powerful supporters. Unable to attract investors since,

> "The public mind was not sufficiently enlightened to induce moneyed men to embark their funds in a project then considered wild and impracticable,"

Stevens set out to demonstrate the feasibility of steam-powered locomotives. He built a tiny machine that he ran on a wooden, racetrack-like oval at Hoboken, New Jersey in 1825.

Scott #2364   ©1987 USPS

By 1830, public conceptions and the investment climate had changed and Stevens secured another charter to build a railroad from Camden, New Jersey, near Philadelphia, to South Amboy, a short water trip from New York City. The Colonel's son, Robert, the Chief Engineer of the company, was dispatched to England to purchase a locomotive and iron rails for the enterprise. During the voyage, Stevens studied the English Birkinshaw rail design and found several shortcomings. Consequently, he designed a new rail with an H-shaped crossection, which he arranged to have fabricated in Wales. (This design evolved into the standard T-rail that continues to be used worldwide.) In addition to making this valuable contribution to railroading, Stevens also purchased a locomotive, the *John*

Bull (Scott #2364) for the Camden and Amboy Railroad. Incidentally, the name *John Bull* was not applied to the engine until after it had entered service.

The *John Bull* incorporated many of Stevens' suggested modifications into an existing Stephenson design of a Planet type locomotive. The *John Bull*, the 44th locomotive manufactured by the Stephenson firm, had a Bury boiler, sometimes called a "haystack boiler" because of its vertical shape and hemispherical top, and four inside-connected, coupled wheels. When delivered, it did not include the pilot, or "cowcatcher," that is shown on the stamp. Upon its arrival in America, it was brought to Bordentown, New Jersey and assembled by Isaac Dripps, a steamboat mechanic employed by the Stevens family. This was a real accomplishment for the 21 year old Dripps and his helpers, none of whom had ever seen a locomotive. The engine arrived in discrete components—a boiler, wheels and axles, and four boxes of assorted parts—without any instructions for their assembly. Even though Robert Stevens was away and not available for consultation, Dripps managed to get it all together and the first test of the machine was a qualified success.

A small contractor's flat car was outfitted as a tender to hold coal and a whiskey keg, mounted upon it, held water that was carried to the pump by a leather hose fabricated by a local shoemaker. After several demonstrations, the *John Bull* was stored until completion of the road, some eighteen months later. (During this period, Stevens arranged to have more engines built on the *John Bull* pattern, some by outside concerns, others in the C&A shops.) After the *John Bull* was placed in service, Stevens felt that a pilot should be added to help guide the engine into curves. His invention, installed in 1833, served the added purpose of sweeping obstacles aside. Its suitability for the latter purpose was demonstrated to David Stevenson, an English engineer, who wrote,

> "The train in which I travelled, while moving with considerable rapidity, came in contact with a large waggon loaded with firewood, which was literally shivered to atoms by the concussion. The fragments of the broken waggon, and the wood with which it was loaded, were distributed on each side of the railway, but the guard (pilot) prevented any part of them from falling before the engine wheels, and thus obviated what might in that case have proved a very serious accident."

The pilot was affixed to the front driver axle and the outside cranks and side rods had to be removed from the locomotive. Thus, the 0-4-0 machine became a 2-2-2 engine. Because the pilot was eight feet long, when it was mounted the *John Bull* was too long for the Camden and Amboy's turntables. The apparatus had to be removed before placing the engine on the table.

The *John Bull* continued to be used as a road locomotive from 1833 into the late 1840s. After being removed from that service it was variously used for hydrostatic testing of new boilers, to haul work trains, as a switching engine, and as a stationary engine to power a saw. Beginning in the late 1850s, it was displayed at fairs and expositions, including the 1876 Centennial Exposition in Philadelphia. In 1893, the *John Bull* was driven under its own power for almost 1000 miles to the Columbian Exposition in Chicago where it assumed a starring role. The engine traveled at about 30 miles per hour but, because of the many stops along the way to show it off, it took a little over five days to make the journey. The John Bull survived to become the oldest original locomotive in the United States and was accorded a place of honor in the Smithsonian Institution at Washington, D. C. In anticipation of its 150th birthday, the locomotive was reconditioned and brought to operating condition and, in 1981, it was taken from the museum and operated under its own power for a short distance over the tracks of the Chessie System. It was then returned to the Smithsonian where it now resides.

Brother Jonathan Locomotive

The early English-made locomotives that were exported to the United States were heavy, rugged, and reliable but were unsuitable for use on lightly-built American track for two reasons. First, the rails were destroyed by the great weight and by the hammering of the unbalanced driving wheels and second, the engines often derailed when they entered curves, an abundant feature on American railways. A means to gently lead or guide the machine through curves was required and the leading, or pilot, truck was the answer.

The function of a pilot truck was already understood in England at the time of the pilgrimages of Allen, Stevens, and Miller yet a number of Americans have been mentioned as its inventors. However, although not its inventor, John Jervis is generally acknowledged to be the first to apply a pilot truck to an American locomotive. He discovered that a recently acquired English machine on the Mohawk and Hudson Railroad, the *Robert Fulton*, pitched and rocked badly and derailed frequently. This situation caused him to consider that although "a rigid frame for the engine machinery" was necessary on a locomotive,

> "It appeared important to provide guiding wheels that should be geared favorably to follow the track..."

By "geared" Jervis meant "arranged" or "mounted" and, in particular, referred to their ability to rotate horizontally. He thereupon designed a locomotive with a four-wheel leading truck, which he termed "a bearing carriage." Jervis was gracious in his praise of Horatio Allen, his protégé, who had earlier proposed such a device.

Scott #2365   ©1987 USPS

Jervis' design, the *Brother Jonathan* (Scott #2365) and originally named *Experiment*, was built by the West Point Foundry. Delivered in 1832, its claims to fame were that it was the first locomotive in the world to be designed with a swiveling, leading truck and it was the first 4-2-0 engine constructed in the United States. The locomotive had five foot diameter drivers and was said to have attained a speed of eighty miles an hour, an improbability considering the lightly-made track of the time.

George Stephenson allegedly proposed the idea of a leading truck to Robert Stevens when they met in England. However, Stephenson never applied the idea to any of his locomotives until 1832-33, when he built the *Davy Crockett* to John Jervis' specifications for the Saratoga and Schenectady Railroad. It is likely that the engine Jervis described in a letter to the *American Railroad Journal* in 1833 was the *Davy Crockett*, which had the same wheel arrangement as *Brother Jonathan*. In part, the letter read,

> "The small (pilot) wheels, with their frame, work on the road the same as an independent wagon; and being geared short, they go round a curve with as much ease as a common wagon, and being leaders, they bring round the working wheels (drivers), and the large frame on which the whole machinery of the engine rests, with as much ease as practicable. By this method it will be seen, the engine may pass a curve with the same ease as a common railroad carriage, having the same weight on the wheels."

The pilot wheels were intended to prevent the

> "front outer driving wheel flange from grinding against the rail and (to) compel it to stand away from the rail, or at least relieve its pressure."

A contributor to *The Knickerbocker* in 1833 described a trip from Schenectady to Albany in glowing terms:

> "The gentleness of the motion (of the train) renders it difficult to estimate its rapidity, which is easily measured, however, by the apparent dizzying flight of the trees and fences."

The odds are high that this traveler was riding behind one of Jervis' improved locomotives, perhaps the *Brother Jonathan*.

"American" Type Locomotive – the Queen of the Rails

Scott #114

Scott #114 was one of a group of eleven stamps known as the "1869 pictorials." Except for three of the issues—images of Franklin, Washington, and Lincoln—the stamps represented important incidents in American history, federal icons, or themes illustrating "the advance from the post boy on horseback to the facilities afforded by the railway and ocean steamship." Most of the 1869 pictorials were withdrawn prematurely because the two-color items were expensive to produce and the public was dissatisfied with the lower values, which were not particularly "interesting or dignified." However, the four lowest values continued to be sold.

Scott #114, a 3 cent denomination, pictured a 4-4-0 steam locomotive and was the most common of the group. The vignette was engraved by Christian Rost and over 386 million were printed by the contractor, the National Bank Note Company. Rost used a drawing of a Baldwin locomotive that was drawn by William Croome and previously used on a $1.00 bank note of the Northwestern Bank of Warren, Pennsylvania.

Prior to 1840, locomotive designers were individualistic inventors who exhibited differing opinions concerning locomotive design. As a result, there were no characteristic locomotives. The period was a time of experimentation and engines were diverse in appearance and capability. That situation was soon to change after the 4-4-0, "American" type, locomotive was originated and further developed. Although a 4-4-0 machine was proposed by George Sellers for the Philadelphia and Columbia Railroad, it was never built and credit for building the first "American" type locomotive was earned by James Brooks. His machine was built in May 1837. English engineers named locomotives of this wheel arrangement "American" types.

It is appropriate that a Baldwin 4-4-0 locomotive be pictured on the first U. S. stamp with a railroad subject. The 4-4-0 locomotive became the most prolific of all types used during the nineteenth century. There were fewer than 600 locomotives in the U. S. in 1840, of which 20 were 4-4-0s. Engines of this type accounted for 85 percent of all locomotives in use in 1870 and, by 1900, about 25,000 "American" type locomotives had been built. At that time, the Baldwin Locomotive Works, one of the earliest manufacturers, was the principal locomotive builder in the country. In total, until it outshopped its last steam locomotive in 1948, Baldwin produced over fifty-nine thousand of all types.

Interestingly, in the early years, Matthias Baldwin could not see an advantage in applying the new four-coupled wheel arrangement. He believed that his single locomotives (with only two driving wheels) were simpler and adequate, but eventually, his customers persuaded him to build 4-4-0 locomotives. The first one he produced was sold to the South Carolina Railroad in 1845.

"American" type locomotives were used for passenger and freight service. For the former, larger diameter drive wheels were used but even so, passenger trains rarely exceeded 35 or 40 miles per hour. There was little demand for much larger and more powerful locomotives and the 4-4-0s were incrementally improved to satisfy most railroad motive power needs until about 1875. Except for the Civil War period, the cost of an "American" type locomotive, the "queen of the rails," was remarkably constant throughout the nineteenth century.

Scott #1897a   ©1982 USPS

Another stamp picturing a 4-4-0 locomotive is Scott #1897a. This offering, a member of the 1981-1995 "Transportation Series," carries the same drawing as Scott #2226, which was issued later. The differences between the two, both of which are of two cent denomination, lie in the lettering. Also, the cents sign was removed on #2226 in order to allow the designers more latitude to exercise their creativity. This led to confusion with higher denomination stamps so it was then decided to add a dollar sign to the more expensive ones. The locomotive on these stamps is represented as dating from the 1870s.

Ultimately, the demand for more powerful machines with larger grates and boilers was the cause of the demise of the eight wheel locomotives. This demand resulted in the development of engines with more driving wheels and trailing trucks behind the drivers that could carry larger fireboxes. Toward the end of the nineteenth century, many measures were taken to prolong the application of 4-4-0s but there were limitations to "scaling up" the machines. Other wheel arrangements were developed for specific tasks. "Ten-wheelers" (4-6-0) and then "Pacific" (4-6-2) types were introduced into freight service and "Atlantic" (4-4-2) types began to be used for hauling passenger trains.

Scott #1573, which was issued over 100 years after Scott #114, depicts a 4-4-0 locomotive that is painted green. It may have been built by the Norris Locomotive Works because that concern was noted for outshopping green locomotives. However, during the years 1850 to 1875, many locomotive builders sold colorful and highly decorated engines, some carrying paintings of women, animals, and castles. But the ornamentation was costly and the nature of the machine's duty and its attendant soot, smoke, and coal dust worked against keeping the decorations in their original, pristine condition. Eventually the railroads adopted black as the preferred color for their locomotives, a color that disguised any dirt.

Scott #1573

Also pictured on Scott #1573 is a diesel locomotive. The diesel locomotive eventually almost monopolized the entire rail motive power market, except for the mass transit arena. Its ascendancy and domination is detailed in later vignettes.

Gowan and Marx Locomotive, 1839

Joseph Harrison, Jr., when he worked for the Norris firm of locomotive builders, played an important role in the building of the *George Washington*, an engine that became famous for demonstrating that a locomotive had the potential to replace inclined planes. Later, Harrison moved to Garrett and Eastwick's shops and, shortly thereafter, became a partner of that concern, replacing Garrett. In 1838, he invented a scheme for locomotive driving wheel equalization (means that allow a locomotive to conform to irregularities of the track) that remained in use throughout the steam era. Harrison's equalizing levers were installed on the *Gowan and Marx* locomotive (Scott #2366).

This engine was built by Eastwick and Harrison for the Philadelphia and Reading Railroad (P&R) in 1839 and was named for a British banking firm—the one that underwrote the Reading's Pottsville, Pennsylvania extension. The engine, classified as a 4-4-0 with a leading truck, was designed so that all of the weight behind the rear driver axle and much of the weight in front of the drivers was carried by the drivers. Nine (long) tons of its total weight of eleven (long) tons was supported by the driving wheels. The feedwater pump was placed inside the cylinder saddle, an unusual, but practical location because the steam within the saddle prevented the pump from freezing.

Scott #2366   ©1987 USPS

Because the P&R was a major carrier of anthracite coal, it had rebuilt all of their engines to burn hard coal to avoid the embarrassment of using wood-burners. Hard coal was not only hard to burn but it also provided an especially hot fire. So, because the requirement applied to new engines as well, the grooved, wrought iron grates of the *Gowan and Marx* were coated with clay to protect them. (Firemen later determined that a layer of ash and cinders insulated the grates from hot coals but required substantial experience and practice to establish the proper amount of ash without exposing the grates.)

To assist in the combustion process, an exhaust blast was generated by steam exhausted from the cylinders and routed to the stack where it escaped into the stack "through a number of small tubes." (As the exhaust steam expanded, it caused a corresponding reduction in pressure in the stack that accelerated the smoke and exhaust gases from the firebox and drew more air over the fire.) The *American Railroad Journal* reported that, "With the aid of this contrivance, the anthracite fire is kept in a state of intense activity, and generates an abundance of steam without the annoyance and danger arising from the smoke and sparks of a wood fire."

Despite the road's best efforts, the *Gowan and Marx* could not burn coal well and it was soon reworked to burn wood. Another attempt was made, in 1855, to refit the engine to use coal but that exercise failed also.

The first train was hauled over the completed Philadelphia & Reading Railroad by the *Gowan and Marx* in December 1839. At a later demonstration, the engine proved it was able to pull 40 times its own weight, the first locomotive to do so, at a speed of about ten miles per hour. (Ten short years earlier, the *Best Friend of Charleston* was required to pull only three times its own weight.) The demonstration was observed by a delegation of engineers from Russia who were seeking ideas and advice for building that country's first railroad. This performance was largely instrumental in the Russians' decision to recommend American methods and machines. As a result of its admirable pulling capacity, the P&R ordered twelve more copies from the Locks and Canal Company. During its working life on the P&R, the engine traveled 144,000 miles.

In 1859, the *Gowan and Marx* was removed from the road's roster and delivered to the Baldwin Works in part payment for a new locomotive. Its ultimate disposition was not recorded.

Singing Wires, Samuel Morse's Contribution to the Railroads

Scott #890, one of the American inventors series, portrays Samuel Finley Breese Morse toward the end of his life, a distinguished and much decorated man. Many of the decorations were conferred by foreign countries in recognition of his invention of the telegraph. The second stamp (Scott #924) issued in 1944, 100 years after the event, commemorates the transmission of the first message sent by telegraph in the United States.

Born in 1791, Morse's education was extensive and upon graduating from Yale College, he studied art for four years at the Royal Academy in England. Not particularly successful as a portrait painter, he later became an art professor at New York University. Eventually, returning home from France on a long sea voyage, he was shown an apparatus for the transmission of electricity over long distances and recalled

Scott #890

that years earlier he had attended a lecture where electromagnetism was demonstrated. His interest aroused, Morse began to investigate electromagnetic telegraphy upon his arrival in New York,

Experiments in telegraphy had been conducted for many years and some authorities credit Sir Charles Wheatstone as the inventor of the telegraph. In fact, one of Wheatstone's instruments was used in a block signaling system installed on the North Midland Railway in England in 1841. But it was Morse (with help from Leonard Gale, Joseph Henry, and Alfred Vail) who devised the first practical instrument in the United States. (It is recorded that Morse conducted a practical model and test of a telegraphic instrument in 1835, predating Wheatstone's invention). Morse's telegraph involved a "sender," essentially a switch that could "make or break" a circuit and a receiver that provided an audible signal as its electromagnet was energized. To complete the system it was necessary for the inventor to devise a code representing letters and numbers. That code still bears his name today. He applied for a patent in 1837, but it was not until 1843 that the United States Congress appropriated funds to test the system over an appreciable distance.

Scott #924

With the federal funds, Morse had a telegraph line constructed from Washington to Baltimore along the Baltimore and Ohio Railroad tracks (the line extended from the Capitol at Washington to the Mount Clare station of the B&O at Baltimore), and upon its completion in May 1844, transmitted a message. The message, "What hath God wrought," was composed at Washington, delivered to Morse and sent to Vail at Baltimore. Vail, without foreknowledge of the content of the message, received it and retransmitted it to Washington. (Incidentally, the very first message transmitted by Morse was sent during the course of his experiments in 1838. That communication, "A patient waiter is no loser," traveled over three miles of wire at his laboratory in Morristown, New Jersey.)

Although the Washington-Baltimore test was successful, Congress—who owned the line—could not decide whether to assume the patent and make the new technology a government operation, like the post office. Eventually, it decided that telegraphy would not be a lucrative business and opted to allow development by private companies.

Because insulation was a subject about which little information was available, the transmissions over Morse's apparatus were subject to the whims of the weather. On rainy days, the signal became extremely weak or nonexistent. Then, line construction was flimsy and it was not unusual for the wire to be broken by high winds. Because only a single line was strung, only one message at a time could be sent or received. Despite these difficulties, the business grew and ultimately many competitors entered the field, precipitating legal actions regarding patent rights that were finally decided in Morse's favor.

The first link to railroads was apparent and grew even stronger as the railroads quickly adopted the telegraph as an invaluable aid to conduct their operations. In 1851, the Erie Railway was the first to employ it for dispatching. In the fall of that year, Superintendent Charles Minot was a passenger on a train that had been halted at a station and directed to wait until an eastbound express had passed. Minot, impatient to continue, detrained and walked to a nearby telegraph office. (The telegraph company was independent of the railroad but, like many at that time, followed the railroad tracks.) Minot directed the telegrapher to wire ahead and, learning that the express had not yet arrived, directed the receiving telegrapher to hold the express train. He then demanded that his engineer run to the next station despite rules to the contrary. The engineer balked at the order and Minot drove the engine himself. Upon arriving at the next station, the express had not yet arrived and Minot repeated the event again.

Before long, other American railroads were using the new technology for train dispatching and, by 1861, the Richmond and Danville Railroad had established a ten person telegraph department. The sharp increase in railroad traffic during the Civil War helped further its acceptance into the everyday operation of railroads (as well as being used for military communication). When block signaling was devised by Ashbel Welch, telegraphy was an integral and essential part of the system. Eventually, the telephone began to supplant the telegraph for general communication, but the latter continued to be used for those messages that required a hard copy at the receiving end until that function, too, was replaced by other devices.

The Railroad Lantern - A Light in the Night

This stamp was issued as part of the Americana series of commemoratives relating to the culture and history of the country. The representation of a railroad conductor's lamp of 1850 (Scott #1612) is one of a group of four stamps depicting various antique lamps. The members of this group were the highest denominated stamps of the entire series and the conductor's lantern, at $5.00, the most expensive of all.

Scott #1612

A railroad lantern is one of the most prosaic pieces of equipment in the railroad inventory yet its value and utility in many circumstances is inestimable. For the want of a lantern, people have died and trains have been wrecked. Again, although its function is obvious, lanterns come in many shapes and sizes, each designed for specific applications. Railroad lanterns comprised a specialized class but even these varied substantially.

According to William Cunningham, the first railroad lantern patent was issued in 1848 with a few others following in subsequent years. After the Civil War though, the flood gates opened and hundreds of lantern patents, covering new shapes and features, were released. One improvement was directed toward a pivoting "bail," or handle, making it more convenient "for the use of railroad conductors." Many involved methods for employing a removable globe, important for cleaning off the carbon residues and accessing some of the interior parts. Lantern guards were specified to protect the fragile glass globes and, in 1865, a hinged lid was featured that simplified globe removal.

The Adams and Westlake Company (A&W) was probably the leading railroad lantern maker in the United States throughout most of the nineteenth century. A&W lanterns were carried by trainmen as an essential piece of equipment when working at night. They frequently were stamped by the manufacturer with the name of the railroad on which they were used.

In the 1890s, lanterns were surprisingly inexpensive measured by today's costs. A&W advertised steel lanterns as cheap as 46 cents! Clear globes were 6 cents each, with colored ones twice or three times as costly. Yet, considering that a trainman might make as little as one dollar a day, the price to him was not trivial. Remarkably, at the same time, brass conductor's lanterns could be had for six and one-half dollars and nickel or silver plating could add several dollars to that price. In 1893, A&W advertised "fancy lanterns" for conductors which could be engraved or otherwise customized as presentation pieces. These could be furnished "as elaborate as may be desired, and to cost almost any amount."

In addition to their use while collecting fares in the "dim, religious light" cast by candles in early passenger cars, lanterns were used for many other routine tasks performed by conductors and brakemen. Signaling motions were standardized so that trainmen could communicate in the dark. An engineer could be directed by a brakeman standing at the last car to release the brakes and proceed. A lantern swung back and forth across the track meant "stop!"

A less routine, but infinitely more important, use for a lantern was to warn the engineer of an oncoming train about a dangerous condition ahead. Lanterns were especially useful in the avoidance of rear end collisions. Such collisions were infrequent and not particularly destructive until the time of the Civil War. Then, traffic increased greatly and, after the war, train speeds increased so that, with the lack of signaling systems and the poor braking systems then in use, the severity of such accidents contributed to more deaths and injuries. When a train broke down or was delayed for any reason, following trains ran the real risk of collision. In such circumstances, a flagman was dispatched from the leading train to walk a reasonable distance back along the track to warn approaching trains of the situation. In most cases, by flag by day or lantern at night, tragedy was averted by this simple precaution. However, there were instances where, despite the taking of adequate precautions, accidents occurred.

Just such a situation occurred in November 1867 when the Cincinnati, Hamilton and Dayton's *New York Lightning Express* was delayed near Lockland, Ohio. The conductor immediately dispatched a flagman down the track to warn the crew of the following train. The engineer of the second train saw the flagman's signals but due to fog and slippery tracks could not stop his train completely. The locomotive of the latter train crashed into a sleeping car of the *Express* and its headlight spilled kerosene that ignited. Five passengers were killed in this accident but the flagman's warning undoubtedly saved many more by slowing the oncoming train. If it had continued at full speed along the fog-shrouded tracks a disaster of monumental proportions might have occurred. Unheralded are those numerous instances where the flagman's lantern prevented a tragedy from occurring. One of these instances in more recent times involved the *Twentieth Century Limited* and is discussed in a later vignette. After a boiler explosion and derailment of cars, wreckage was strewn over all of the main line tracks. One of the survivors, a mail clerk, ran down the track and waved his lantern to halt an approaching freight train from involvement in the accident.

There is one story...a ghost story at that...involving a lantern that was not the cause or prevention of an accident. In the same year that the *Lightning Express* was struck, a conductor named Joe Baldwin, with lantern in hand, attempted to recouple his train at Farmer's Turnout (now Maco), North Carolina. The balky link and pin couplers required him to stand between the cars to effect the coupling. In conducting the operation he was decapitated. From time to time since then, numerous witnesses have claimed to have seen a mysterious light appear along the tracks. Sometimes, a second light was evident and it would approach and meet the first light. The local residents believed that the light was from Baldwin's lantern, visible as he took nocturnal walks along the tracks in search of his head. The light appeared from time to time and several trains were stopped because their engineer had seen the ghostly light. The railroad, the Wilmington, Manchester and Augusta, changed its signaling conventions and had its brakemen use two lanterns, one green and one white, to avoid any confusion with Joe's two white lights. The vision continued and no acceptable explanation has yet been offered that would contradict the tale of Baldwin's ghost.

Union Stations

Scott #1161 portrays Robert A. Taft, senator from Ohio and presidential hopeful. Taft was a lawyer, the son of William Howard Taft (Scott #685), ex-president and Chief Justice of the Supreme Court. Like his father he was devoted to public service and, as an adjunct to his law practice, was involved in numerous corporate problems involving urban affairs. One involved the poor service delivered by the Cincinnati Traction Company. As a mediator between the operator and the city, he succeeded in getting the parties to agree to changes that reduced fares, improved service, and assured dividends to stockholders.

The one notable area concerning railroads in which Robert Taft was involved had to do with the confusion and inconvenience caused by the fact that Cincinnati had five widely separated passenger terminals served by seven railroads. Civic leaders had long pressed for a single terminal but there was no incentive for the individual railroads to go to the expense of consolidating service by building a "union" terminal. To appreciate the seriousness of the problem, one must look back to the early days of railroading.

Scott #1161

The multiplicity of terminals in any city was ultimately wasteful of scarce, expensive land for the structure and its approach tracks and inherently dangerous because there were so many more opportunities for accidents with pedestrians and wagons. For the traveler, it was as though an unbridged river existed that prevented through travel. Probably, the most acute example of redundancy was at Boston. There, between 1834 and 1855, eight different railroads entered the city and each operated out of its own terminal. Four of the depots were concentrated in the "North End" but the others were separated from these. Eventually (by 1900), the terminals at Boston had been consolidated into two large "union" stations. In Chicago, a similar situation existed but, significantly, the twenty railroads entering the city during the nineteenth century shared seven stations. So, early on, the advantages and economies to be obtained by consolidating the passenger facilities of the railroads entering a particular town were recognized.

The distinction of being the first union terminal in the United States belongs to the Romanesque building designed by 22 year old Thomas Tefft and erected in 1848 at Providence, Rhode Island. (A barn-like station built by the Indianapolis Union Railway has been reported to be the first "union depot" in the country but it was built in 1853.) Tefft's station was an architectural masterpiece and 40 years later it still was considered to be one of the twenty most distinguished buildings in the country.

During the ensuing years of the 19th century, other railroads collaborated to build union stations to relieve traffic, noise, accidents, and cost. Yet, by the end of that century, many railroads had never moved to eliminate the problem. Instead, transfer services were established to "transfer railroad passengers and their effects" between terminals (see vignette titled, *"Railroad Station Transfer"*).

But, back to Mr. Taft. In 1923, he was invited to join a group of citizens, headed by George Crabbs, who organized the Cincinnati Railroad Development Company. The objective of this group was to locate a suitable site for a union station and to bring the tracks of the seven local railroads into it. Taft was intimately involved with the undertaking, negotiating with the Interstate Commerce Commission and the appropriate railroad officials. By 1927, agreement was reached and the Cincinnati Union Terminal Company was formed to build a terminal that would accommodate 200 trains per day. Over the next six years an Art Deco building was erected on the west side of the city—the delay occasioned by the difficulty of raising funds during the depression. The same depression caused a precipitous decline in railroad passenger traffic and, except during the World War II years, the station never realized its full potential.

One remarkable feature of the building is the large interior mosaic tile mural that reaches around the circular rotunda. It depicts the development of the country and the Ohio River Valley in particular and the importance of transportation to that development. The mural was an important factor in a drive to rehabilitate and recycle the station, which now operates as a museum center with three distinct museums and an OMNIMAX theater as well as the Amtrak station.

RAILROAD ADOLESCENCE
(1850-1875)

Railroad Land Grants

Scott #1115 was issued to commemorate the hundredth anniversary of the Lincoln-Douglas debates. This stamp was chosen to illustrate this vignette, not because of those debates of 1858 but because the two debaters, Abraham Lincoln and Stephen Douglas, were both intimately involved in the legislative process that resulted in the first federal land grants to a railroad.

The idea of land grants to help finance the construction of railroads originated in the eighteen thirties but was first applied in Illinois. Abraham Lincoln was an influential member of the Illinois legislature and an enthusiastic supporter of a "(Illinois) Central Railroad." In 1837, the state legislature passed the Internal Improvement Act which authorized the construction of over 1300 miles of state-owned railways. The plan was overly ambitious and expensive and support for it collapsed. In 1842, a new proposal was advanced wherein the railroad would be privately owned and, since it would be part of a larger network, federal funds, including land grants, would be sought. In 1848, a bill was introduced by Senator Stephen A. Douglas, another vocal and committed supporter of an Illinois railroad, in the United States senate. Lincoln, by this time a member of the U. S. House of Representatives, attempted but failed to secure passage of Douglas' bill in the lower chamber. Douglas then introduced a new bill, which granted alternate sections of land, six miles wide on each side of the proposed railroad. This legislation was passed by both houses and on Sept. 20, 1850 it was signed by President Millard Fillmore

Scott #1115

(Scott #818), one of the first of his official acts after assuming the presidency two months earlier.

With a precedent established, it was almost a foregone conclusion that land grants would be offered to the builders of the Pacific Railroad. A transcontinental railroad had been discussed since 1832 and many different routes had been suggested. The most vocal promoter, Asa Whitney, asked the Congress "for a grant of the public land, sixty miles wide from Lake Michigan to the (Pacific) Ocean."

Many years were to be spent in generating enthusiasm for the idea, surveying possible routes, and arguing about the route to be taken. Concerns that the new western regions, Oregon in particular, might seek independent status was a positive force in favor of the road but arguments over the route to be followed militated against action. After annexations of Mexican land and the Gadsden Purchase made an extreme southern route possible, southern legislators fought for that line while easterners favored a central, or more northerly, route. The arguments were not resolved until the Civil War saw the resignation of the vociferous southern voices from Congress.

Largely through the efforts of Thomas Hart Benton, the eloquent senator from Missouri, the Pacific Railroad Act was passed by Congress in 1862. Officially labeled "AN ACT To aid in the construction of a railroad and telegraph line from the Missouri River to the Pacific ocean, and to secure to the government the use of the same for postal, military and other purposes," it authorized construction along the mid-section of the country, "from the Missouri River to the navigable waters of the Sacramento River." President Lincoln signed the act into law on July 1, 1862. The companies organized to build it, the Union Pacific and the Central Pacific Railroads, were to be given monetary loans and a four hundred foot wide right of way and areas for other specific railroad use. In addition, alternate sections of land, ten mile wide on either side of the right of way for each mile of track laid, were granted.

Like much legislation of the time, the acts of Congress that granted land to the railroads were poorly written and this fact led to continuing abuses. Thus, by 1871, as a result of corruption and scandal involving the grants and near-illegal financing schemes, land-granting was in disfavor. Some of the public outrage may have been precipitated by largely distorted railroad maps that were distributed by speculators offering lands for sale. For example, John W. Amerman's 1856 book entitled, *The Illinois Central Railroad Company Offers for Sale Over 2,000,000 Acres Selected Farming and Wood Land*, describes the railroad by a heavy black line that exaggerated the actual amount of property that it owned.

One author stated that although 50 roads had received land grants by 1860, he believed that most of these would have been built even if the subsidies had not been provided. Most railroads built after 1872 did so without the benefit of land grants, a situation which some authorities contended produced a better railroad. The result, observed by Folsom in *The Myth of the Robber Barons*, was that "those who got federal aid ended up being hung by the strings that were attached to it." In other words, the aid was dependent upon the number of miles completed, a criterion that encouraged rapid, not high-grade, construction. A resulting road had more numerous and steeper grades, required more maintenance, and suffered more accidents—all elements that ate into the road's profits.

In total, the federal and state governments distributed over 214,000,000 acres to American railroads via land grants. Contrary to general opinion, the land grants proved to be economically sound investments. In exchange for the grants, railroads were required to charge the government preferential rates. This arrangement saved the government over one billion dollars until it ended in 1946. Furthermore, as soon as the railroad was built, the value of the lands that the government had reserved for itself (the alternate sections) increased in value.

Abraham Lincoln: The Most Famous American Railroad Employee

Abraham Lincoln is represented on more than 30 United States stamps which mostly show a bearded Lincoln. However, for the greater part of his life, Lincoln was clean-shaven. After he was nominated for the presidency for the first time (1860), a young girl in Westfield, New York, Grace Bedell, saw his portrait. She commented that she thought Mr. Lincoln would look more handsome with a beard and wrote to him with that suggestion. Lincoln was taken by the girl's candor and obviously agreed with her because he later grew a beard. On the trip to his inauguration, his train passed through Westfield and he had the opportunity to thank Grace personally. Because this section of this book is concerned with Lincoln's railroad associations before he became president, Scott #1113 (a stamp portraying a beardless Lincoln, inspired by a portrait painted from life in 1860 by George Peter Alexander Healy shortly after Lincoln's election to the presidency) was chosen to illustrate it.

Scott #1113

Abraham Lincoln was retained as an attorney by the Illinois Central Railroad from 1851 until 1860, when he was nominated for the presidency of the United States. Among other efforts, he offered opinions on the constitutionality of certain provisions of the Railroad's charter; however, his greatest contribution involved defending the road in the McLean County tax case. Although the railroad's charter provided for payments to the state from earnings in lieu of taxes, county tax collectors adopted the position that the road could be assessed and held liable for county taxes in its operating territory. This was a real threat that, had Lincoln not been successful, would have led to the railroad's insolvency. Lincoln also litigated several "right of way" cases for the Illinois Central, cases that dealt with encroachment, trespass, and property damage.

The first railroad bridge across the Mississippi River extended from Rock Island, Illinois to Davenport, Iowa. Built in 1856, the 1,562 foot long crossing connected the Mississippi and Missouri and the Chicago and Rock Island Railroads. The river divided into two channels separated by an island at that point. The main bridge, comprised of five Howe trusses and a swing draw span, joined the island to the Iowa shore. The eastern channel was spanned by three Howe trusses. The swing drawbridge segment, 286 feet long, was the longest drawbridge in the country at the time. Despite its huge size, it could be "opened or closed by two men in one and a half minutes."

Though it was an ambitious undertaking, most of the problems associated with the bridge's construction were political, rather than technical. Steamboat operators had enjoyed a monopoly regarding river transportation and they strenuously objected to the erection of a bridge that was "unconstitutional, an obstruction to navigation, (and) dangerous." After all of the objections had been overcome, including Jefferson Davis' original refusal to permit a span at that point, construction began.

John B. Jervis, of earlier railroad fame, was hired as a consultant for the project and the bridge was completed in April 1856. Although sound, travelers dreaded the crossing because, in the words of one,

> "The structure has a very unsubstantial appearance, and, as it creaks and sways as the train passes over it, the contingency of an unwelcome descent into the deep and rapid stream beneath is one which flashes over the mind."

Suspension chains, which also provided additional stability, were later added to strengthen the trusses.

Two weeks after its opening, the riverboat *Effie Afton* smashed into a supporting pier and caught on fire; the fire spread and destroyed one of the Howe truss spans. The steamboat's owners, still smarting from having to accept their new competitor, sued the bridge company. Their contention was that unusual and unmanageable currents and eddies were produced around the piers that made ship steering difficult. There were rumors that the collision was intentional but this was never proven. Abraham Lincoln was engaged to defend the bridge company and based his argument on the fact that people and goods had as much right to cross the river as to travel along it. Though the jury could not reach a verdict in the lower court, the Supreme Court eventually heard the case and rendered its verdict in favor of the bridge company.

In 1872, a new iron bridge was built to replace the original bridge and, in 1900, a new steel truss bridge with a 442 foot long swing span superseded the replacement.

Andrew Carnegie: Immigrant, Industrialist, Philanthropist, and Railroad Man

Appropriately, on this stamp (Scott #1171), Andrew Carnegie is shown turning the pages of a book. Although well known as a captain of industry, his everlasting legacy was the scores of libraries established through his generosity. Less well known however, is the fact that his early years involved considerable railroad association in positions ranging from telegrapher to division superintendent of the great Pennsylvania Railroad.

Carnegie immigrated to the United States with his family when he was twelve years old. A year later, along with his father, he was working in a

Scott #1171

nearby textile mill tending the steam engine that powered the plant. Soon thereafter, he took a job as a messenger boy for a local telegraph office. At that time, the code of incoming messages was impressed on paper tape and later translated into handwritten copy. Carnegie learned of a new technique of reading the code directly from the audibly different sounds of the dots and dashes, and it was said that he became the third person in the country to acquire this skill.

His capabilities brought him to the attention of Thomas Scott, the superintendent of the Western Division of the Pennsylvania Railroad. In 1853, not yet 18 years old, he was hired as a telegrapher and later promoted as secretary to Mr. Scott. In that capacity, he gained broad and invaluable experience in railroad operations. A few years later, just one month past his twenty-fifth birthday, Andrew Carnegie was promoted to Scott's old position, superintendent of the Pennsylvania's Western Division. (Scott, meanwhile, had become a vice-president of the road.)

When the Civil War erupted, there was a fear that the seat of the Union's government, Washington, D.C., would be invaded and occupied by Confederate forces. Surrounded by Virginia, a secessionist state and Maryland, with many southern sympathizers, the possibility was real. Scott was recruited by the Secretary of War to keep railroad and telegraphic communication open and his first call was to Carnegie, requesting a force of experienced railroad men to repair and maintain lines into the capital. Carnegie's workers completed the task and he was among the troops that were rushed into Washington to defend the city. During the next few months, he supervised a number of other railroad projects that were essential to the war effort and narrowly escaped capture after the first Battle of Bull Run.

According to Carnegie, he was approached in 1858 by Theodore Woodruff, an early innovator in sleeping car development. Woodruff had invented a unique sleeping compartment that accommodated four passengers. It was rumored that Woodruff conceived the idea after he fell from the top of a freight car. He built a model which was adapted into a full size car by the Wason Car Company. This car was shown to several roads, including the New York Central, which, through rights granted to Webster Wagner, used Woodruff sleepers on its lines. Carnegie brought Woodruff's idea to higher officials of the Pennsylvania Railroad, who made a decision to support the adoption of sleeping cars on the road. This version of the Carnegie-Woodruff relationship was hotly disputed by the latter, who pointed out that he, Woodruff, had already approached the Pennsylvania Railroad management and arranged for them to use his cars.

In any event, whether for his assistance in the adoption of Woodruff cars on the road or because Tom Scott extended the favor, Carnegie paid $217.50 for a one-eighth interest in the Woodruff firm. That small investment returned more than $5,000. per year profit and enabled him to participate in many other enterprises. These later investments in telegraph, iron, oil, and locomotive companies and in banking shares became the foundation of a great fortune, and were the reason for his withdrawal from the Pennsylvania Railroad. Although offered the job of general superintendent, he refused, intending to devote his full time to the management of his personal holdings.

But he was not yet finished with railroading. In 1869, he and George Pullman formed a partnership between the Woodruff and the Pullman companies. The new firm, the Pullman Palace Car Company, soon dominated the sleeping car market. Succeeding ventures in bridge building and iron mills involved railroading peripherally...many dangerous wooden railroad bridges were fire hazards and were inadequate to support the larger and heavier locomotives and the war had caused enormous destruction of railroad property, rails particularly, that required replacement. Carnegie prospered in both undertakings. Another enterprise directly associated with railroading, an axle company, also succeeded.

Incidentally, one enterprise which Andrew Carnegie misjudged completely was a by-product of his investment in the Columbia Oil Company, a participant in the Oil Creek field (see "*Moving Liquid Gold*," a vignette in this book). Carnegie and his associates were convinced that the oil field would be depleted quickly by the gushers that were pumping oil at a furious rate. They believed that if they could store a large amount of oil it would become extremely valuable when the field petered out. Accordingly, they had a huge, unlined hole dug, sufficient to hold one hundred thousand barrels of crude. Seepage loss was replenished by added oil. The field did not play out and the seepage of oil was greater than anticipated so the scheme was abandoned.

Later, Thomas Scott prevailed upon his protégé to travel to Europe to sell railroad bonds. While he was in Europe, Carnegie realized the potential of steel as a replacement for iron and, upon his return to the United States, he determined to launch a steel making company. This latest venture also proved to be the most profitable and secured for him a prominent place in the histories of this country's great industrialists. The Panic of 1873 presented him with serious financial problems. He was compelled to sell his Pullman stock to cover the continued construction of his steel works but regretfully, his greatest loss may have been the friendship of his long-time mentor and friend. When Scott asked him to guarantee loans that he had negotiated to build the Texas and Pacific Railroad, Carnegie, short himself, refused.

Andrew Carnegie, who believed that a rich man should distribute his wealth during his lifetime, practiced what he preached. He donated money to hospitals, universities and municipal projects but was to be remembered best for his establishment of libraries. As a young boy he had taken advantage of Colonel James Anderson's offer to lend books from his personal library to any working boy and, in his own words, decided that "if ever wealth came to me, it should be used to establish free libraries." In his lifetime he built 2,811 free public libraries worldwide and every state in this country, with the exception of Rhode Island, had at least one Carnegie library.

Within the "Range of Our Sure and Easy Guardianship"

Scott #1028 commemorates the hundredth anniversary of the Gadsden purchase from Mexico, an acquisition ratified by the Senate in 1854. The large (45,535 square miles) triangle of land lay south of the Gila River and was annexed to the Arizona and New Mexico territories. It was the last addition to the contiguous continental United States. The stamp shows a pioneer group in a covered wagon pulled by oxen passing through the desert and surrounded by cactus plants; an outrider is nearby. A map of the acquired area is also provided on the stamp.

References to the Gadsden purchase were made in two other vignettes in this book concerning land grants and the transcontinental railroad. The context of these references involved the fact that although a southern route for a Pacific railroad was one of those considered, some of the land on that route was within the borders of Mexico. (The thought of building a transcontinental railroad across a narrow neck of Mexico had been advanced since mid-century. Mexico had granted concessions to Americans to build a railroad across the Isthmus of Tehuantepec at the southern end of the country as early as 1849 and Cora Montgomery, in an article published in *The Merchants Magazine and Commercial Review*, declared that building at that location was within "range of our sure and easy guardianship.")

Scott #1028

Coincident with arguments about Pacific railroad location was Mexico's annoyance that the United States had not protected it against border incursions by American Indians as required by a provision of the treaty of Guadalupe Hidalgo that ended the Mexican War. Thus, instructed by President Franklin Pierce (Scott #819), James Gadsden, his minister to Mexico, negotiated the purchase of a tract of land in northern Mexico in 1853. This parcel was seen as the solution to (or at least a way to ameliorate) both problems. Now, the border was moved further south and an all-American southern railroad route became possible. (Gadsden was a fortuitous choice to deal with the Mexicans because he had long been a promoter of railroads that would serve Southern interests. He was a past president of the Louisville, Cincinnati and Charleston Railroad and had advocated a Pacific railroad controlled by the South at various commercial conventions.)

In the same year that the Gadsden Purchase was negotiated, the U. S. Congress funded a survey of western areas, north, central, and south to determine the best route for a railroad. Jefferson Davis (Scott# 2975f) was Secretary of War in the Pierce Administration and because the survey was to be conducted by military engineers, it fell to Davis to implement the legislation. Five route alternatives within the three regions were investigated. When the results were made known, Davis recommended that the southern route be chosen. His reasoning was questioned by critics who suggested that, being a Southerner, he naturally favored a southern route. Yet, it is just as likely that he was supporting the Army's position that a railroad would settle the area near the Mexican border and, over time, would reduce their encounters with Apache and Comanche Indians. Most probably, he saw the southern alignment as more favorable because of climate, fewer grades, least expense, and shorter length. In the end, a Congressional committee recommended that the road be built over the northern or central routes (which were favored by easterners).

Although a majority in Congress was always in favor of constructing the transcontinental railroad, the continuing disagreement over the route made it impossible to begin planning or constructing it. Finally, when the Southern representatives withdrew from Congress at the commencement of the Civil War, a consensus was reached and a bill was enacted authorizing construction along the central route. Yet, Gadsden's acquisition proved to be invaluable when the southern route was developed by the Southern Pacific Railroad as its Texas-to-California "Sunset Route" which opened in 1883.

Spanning the Niagara Gorge

The stamp depicting the Niagara railroad suspension bridge (Scott #961) was copied from a print by H. Peters and first placed on sale at Niagara Falls, New York. The bridge was completed in 1855 but the idea of a bridge across the deep chasm of the Niagara River originated much earlier when Major Charles B. Stuart suggested a "hanging bridge" at that location. Stuart's suggestion languished until 1845 when a bridge company was established to erect it. A flamboyant engineer, Charles Ellet, who was also a pioneer in long suspension bridge construction, was chosen to design and build the Niagara bridge.

Ellet intended to fire the first line across the gorge via rocket but, instead, sponsored a kite flying contest among local boys to make the initial connection. This was done by Homan Walsh and from his first light kite string successively stronger lines were pulled over, culminating in a strong iron cable. Ellet attached a basket to the cable and drew himself across the span. A temporary, eight foot wide, span was finished in 1848 and, true to form, Ellet rode a horse across the narrow way. Theatrics aside, the bridge directors became dissatisfied with progress of the project and a dispute regarding the authority to collect fares ensued. They sacked Ellet and, in 1851, asked John Roebling to assume direction of the construction. Roebling had pioneered the development of wire rope, a product that was made by twisting small diameter wires together into a small diameter cable and then twisting many such cables together into a strong, large diameter cable. Wire rope was ideal for the main supporting cables of a suspension bridge.

Scott #961

Roebling's bridge, over 820 feet long between towers, was begun in 1851 and took four years to complete. It had a double floor, separated by wooden trusses eighteen feet high, which carried rail traffic above and road traffic below. Although the truss structure added considerable stiffness to the bridge, Roebling ran diagonal stays from the tower tops to the roadway to increase its strength. Such stays were a trademark of Roebling's suspension bridges (see Roebling's classic, the Brooklyn Bridge, depicted on Scott #2041 and discussed later).

The first locomotive was driven across the span in March 1855 and the first train, weighing about 120 tons, used it on March 14th. The roadway below had been finished a year earlier. Except for some vibrations, the bridge was more than adequate for the load. At a later time, Mark Twain, (Scott #863) would write in a short story, *A Day at Niagara*,

> "Then you drive over to Suspension Bridge, and divide your misery between the chances of smashing down two hundred feet into the river below, and the chances of having the railway-train overhead smashing down onto you."

Train speed was limited to five miles per hour and later lowered to three miles per hour. Because suspension bridges were seriously affected by vibratory forces, the bridge directors banned movements that involved a regular cadence. Travelers using the lower deck could be fined for marching over the bridge in regular step. Marching musical bands and trotting horses were not allowed.

John Roebling understood that the bridge's "weight, girders, trusses, and stays" were important and that each element contributed to its stability. Regrettably, some later bridge designers "forgot" how to stiffen a suspension bridge properly. A notable example was "Galloping Gertie," a highway suspension bridge across Tacoma Narrows in the state of Washington, which collapsed in 1940 as a result of wind loads that set up ever-increasing vibrations.

Scott #297

By 1880, trains had become so much heavier that iron and steel were substituted for the wooden trusses. The wire rope cables had been thoroughly inspected a few years earlier and found to retain their original strength. In 1886, the stone towers of the bridge were replaced by steel towers to extend the bridge's life but by the mid-1890s, the capability of the bridge to support the immense weight of trains was questioned and before the end of the decade, the Niagara suspension bridge had been supplanted by the Grand Trunk Railway's Niagara Railway Arch Bridge.

The latter bridge was also represented on a stamp (Scott # 297) issued in 1901. The scene shows streetcars on the upper deck of the bridge. Work was begun on this structure, designed as a graceful arch bridge, in September 1896. It was built exactly on the site of Roebling's bridge and took shape from each side of the gorge, using the stone towers of the earlier bridge to carry cables that supported the ends of the arch during construction. The arch of the new bridge was built under and around the decks of the old bridge. In this way, traffic continued to cross the original bridge without interruption, halting only while sections of the railway track were replaced, their support transferred from old to new bridge. Parts of the old bridge were carefully removed with the intent to use them elsewhere but this plan was not fulfilled. The new, double deck bridge was officially opened in September 1897. On January 26, 1938 the arch bridge was closed because a massive ice jam had lodged against its abutments. Two days later, the ice pushed the bridge off its abutments and it fell into the gorge.

Johns Hopkins: Savior of the Baltimore and Ohio Railroad

Johns Hopkins, portrayed on Scott #2194, a $1.00 stamp issued in 1986, was primarily noted as a merchant and philanthropist. Less known was his association with the Baltimore and Ohio Railroad as a promoter, financier, and director.

Johns Hopkins was born into a Quaker family in 1795. When he was twelve years old his family, following the position taken by the Society of Friends, freed their slaves. This changed the young boy's life: where before his major responsibility had been caretaker for his younger siblings, now he was required to contribute various manual tasks on the plantation. That need cut his formal education short although he did continue his studies at home. Recognizing his

Scott #2194   *©USPS 1989*

business abilities at the age of seventeen, his uncle asked that he come to work with him in a wholesale grocery business at Baltimore. After seven years with his uncle's firm, Hopkins opened his own business, well-capitalized by his uncle and others. Thanks to his ability to understand men and a keen business sense, the business prospered substantially and Hopkins became one of the wealthiest citizens of Baltimore.

Unsurprisingly, he was an early investor in the Baltimore and Ohio Railroad. As a merchant in Baltimore, he dispatched Conestoga wagons laden with goods locally and across the Alleghenies to the new states beyond. Thus, he was quick to foresee lower shipping costs and faster deliveries that a railroad could offer. He invested in the fledgling company to the extent that he shortly became, after the state and city, the company's largest stockholder. His control of 15 to 17,000 shares led to appointment to director in 1847. In 1855, he became Chairman of the

Finance Committee, a powerful position that gave him much leverage within the company.

The B&O came upon hard times during the Panics (recessions) of 1857 and 1873. For example, a new passenger and freight station in downtown Baltimore was recognized as a critical need to serve the B&O's increasing business in the 1850s. Work was begun on a magnificent three-story brick structure, the Camden station, in 1856. Although it was in use the following year, the Panic of 1857 (and the Civil War) affected its completion. Not until eight years later, toward the end of the War, was the station completed as planned.

During the difficult days of the first panic (1857), Hopkins was appointed to a special committee that was established to examine the company's financial accounts. He and John Garrett supported an arrangement to pay a dividend on the stock, an action that precipitated legal action by the City of Baltimore and the State of Maryland, large holders of B&O stock. The governmental entities were concerned for the financial health of the depleted treasury. But it was Hopkins who stepped forward and pledged his private fortune in the amount of about one million dollars to maintain the road's credit standing. A contemporary spoke of, "the material assistance he granted to the Baltimore and Ohio Railroad in the hours of darkness which shrouded that corporation prior to 1857." In 1873, through his individual efforts he again protected the road and the City of Baltimore from the financial turbulence that was disastrous at Philadelphia and New York.

Maryland, a border state during the Civil War, had numerous Southern sympathizers, some of whom sat on the B&O's Board of Directors. Hopkins worked with John Garrett, then president of the road, to counter the sympathizer's proposals and to put the railroad at the disposal of the Union. Because the B&O was in the area of military operations for much of the war, it suffered serious losses of engines and other property and required exceptional determination to maintain some degree of normalcy in moving men and supplies. Yet its cooperation with the Union forces proved invaluable and speeded victory. Johns Hopkins deserves much credit for establishing this cooperative posture.

A resolution drafted by the Mayor and City Council of Baltimore in 1873, the year of his death, expressed their thanks that, "Johns Hopkins has nobly contributed to the future welfare and happiness of our people and should receive every evidence of public appreciation and gratitude."

Johns Hopkins had contracted cholera when he was younger and, at a later time, witnessed another cholera epidemic in the city of Baltimore. This experience, particularly seeing poor victims without recourse to medical assistance, convinced him of the need for a hospital (a vision that expanded to include a college) that would accept all needy individuals. His generosity resulted in two great institutions that prospered and, to this day, rank among the best...The Johns Hopkins University and The Johns Hopkins Hospital. Alas, a third great institution that was also a recipient of his sagacity and munificence, the Baltimore and Ohio Railroad, has lost its identity in a latter day consolidation with other regional railroads.

Palaces on Wheels

A. Philip Randolph, who was instrumental in the founding of the Brotherhood of Sleeping Car Porters, is shown on Scott #2402. Scott #Q9 depicts passenger and freight cars at the Pullman Manufacturing Company plant at Chicago, Illinois. Together they represent the development of the sleeping car and its operation in this country.

In 1819, even before uncomfortable railroad coaches were available, Benjamin Dearborn suggested the concept of sleeping cars. When the first railroads did appear, trips were short, rarely requiring overnight travel. But before long, the need for sleeping accommodations became obvious. The first sleeping car was placed into service between Chambersburg and Philadelphia by the Cumberland Valley Railroad around 1837. This car was divided into four compartments, with the two center ones fitted with three padded shelves on each side of the car. Within ten years, sleeping cars were in use by at least eight railroads in the United States.

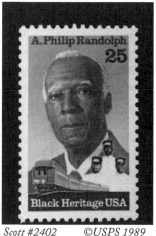

Scott #2402   *©USPS 1989*

In 1854, Theodore Woodruff invented a sleeping compartment that provided private quarters for four people. His demonstration car was well-received and eventually sold to the Ohio and Mississippi Railroad. Woodruff went on to establish a company that provided sleepers to several roads. Other names have also been mentioned in connection with early sleeping cars but the individual who became best known in the sleeping car industry was George M. Pullman. A cabinet maker, Pullman was involved in several other enterprises before he exhibited an interest in the sleeping car business. When he did, he entered into a contract with the Chicago and Alton Railroad to convert two of their day coaches to sleeping cars. Pullman and Leonard Siebert, his assistant, arranged the cars into ten sleeping sections. Each section had an upper and lower berth. Pullman's car was first operated between Bloomington, Illinois and Chicago in September 1859.

Scott #Q9

Before this car was placed on the rails, passengers had to make up their own beds. George Pullman, however, believed that trained employees should cater to their clients needs and hired J. L. Barnes for that task. This was an inspired concept because it accelerated the use of sleeping cars by women, children, and invalids. Cleanliness was another important factor in Pullman's success.

The early Pullman cars were rude and elementary so he undertook the effort to build better and more finely appointed ones. One of these, the *Pioneer*, was substantially better. Its drawback was that was too wide for use on standard gauge railroads. When President Lincoln was assassinated, the Chicago and Alton was asked to carry the family in the *Pioneer* on the last leg of the funeral journey from Chicago to Lincoln's resting place in Springfield, Illinois. The road immediately made the necessary changes to the right of way to allow the car to pass.

Pullman went on to expand his presence in the sleeping car field through mergers and acquisition. By 1872, over 500 "palace" cars were operating nationwide and Pullman's factory was producing three per week. Twenty years later the Pullman Company controlled 2,239 cars.

George Pullman was a paternalistic individual who was concerned about the welfare of his employees and when he consolidated his manufacturing facilities near Chicago he decided to establish a planned community. Pullman, Illinois had homes for employees, stores, and theaters and was intended to be "aesthetically ennobling." Yet, some critics felt that he treated most of his employees poorly. Hubbard wrote, "Some 12,000 of them lived in slums on the fringe of his model city...(whose)...civic center was a handsome showplace occupied mostly by company officials, while many of the workers' wooden shacks did not have running water or individual toilets." Pullman died in 1897 but his company prospered and became the predominant sleeping car operator in the United States.

After World War One, the Pullman Company strongly resisted the efforts of union organizers to organize its operation and, to forestall them, the company created a company union which it could control. One outcome was that A. Philip Randolph became an important labor leader, a distinction that was thrust upon him by the porters who wanted an independent union. Randolph was chosen because he had a record of championing African-American rights, was an excellent orator, and because he was not a porter and thus, immune from Pullman vengeance. Established in 1925, the Brotherhood of Sleeping Car Porters clashed with the company for over a decade. In 1937, aided by legislation sympathetic to unions and affiliation with the American Federation of Labor, the Brotherhood negotiated a contract with the Pullman Company and Randolph was recognized as one of the first black labor leaders in the United States. He went on to become a notable pioneer in the burgeoning civil rights movement of the 1940s and 1950s.

Carrying Cows

The dominant feature of Scott #1328 is a Hereford steer, an icon of the west. This stamp offers an opportunity to discuss the transport of cattle by the railroads.

Long before specialized stock cars were devised, cows (and other livestock) were carried in open burthen cars. In the 1830s, the Baltimore and Ohio Railroad owned many of these, some of which were partitioned into separate stalls. The open cars presented a formidable challenge to a brakeman, who had to climb through the animals to pass from car to car. Closed cars then came into use and ventilation was achieved by simply cutting holes in the roof. A little later (1850s), cows (and other livestock) were carried in so called "combination cars," which were really box cars with features that allowed ventilation. The application of such cars yielded a high utilization factor because they could be used for bulk commodities such as grain, general merchandise, fruit shipments or cattle.

Scott #1328

Around the late 1850s and early 1860s, stock cars of a more recognizable design, with slatted sides and interior fittings for feeding animals, began to appear. Lee Swearingen was awarded the first patent for an improved stock car in 1860. However, these cars still fell short of what was needed for safe and humane livestock shipment. Animals were not watered enroute and it was not uncommon for many to die. In one instance, an observer noted a cattle shipment where,

> "...there were some dead, others in a dying state...Some were prostrate under the feet of the rest...The causes...was (sic) obvious. The weather was intensely hot...the cattle crowded together...and not having been allowed to drink...were dying of thirst."

To avoid this situation, a shipper occasionally had an employee ride the cars and provide food and water to the animals. Yet, in general, stock transport by rail continued to be inhumane and losses were relatively high (some 10% died during passage).

The United States Congress addressed the problem and, in 1873, passed legislation that prohibited livestock confinement to cars for more than 28 hours before being removed and watered. Many inventors also applied their talents to the problem, with some seeking to win a $5,000 prize offered by the American Humane Association for the best design. What was really needed, though, were feeding and watering appliances built as features on the car. Such devices eventually were added to basic stock cars and in the 1870s, the "Palace" stock car appeared. The name was copied from Palace Pullman cars and implied superior accommodations.

The mid-1870s saw the further development and application of the "Palace" stock car, although the reluctance of railway officials "to carry cattle in palace cars, packed in as loosely as hyenas and tigers in a traveling menagerie, while a rival road, by prodding and tail twisting, carries twice as many in the same number of cars of the common kind" took some time to overcome. Yet, before the end of the nineteenth century, builders were manufacturing stock cars that met the demands of the loudest critics of inhumane animal care.

Stonewall" Jackson Deceives the B&O Railroad - True or False?

Scott #2975s   ©1995 USPS

A good part of the territory in which the Baltimore and Ohio Railroad operated lay in the path of the warring armies during the Civil War. Consequently, it was the object of many destructive forays but one of the most audacious ones was exemplified by Colonel T. J. "Stonewall" Jackson (Scott #2975s), devised and conducted while he was in command at Harpers Ferry in May 1861. According to the story, Jackson occupied a sector through which heavy B&O traffic passed, day and night. Jackson complained to the management of the railroad of the disruption to his operations and insisted that train movement in his sector be limited to two hours each day. When the railroad complied, Jackson blockaded the tracks at Point of Rocks, Maryland and at Martinsburg, Virginia, trapping the many trains that were between those two points. He could not move the locomotives south because track and bridges could not carry the heavy "camel" locomotives and part of the route was incomplete. Jackson destroyed most of the engines and all of the rolling stock—mostly loaded coal cars that burned for weeks afterward. He did attempt to move some of the locomotives, hauled by horses and men, and some of them did reach the Manassas Gap Railroad.

James Robertson, a recent Jackson biographer, branded the tale a myth. He contended that Jackson "had no orders to disrupt the B&O completely" because the Confederate hierarchy would not have countenanced such a raid while they were still courting Maryland, trying to bring the state into the Southern fold. He was also firm in his opinion that the B&O management would not have been duped by such a pretext and would not have allowed trains to run on excessively tight headways. Robertson attributed the fabrication of the story to Captain John Imboden and its propagation to Jackson's biographer, G. F. R. Henderson, and then to numerous other historians and writers. Farwell, in his book *Stonewall*, reinforced Robertson's assertions by stating that Jackson never reported this incident to Lee and that it was promulgated by no one other than Imboden. It could be that the tale was built on the account of the action at Martinsburg a few weeks later that is described below.

On June 20, 1861, Jackson's troops entered Martinsburg, Virginia where, following orders, Jackson had the railroad's yards and buildings destroyed. Fifty-six locomotives and over three hundred coal cars were burned or otherwise ruined, some being pushed into the Opequon River. Reflecting on what to him was a waste, Jackson called upon railroad engineers to develop a plan to move some of the least damaged engines to the tracks of the Manassas Gap Railroad. Thirteen (or fourteen) engines were chosen, disassembled, then transported by forty-horse teams to Strasburg, from whence they were moved to Richmond. At Richmond, the machines were reassembled and put to use by Southern railroads that were in need of motive power. In this recounting of the story, there is no mention of Jackson's deception and trapping of locomotives along the line but many other facts coincide.

On the other hand, Henderson's account of the trapping incident, in the form of a narration by Imboden, who related that he took part in the operation, is minutely detailed, down to the identity of the troops sent to Martinsburg and the specific times of day that the trains were permitted to roll. Henderson concurred with Robertson that the Confederacy would not have countenanced destruction of the rail line at that time in the war but contended that Jackson, on his own authority, decided to capture the rolling stock. Destruction of the coal cars was a legitimate act of war against the government in Washington, which was accumulating supplies of that commodity on the seaboard. Imboden recounted that Jackson first made a request to limit all east bound trains only. He then waited "several days" and made a further request to limit west bound traffic also before he sprang his trap. This detail, that is, the embellishment of a hiatus in Jackson's orders, adds some authenticity to the Henderson/Imboden account.

Finally, Hungerford, an authority on the Baltimore and Ohio Railroad, contended that Jackson did indeed capture four small locomotives from Harpers Ferry and moved them overland, using the ruse described above. That author goes on to state, "Jackson undoubtedly would have repeated it (the stratagem), had it not been that Harpers Ferry was beginning to be untenable for him." Hungerford then describes Jackson's actions at Martinsburg and the movement of further locomotives to the tracks of the Manassas Gap Railroad.

The reader should be aware that the accounts mentioned above were derived from secondary sources. Unfortunately, the best available primary sources, such as the B&O Railroad Directors' Minute Books, the B&O Annual Reports, and Official Records of the Union and Confederate Armies do not substantiate either version.

That the road was closed in May 1861 is a fact confirmed by accounts in the B&O's Annual Report to the Board and Stockholders. (This report was not published until October 1, 1863.) In it President Garrett states that "On May 28, 1861, general possession was taken by the Confederate forces of more than one hundred miles of the Main Stem, embracing chiefly the region between the Point of Rocks and Cumberland." John L. Wilson, the Master of the Road, stated that trains continued to run until May 25, 1861 when the tracks at Point of Rocks were closed. No mention was made in these statements about captured locomotives. But Thatcher Perkins, the Master of Machinery, did affirm that 14 locomotive and tenders were taken and transported South during the 1861 fiscal year.

The Great Locomotive Chase

The *General*, depicted on Scott #2843, was one of the most famous of all American locomotives. Its story is at once the most thrilling and, probably, the best known railroad war story. Headlined by the *Southern Confederacy* newspaper as "The Great Locomotive Chase," the account received country-wide attention and became the subject of countless articles, books, and a motion picture starring Buster Keaton.

James Andrews, a Union spy, along with 21 soldiers, was charged with infiltrating Confederate lines, seizing a train, and proceeding north toward Tennessee, burning bridges and creating havoc behind them. This objective was to support a Union army advance on Chattanooga by denying the railroad to Confederate reinforcements.

Scott #2843   ©1994 USPS

Early on April 12, 1862, a Western and Atlantic (W&A) Railroad train, drawn by the locomotive *General* arrived at Big Shanty, Georgia, for a twenty minute breakfast stop. Passengers and crew retired to the lunchroom, leaving the train unoccupied. Andrews and his men, loitering nearby, immediately boarded the train and drove it away. W. A. Fuller, the conductor of the stolen train, along with the train's engineer and a shop manager took off in pursuit on foot! Two miles down the line, the chase party came upon a work crew with a hand car. Commandeering the hand car, Fuller's group continued the pursuit and eventually they reached Etowah Station where they found the locomotive *Yonah* under steam. Recruiting armed volunteers, Fuller again took chase with the Yonah.

Farther along, they found the track blocked by several trains and another locomotive. Anxious to continue the pursuit, Fuller chose to follow on the engine *Shorter*, a less capable machine than the *Yonah* and the distance between pursued and pursuer increased. Furthermore, they encountered missing rails, torn up by Andrews to hinder pursuit, and Fuller was compelled to take to his feet again. Soon he came upon the locomotive *Texas* and he persuaded its engineer to follow the *General*. Running the train backwards, Fuller guided the engineer by hand signals from the first car until they came to a switch where they could detach the cars from the train.

With his band augmented at the next station, Fuller's engineer drove the *Texas* recklessly. Approaching a curve,they saw that an inside rail was missing! Reasoning that the engine would bear upon the outside rail of the curve, Fuller called for more speed and the *Texas* passed through the curve safely. (Some accounts of the chase do not mention this incident, others state that the rail was loosened but not removed, and Abdill attributes the happening to an entirely different episode, which occurred on the Baltimore and Ohio Railroad near Harper's Ferry. However, the missing rail rendition was recounted by William Pittenger, one of the Union participants in the action. Pittenger claimed that he had helped to remove and lift the rail onto their train and thus accepted Fuller's version that the *Texas* passed over a missing inside rail.)

Although Andrews made further attempts to delay his pursuers, he eventually ran out of wood at Ringgold, Georgia, only 15 miles from Chattanooga, but 86 miles and 8 hours since the chase began. The raiders took to the woods but all were captured. Andrews and seven of the group were executed, eight escaped from prison camp, and six were exchanged. The Union survivors became the first recipients of the Congressional Medal of Honor (Scott #2045). Ironically, the eight executed soldiers did not receive medals.

As for Fuller, a member of Andrew's party praised him later saying,

> "...his energy, skill, and daring shine in such brilliant colors...With a conductor of less energy in the place of this man, the probabilities are that we would have had the whole day uninterruptedly for the accomplishment of our task."

Fuller received the thanks of the Georgia Legislature for his actions that day. That assembly also voted to present him with a gold medal but, as he remarked later, "Gold was so scarce in the South that it was hard to find enough for a medal...I got nothing."

After its recapture, the *General* continued to work on southern rails and in 1864 helped move Confederate supplies and wounded at the Battle of Kennesaw Mountain. Damaged during the retreat from Atlanta, the engine was rebuilt in the W&A shops where it was converted to a coal burner.

As a postscript to this story, the engine was stolen once more a century later. Its owner, the Louisville and Nashville Railroad, displayed the engine at Union Station in Chattanooga. In 1961, they planned to exhibit it nationwide on a tour commemorating the hundredth anniversary of the great chase. Because some residents of Chattanooga protested its removal, the railroad arranged to cut the station fence one night and took the engine. This action was the cause of a three year court battle that ended at the United States Supreme Court. The judgment of that court was to uphold the railroad's ownership of the engine.

The *General*, designed by William Hudson and built by Rogers, Ketchum and Grosvenor in 1855 for the Western and Atlantic Railroad, was a 4-4-0 engine weighing a little over 25 tons. This unremarkable machine, much like scores of other 4-4-0 locomotives in the country (see vignette titled " '*American' Type Locomotive: Queen of the Rails*"), became famous because of its part in this drama.

The *Texas* was of the same approximate size and power. Although the *Texas*, constructed by a different Paterson, New Jersey builder, Danforth, Cooke and Company, was but one of the locomotives used by Mr. Fuller to run down the *General*, the others are rarely mentioned. It was a good steamer and probably deserved its prominence because the tale might have ended differently if it had not been used. Yet, the success of the chase was due less to the capabilities of the various pursuing engines than to the tribulations attending Southern railroads—heavy traffic on single tracks and late trains—and the stubbornness and resourcefulness of W. A. Fuller, the conductor of the captured train.

Both the *Texas* and the *General* have been restored and are now exhibited in Georgia.

Emigrants to the West

Two stamps that include trains are Scott #1669, which was issued as one of the Bicentennial issue of state flags, and Scott #1506, which recognized rural America. The former shows the great seal of the state of Nebraska, which includes a train hauled by a steam locomotive traveling westward through mountains, and the latter shows a prairie covered with winter wheat. Numerous other stamps celebrate the anniversary of statehood or territorial status of other midwestern and western areas that saw a large influx of immigrants, many of whom came by rail. Two in particular (Scott # 1060 and #2403, not shown) celebrated the hundredth anniversary of the Nebraska Territory and North Dakota statehood. These two stamps depicted "The Sower" and a grain elevator, respectively. The agricultural themes were representative of these states and the principal attraction for immigrants that came to settle there. The railroad brought them.

Scott #1669

Settlers were moving west in fairly large numbers before 1850, but the passage of the Homestead Act (Scott #1198) in 1862 accelerated that movement by distributing public lands to those who would work it. Coincident with that legislation, or even somewhat before it was enacted, railroads were encouraging immigration (into the country and then settlement in western states). To carry these individuals and families, special cars were placed into operation. Known as "emigrant cars," (denoting their use for emigrants from Europe or the eastern states) these vehicles were generally less comfortable or well-appointed than the road's regular rolling stock. On the Western Railroad in Massachusetts, emigrants were carried in ordinary freight cars but the first emigrant cars were built for the Utica and Schenectady Railroad in 1836 which saw them as inexpensive passenger cars.

Around 1855, two roads, the Illinois Central and the Michigan Central, realized they had substantial emigrant traffic to western farmlands. At the same time, their railroads were bringing grain and other agricultural products in an eastbound direction. Obviously, to use passenger cars for the former and freight cars for the latter would mean that each would make the return trips empty. To achieve high car loadings, they fitted their grain cars, which were essentially box cars with additional ventilation, with removable seats for the westbound trip. These accommodations were spartan but not inhuman despite one writer's opinion. That author railed against the "callous" treatment of emigrant passengers who were given "neither heat, water, food or sleeping accommodation" en route. However primitive and uncomfortable, they were not much worse than ordinary coaches and, in fact, were superior in some ways. Most emigrant cars were equipped with stoves; their occupants carried their own food (cook stoves were never available to the ordinary passengers). Then too, sleeping cars were unknown before the 1860s and, even then and later, were used by only a minority of the traveling public.

Scott #1506

Robert Louis Stevenson, who traveled on an emigrant train when he was in this country saw the emigrant car as a "flat-roofed Noah's Ark" on wheels and noted that

> "Equality, though very largely conceived in America, does not extend so low down as the emigrant."

Emigrant cars acquired the nickname "Zulu cars," a disparaging term whose roots were in England where, after the British had defeated the African Zulu tribes, they hired some of the native warriors to make an exhibition tour of England by rail.

Yet not all emigrant cars were rude and uncomfortable. The Central Pacific Railroad built emigrant cars with upper and lower berths that were similar to, but not as well finished, as their first class sleepers. In the west, "families and unmarried women were assigned one car, single men to a second and Chinese to a third." One article stated that emigrants on the "Pacific railroads" were "carried on the express freight train, and make the trip in less than ten days." Often, however, their car was included in a freight train making for a longer trip, mitigated only by the camaraderie of the group and the anticipation of reaching the rich farmlands ahead.

Special emigrant accommodations continued into the twentieth century as disclosed by a photo of a New York Central car built in 1901, essentially a box car with passenger car trucks, that was lettered "Emigrant Baggage Car."

Scott #1198

The Little Red Caboose

The Random House and the Oxford English Dictionaries etymologize the word "caboose" and establish that it originally referred to a kitchen on the deck of a ship. A number of foreign words...the Dutch *kabuis*, the Swedish *kabysa*, and the German or Greek *kabuse*...meaning "little room or hut," support this definition. Many slang expressions for cabooses have found their way into railroading lingo, some affectionate, some disparaging; two common ones are "crummy" and "hack." Scott #1905 pictures a lumber company's caboose number 5.

In the 1840s the Auburn and Syracuse Railroad employed a box car to carry tools and supplies that could be used by the train's conductor. Soon thereafter, makeshift cabooses, some constructed by erecting a shed or shanty on a flat car, were built by train crews. More common though were box car conversions into which windows and doors were cut and bunks and cookstoves installed. None of these had the most recognizable feature of a caboose—the cupola.

Scott #1905 ©*1984 USPS*

There are two different origins of the addition of cupolas to freight cars. One tale attributes the cupola to employees of the New York and Erie Railway at mid-century. Trackside at Suffern, New York, telegraph line workers were operating out of a box car. One of these men built a belfry-like addition with windows through the roof above the car. Although not a caboose per se, this cupola provided a 360 degree observation field around the car.

The second story is more interesting and probably is the first instance of a cupola on a car that was being used as a caboose. In the 1860s, T. B. Watson, a conductor on the Chicago and Northwestern Railway, was using a box car with a damaged roof while on a run in Iowa. In this car he piled a number of boxes upon each other and sat atop them. From his perch, his head projected through the hole in the roof from whence he could see his train and the surroundings. This scheme worked so well that his idea was applied to two conductor's cars that were being built by the road.

A famous caboose, probably the most famous, is the one in which the Brotherhood of Railroad Trainmen was organized in 1883. This car is preserved at Oneonta, New York, where the organizational meeting of the union was held by employees of the Delaware and Hudson Railroad.

The location of the cupola along the length of the car was variable. Some car builders preferred it to be located at the center but all locations, from center to extreme end, have been used. Many cabooses had a "possum belly," a locker below the car for tools and supplies that might be needed by the crew. Crews sometimes carried scrap iron in the caboose to increase its weight; a heavier car rode better and its brakes worked more effectively. Brake handles could be found at either end of the car and occasionally in the cupola. Many times, it was possible to stop an entire train using the interior brake alone.

Although the original concept of a caboose was to serve the conductor only as an office and shelter during a trip, that purpose was enlarged to include the entire crew (except the engineer and fireman). Some cabooses accommodated four or five men for an entire week; they prepared meals and slept in the car. Frequently, on a railroad that had little passenger traffic, the caboose was used as an "accommodation car" to carry paying passengers.

Many poems and stories have been written about the little red caboose such as,

"Oh, the brake wheel's old and rusty, the shoes are thin and worn,
And she's loaded down with link and pin and chain,
And there's danger all around us as we try to pound our ear
In the little red caboose behind the train."

Yet, such lines to the contrary, not all cabooses were painted red. Some assumed the livery of the railroad, others used bright, reflective colors that reduced the temperature within. But, although cabooses have virtually disappeared from usage, they have a place in the heart of railroaders and are remembered fondly by them.

Mail by Rail

As might be expected, the postal service memorialized its long association with railroads on numerous stamps. Mail was carried on the earliest railroad trains; the South Carolina and the Camden and Amboy Railroads transported mail in the early 1830s. Generally, mail on these roads was handled in the same manner as other freight. The Baltimore and Ohio Railroad, on the other hand, operated a dedicated mail car between Baltimore and Washington before the mid-1830s.

Scott #C66

In 1838, the Philadelphia, Wilmington and Baltimore Railroad prepared a "travelling post office," a mail car that closely resembled later Railway Post Office (RPO) cars. In it, a postal clerk received letters at stops during the trip, sorted them, and delivered them at the proper stations. Some popular accounts trace the introduction of in-transit sorting to a clerk, William Davis, on the Hannibal and St. Joseph Railroad. He presumably

Railroad Mail Car
1920s
Presorted
First-Class

21 USA

Scott #2265   ©1988 USPS

rode the westbound mail car and was charged with removing the extra-cost California-bound mail that was to be carried by Pony Express (Scott #894 and #1154, not shown) from St. Joseph, Missouri. Yet, there are inconsistencies with the dates claimed for this account because by the time that the first railway post office car was placed into service on the road (1862), the Pony Express had been disbanded (1861). In any event, sorting on specially fitted mail cars on a regular basis was conducted during the Civil War.

The Postmaster General, Montgomery Blair (Scott # C66), a Lincoln appointee, is usually credited with the establishment of the Railway Mail Service but its basis lay in a scheme worked out by George Armstrong, the assistant postmaster in Chicago. Armstrong was concerned about "choke points" that had developed at various distribution points in his region. His plan to alleviate the problem, which included the concept of en route sorting, was endorsed by the Postmaster General, who directed him to "test by actual experiment...the plans proposed by you for simplifying the mail service." A trial run between Chicago and Clinton, Iowa on the Chicago and Northwestern Railway was conducted using a car fitted with letter cases with pigeon holes to receive the pieces of mail. The test was eminently successful and the idea was adopted elsewhere. By 1871, railway post office cars were being used by fifty seven railroads over more than fourteen thousand miles of track.

Frank H. Galbraith was a railway postal clerk who designed maps with pictorial representations that were intended to aid instruction of new sorting clerks and reinforce memorization of post office names. For example, found on Galbraith's map was a drawing of a frog at the town of Hopkinton. Other coded locations were Worth (dollar sign),

Scott #2781   ©1993 USPS

Robins (robin); Balltown (ball), and so forth. Caricatures of famous people were used for some post offices.

Scott #2265 shows a mail car of the 1920s, RPO #49, and Scott #2781 includes a similar car. But these cars, in their interior accouterments, differed little from RPOs of the 1800s. One of the latter was described in an 1873 issue of *Scribner's* magazine:

"One end of this car was taken up by a semicircle of boxes or large pigeonholes, receptacles for newspapers and packages, each of which bore a label with the name of a station on the route...At the opposite end of the car were a number of smaller receptacles for letters, to the number of several hundred, all arranged in a certain order, and labeled with the names of stations and connecting routes. In the middle was an apartment for use of the clerks...The remaining part of the car was set apart as storeroom for the mailpouches, bags and packages, containing the through mail from San Francisco to Ogden, and further east, or vice versa, which does not require assorting on the road."

But appearance notwithstanding, progress was made over the fifty years for the safety of the clerks. The major improvement was the change to steel cars, an improvement mandated by the Post Office Department about the turn of the century that probably hastened steel car application in general. Postal worker locations were optimized in relation to the fittings in order to minimize the effects of accidents. Because they were usually included in speedy passenger trains, RPOs were equipped with carefully designed springs. These were essential to reduce swaying and vibration, important to the clerks who spent most, if not all, of a trip on their feet while tossing mail into bins.

Movement of packages by the Postal Service was a relatively recent innovation, established in 1913. At that time, special parcel post stamps were issued. Before that, packages were handled by individuals or companies organized for that purpose. An early express company operated on the Providence and Worcester Railroad since its inception in 1834. Two years later, a teenager, William Hayden was hired to deliver small packages in the cities of Boston and Worcester by a conductor who carried them on the railroad between the two points. A few years later, Hayden was succeeded by William Harnden, who then established his own express business between Boston and New York. At first, a single carpet bag was sufficient for his needs but as his business grew, he added offices and employees. Upon his death, his firm was merged into the Adams Express

Company. Other famous names followed in the railway express field, including Butterfield, Wells, and Fargo, whose stagecoaches played starring roles in many motion pictures of the twentieth century. The Overland Mail Company was organized by Wells, Fargo in 1857 to carry United States mail.

A parcel post stamp (Scott #Q5) shows a steam locomotive and mail and passenger cars approaching a mail crane. Mail cranes were devised to hold a special mail-filled pouch in position to be snatched up by an arm on a speeding car. Picking up mail "on the fly" avoided the necessity for stopping, an important consideration, especially for fast passenger trains. One simple apparatus was "Ward's catcher." In practice, the pouch was drawn into a wasp-waisted configuration and held, top and bottom, in a crane at trackside. A fork-like catcher was mounted on the mail car and one arm of the fork intercepted the sack at its constriction. The sack then slid along until it was grasped firmly between the two arms from whence it could be drawn into the car (Scott #Q3). The postal clerk had to be sharp-eyed and agile to manipulate the catcher, particularly during inclement weather, while the train was running at speed, simultaneously avoiding damage to station protuberances or other structures alongside the track.

Scott #Q5

Scott #Q3

Significantly, when the Postal Service issued a stamp to celebrate the dedication of a new, automated mail facility at Providence, Rhode Island (Scott #1164), it included the image of a freight train passing by. Thus, it recognized the long association with railroading even as it heralded a new era with the opening of its first automated post office. Less than two decades later (1977), an earlier technological achievement of the Postal Service, the Railway Post Office, sounded its last hurrah. The last run of an RPO car was made between Washington, D.C. and New York City.

Scott #1164

Railroad Navies

Scott #2466 depicts a ferryboat of the 1900s underway. This particular boat is carrying wagons as well as passengers and though no obvious railroading affiliation is evident, the image was based on a railroad-operated ferry. The artist, Richard Schlecht, used photographs of two existing ferryboats as models. Primarily, the Pennsylvania Railroad boat *Newark* (launched 1902) was his inspiration although he also referred to photos of the *Chicago* (launched 1901), another Pennsylvania Railroad ferry. Although the two boats were nearly identical, it was decided not to identify the boat on the stamp as the *Newark*, as originally planned. The original engraving depicted a heavy black space as the opening to the vehicle deck so the Bureau of Engraving and Printing added a latticed gate and some interior detail. The prototype was painted in the road's distinctive livery color, Tuscan red, with gold lettering. The vista from behind the latticed gate of a ferry is presented on John Sloan's painting "The Wake of the Ferry" (Scott #1433).

It was the case that many railroads operated "navies" comprised of various types of vessels from lighters to tugboats to ferries. The latter were numerous and used in those locales where a significant body of water had to be crossed and the construction of a bridge was not feasible or too expensive. New York City immediately comes to mind, where the city—the terminus for several railroads that approached from the west and south—lay on the far side of the broad Hudson River estuary.

Scott #2466 ©*1995 USPS*

66

Camden and Amboy Railroad travelers journeyed via boat from South Amboy, New Jersey to New York City as early as 1833. By the 1860s, the major railroads with terminals on the west shore of the Hudson had large, side-wheel ferryboats in service to bring their Manhattan-bound passengers across. The New York, New Haven and Hartford Railroad, which entered New York City from the north, ran its cars onto ferries at a Harlem River site and then brought them to New Jersey docks. Once the cars were landed there, they were routed directly west or south without the need for passengers to leave the train. The Long Island Railroad enjoyed a convenient geographic position on the east side of the Hudson but, like the New Haven road, connections were made with New Jersey railroads via ferry. The Pennsylvania Railroad completed a trans-Hudson tunnel directly to its terminal in mid-town in the early 1900s but continued to ferry freight by lighter or barge. Lesser roads, denied access to the tunnel, continued to use passenger ferries until the mid-20th century. Freight car floats operated even longer.

There were many other instances, like the New Haven road example, where ferries were used to carry entire trains of passenger cars across water to accommodate passengers and avoid mid-trip changes. One of these involved the Central Pacific Railroad, which installed a car ferry between Benecia (the one-time capital of California) and Port Costa. The ferry and trackage from the crossing point to Sacramento replaced slow and dangerous river steamers that had been previously used. The ferry service continued until 1929.

Again, there were places like the northern areas of the Great Lakes which, lacking population or industry, could not support a railroad. There, railroad ferry services (Scott #1069) that carried bulk commodities were established. In this northern region sub-freezing weather was to be expected and the Straits of Mackinac, connecting Lake Michigan and Lake Huron, were ice-packed in winter. Car ferries with ice-breaking capability were employed to clear a passage. In 1897, the Flint and Pere Marquette Railroad built the *Pere Marquette*. With four tracks on a 350 foot long lower deck, she was the largest seagoing, ice-breaking car ferry afloat. The *Pere Marquette* could carry 30 freight cars or 16 passenger cars on its deck. Passengers were accommodated in rooms above. This ship operated until the mid-1930s.

One railroad, the Chesapeake and Ohio, sought to capitalize on a growing transportation business. In 1893, it organized a steamship line which carried freight between Newport News in the United States and Liverpool, England. While not a ferry service per se, this was an early instance of a railroad branching out into an ocean-going carrier.

Moving Liquid Gold

Although petroleum (literally "rock oil") had been used for thousands of years for cooking, heating and other sundry applications, it was available in small quantities only. Oil was found in seeps, where the oil had oozed to the surface. In addition, the Chinese drilled oil wells for several centuries before the birth of Christ. These were minor efforts: the first systematic oil drilling on a large scale began at Titusville, Pennsylvania. There, in 1859, Edwin L. Drake, an ex-railroad conductor, drilled 70 feet and struck oil. Scott #1134 was issued to celebrate the one hundredth anniversary of that occasion.

When oil was discovered in Pennsylvania, the implications for railroading were not immediately evident. Only 2,000 barrels of oil were recovered in 1859 and the transport of this amount of oil to markets posed no problem. It was moved in the same manner in which liquids had been transported for hundreds of years — in wooden barrels. But by the following year, production had jumped to half a million barrels and increased steadily thereafter and the production resources of the cooperage industry were overwhelmed.

Scott #1134

An early solution to the problem involved bringing the oil to a waterway near the oil fields in Pennsylvania by wagon (in barrels) and, later, by pipeline. There, it was pumped into tin lined tanks on specially built barges, which carried their cargo to refineries built at Pittsburgh. Soon, horse-drawn wagons were inadequate, so the Oil Creek Railroad was built to connect the oil fields with the Atlantic and Great Western Railroad, a through road. Barrels continued to be used until it became clear that this method was totally incapable of doing the job. The tin compartment idea was translated to a box car in 1863 but, despite serious interest, the car could not be loaded or unloaded quickly or easily.

Within two years, two different tank car designs were being applied. One, invented by Charles P. Hatch, employed three iron-banded wooden tubs which, fully loaded, could carry 3,500 gallons. The second, built by well-owner Amos Densmore, employed two 1,700 gallon wooden tubs. In each case the tubs were mounted on flat cars. Obviously, these near-identical designs were an improvement over the multitude of small barrels that they replaced but both suffered from the same fault. When filled to the top, the contents often overflowed due to thermal expansion. This problem was alleviated by a "small Pennsylvania firm of car builders (who) conceived the idea of putting a 'cupola' on the tank." This was the first instance of the use of a tank dome, and it established the dome design on all tank cars that followed. Eventually, however, it was found that an expansion dome was really unnecessary. In the mid-1950s, engineers discovered that a partially filled tank would accommodate expansion, yet the stresses due to liquid surges were lower than if the tank were completely filled.

Soon (1868), a cylindrical, wooden tank that was mounted horizontally and fitted to a saddle on a flat car was developed. A year later, the first horizontal, riveted iron tank car entered service. This tank had a 3,400 gallon capacity and was mounted on its own wooden underframe instead of on a flat car. From that point forward, the iron tank car predominated and a short two years later William Gray Warden of Philadelphia invented a tank car that incorporated many of the features of modern tank cars.

John D. Rockefeller, whose fortune was built on his Standard Oil Company, testified that

> "We soon discovered, as the business grew, that the primary method of transporting oil in barrels could not last. The package often cost more than the contents, and the forests of the country were not sufficient to supply the necessary material."

Through various railroads and fast freight lines, Standard Oil came to dominate and control the supply of tank cars and to deny them to his competitors. While Standard Oil had an adequate supply of modern tank cars, Rockefeller could watch his competitors being compelled to ship their product in barrels. Some developed racks within boxcars to hold the barrels but this, at the time a necessary expedient, was a step backward.

By 1900, steel cars were introduced and most petroleum and petroleum derivatives came to be transported in such cars. Substances like paraffin and asphalt required special heating pipes to reduce the viscosity of the commodity for loading and unloading. Tank cars were used to carry oil in the United States well into the twentieth century until they were mostly replaced by long-distance pipelines.

Dinner in the Diner

Johnny Mercer (Scott #3101) wrote the lyrics to "On the Atchison, Topeka and the Santa Fe". The song was written in 1944 and sung in the motion picture *The Harvey Girls* by Judy Garland. The real Harvey Girls were waitresses employed by Fred Harvey in the clean and appetizing restaurants that he established to serve railroad passengers. The first "Harvey House"

Scott #3101   *©1996 USPS*

restaurant on the Kansas Pacific Railroad used male waiters but Harvey soon substituted women for the men. Unlike the "greasy spoon" restaurants that preceded his establishments, Harvey House food was tasty, well-prepared, and reasonably priced but served at a furious rate. The waitresses had to accommodate all of the diners during a short (usually about 30 minutes) food stop.

One of the earliest reference to meals for railroad passengers was included in a memorial to Congress in 1819 and a proposal for a dining car was made in the pages of the *Journal of the Franklin Institute* in 1829. In 1836, the *Victory*, a passenger car, was in service. This car had storage for edibles at its end and food service was offered to passengers. In 1853, meals were provided on some Baltimore & Ohio Railroad (B&O) trains but the food was not prepared on board. These few instances aside, most early railroad passengers either carried their own food or ate at scheduled meal stops. The latter usually provided sorry offerings as witnessed by an editorial in the *Raleigh Progress* during the Civil War that rejoiced in the fact that one of the North Carolina Railroad's restaurants was compelled to close down. The journalist wrote:

"Many a weary traveler will thank the fates for this for now he will retain his money and his hunger will go unappeased, while before he parted from his money and still went hungry."

The first railroad to serve food cooked on board was the Great Western Railway. This dining car, the *President*, with a kitchen located at one end, was a modified sleeper built by the Pullman Company in 1867. Meals were carried to passengers at their seats. The following year, the Chicago and Alton Railroad contracted with the Pullman Company to run the *Delmonico*. This sixty foot long car, named for the deservedly famous food establishment in New York City, was the first car used exclusively for dining. It had two dining rooms, one on either side of an eight foot square galley.

Although dining cars were generally unprofitable, long trips required their use; the alternatives were food stops that affected schedules negatively. Dining cars were first featured on midwestern roads; in the east, the first dining car was introduced by the B&O in 1881. On western roads, food stops at lunch rooms were the rule and several western roads colluded against providing dining car service over some routes. When the Northern Pacific Railroad added diners, it precipitated the "Great Dining Car War" of 1888-89 when competitors tried to outdo each other, a situation that led to high monetary losses. Finally, the roads agreed to continue service but at a more prudent level.

Despite being substantial money-losers, dining cars were almost always carried on long distance trains to oblige passengers until the mid-20th century.

National Grange

Scott #1323, a reproduction of an 1870 Grange poster, was issued to commemorate the 100th anniversary of the founding of the National Grange. It shows a farmer carrying a scythe and, in the background, a mill and a railroad train on a viaduct. The Granger movement grew out of a farmer's lodge, the National Grange of the Patrons of Husbandry, which was established in Washington, D.C. in 1867 to promote better farming practices. Each local unit was called a "Grange" and, in addition to their educational objectives, there was a strong social flavor to their meetings. By the end of 1869, there were 37 active Granges and that number reached a maximum of about 20,000 in the middle 1870s. At the latter time their membership numbered about 800,000 (some say 1,500,000).

From their initial social and educational interests, Granger involvement moved into the economic and political sphere. Their connection with railroads grew out of quarrels involving the operation of grain elevators and the unfair rate structures then used by the railroads in the Granger region. That region, the grain-growing states, extended from North Dakota on the north to Kansas on the south and from Illinois at the east to Nebraska at the west. Four large railroads served this area: Chicago, Burlington and Quincy; Chicago & Northwestern; Chicago, Rock Island & Pacific; and Chicago, Milwaukee & St. Paul. These roads repre-

Scott #1323

sented about a third of all the railroad mileage in the region and, before rate regulation, they established discriminatory pricing policies. Where competition was non-existent, they charged higher rates, often for much shorter hauls. Where competition did exist, at least in the case of the first three roads, they colluded to set high rates and then split the profits through an arrangement called the Iowa Pool.

In his book, *The Routledge Historical Atlas of the American Railroads*, John Stover describes a poster that hung in Grange Halls and summed up the Granger attitude. Eight men are depicted: the parson says, "I pray for all;" the merchant, "I trade for all;" the lawyer, "I plead for all;" the statesman, "I legislate for all;" the physician, "I prescribe for all;" the soldier, "I fight for all;" the railroad owner, "I carry for all;" and the farmer states, "And I PAY for ALL."

To redress the abuses, the Grange sponsored local and state-wide legislation (the so-called "Granger Laws") to regulate railroads. To achieve this end, the movement became highly political, striving to elect Grange-controlled individuals to influential office. Where existing political parties thwarted their efforts, the Granges ran, and often elected, independent candidates. Although many of the laws that they introduced were poorly written, with many "loopholes," and were soon repealed or modified, the

Grangers maintained legislative and judicial pressures on the railroads. The extension of the essentially regional regulations into federal interstate commerce and subsequent legal decisions eventually led to the passage of the Interstate Commerce Act of 1887, the federal legislation that was so consequential to American railroads.

As a result of their strength and success, the Granger Movement embraced a number of cooperative business ventures that, ultimately, could not compete with private concerns. These failures were instrumental in the demise of the movement beginning in the late 1870s. However, the Patrons of Husbandry survived as a lodge organization and continued as an effective political power.

Walter McQueen – From Old Puff to Jupiter

Walter McQueen became a notable locomotive designer but had a disappointing start in the business. His first engine left a lot to be desired. Her steam joints were leaky, a condition that prevented the development of decent power and caused her to be nicknamed "*Old Puff.*" She was sold to the Ithaca and Owego Railroad in 1840 where, allegedly, "...horse traders occupied the rear car of *Old Puff's* train, leading their stock at a walk beside and behind." On her 27 mile long daily run (scheduled to take 4

Scott #2844   ©1994 USPS

hours), stops had to be made to tighten the joints, a situation that allowed her to be on time only three times in two years. On one of those occasions, the engine could not be stopped at the end of its run and went right past the station. A short time later, *Old Puff* derailed and went through the side of a bridge. Her engineer died in this accident, the bridge was wrecked, but the engine was retrieved from the water below. At this point, prudence prevailed and *Old Puff* was replaced by a horse. *Old Puff* was moved to Scranton where, in 1851, she was used to help build the Lackawanna and Western Railroad. Four years later, she was retired and used thereafter at Scranton for stationary water pumping service.

Fortunately, McQueen's later offerings were of much better quality and, by 1850, Walter McQueen was Master Mechanic for the Hudson River Railroad. The building of this road was delayed for about a dozen years because it was realized that train travel could not compete with the luxurious and relatively fast steamboats that traveled between New York City and Albany. By 1845 though, track construction methods, using heavy rail and abundant ballast, had improved so that 50 mile per hour speeds could be achieved. The locomotives that were purchased for the road were not sufficiently powerful so the management turned to their master mechanic for an engine that would meet their needs. McQueen produced four express engines in time for the road's opening that met all of their specifications. These successful locomotives were followed by two even larger ones. All of these McQueen locomotives were conventional 4-4-0 types and displayed no unusual design features but they were speedy.

Meanwhile, a locomotive factory came into being at Schenectady, New York. There, several local businessmen persuaded the Norris brothers of Philadelphia to establish a plant. The first engine produced, named *Lightning*, was a powerful, fast machine but tended to pound a track unmercifully and was soon retired. In 1852, Walter McQueen was hired as Chief Engineer of the Schenectady Locomotive Works (which, upon merger with seven other engine makers, became the American Locomotive Company in 1901). McQueen worked at Schenectady for 41 years, where he became a well-known and highly respected designer and attained a vice-presidency. Machines coming from Schenectady's production lines were called "McQueen Engines."

Unquestionably, the most famous of Schenectady's early engines was the *Jupiter*, a 4-4-0 engine built in 1868 and represented on Scott #2844. The *Jupiter* earned her fifteen minutes of fame as one of the two locomotives involved in the ceremony celebrating the completion of the first transcontinental railroad. She was a passenger engine, painted in blue and red with elaborate gold trim and numbered 60 on the Central Pacific Railroad's roster. At the ceremony, the *Jupiter* was driven face to face with the Union Pacific Railroad's number 119. The two locomotives were uncoupled from their trains and then inched forward until their pilots kissed.

Then, *Jupiter* was backed up a short distance and #119 edged forward until it crossed the point where the rails laid from east and west met. This *pas de deux* was then repeated with *Jupiter* crossing the junction. The symbolism provided a powerful finale to the construction of the Pacific Railroad and was immortalized in the few words written by Bret Harte (who is depicted on Scott #2196):

> What was it the engines said,
> Pilots touching—-head to head,
> Facing on the single track,
> Half a world behind each back?

Jupiter continued to work into the twentieth century.

Spanning the Continent: The First Transcontinental Railroad

Scott #922 portrays the Central Pacific Railroad (CP) locomotive *Jupiter* and is copied from a mural by John McQuarrie that is in the Union Pacific Railroad (UP) station at Salt Lake City. It commemorates the 75th anniversary of the completion of the first transcontinental railroad. The *Jupiter* was built by the Schenectady Locomotive Works and it, along with the UP's engine #119, played a starring role at the completion ceremony on May 10, 1869. Interestingly, the ceremony had been scheduled for May 8th, but heavy rains damaged the Devil's Gate Bridge and #119 could not get through. Of the two locomotives, the *Jupiter* was the more elegant. A passenger locomotive, it was painted blue and crimson with gold leaf trim. #119 was an unremarkable freight locomotive without a fancy paint scheme. The stamp was first placed on sale at Omaha, Nebraska, Ogden, Utah, and San Francisco, California, present-day large cities near the termini and the meeting point of the railroads.

Scott #922

In 1890, the Superintendent of the Census announced that there was no longer a frontier in the United States. Arguably, the most important contributor to the veracity of this fact was the transcontinental railroad. Before its construction, the western territories, except for the Pacific coastal region, were largely unsettled. But twenty years later, the railroad had brought migrants, attracted by cheap land, and had stimulated the establishment of towns and many of the fruits of civilization. No other single event of the period can be said to have developed the vast open reaches of the west as quickly or as thoroughly. To describe such a monumental undertaking in a short vignette is all but impossible. Scores of books have been written about this accomplishment and authors still find new unpublished material to document.

Probably the first suggestions for a transcontinental railroad were published as early as 1832 in the Ann Arbor *Emigrant* and the New York *Courier and Enquirer*. But it was Asa Whitney, a New York merchant, who was to become famous for his promotion of a Pacific Railroad. Beginning in 1845, he solicited action from an unresponsive U. S. Congress, but to no avail. By the late 1840s though, Congress began to be aware of the importance of good communication with the far west. The fear that the Oregon territory would establish an independent state was an early consideration. The acquisition of extensive southern lands after the Mexican War (and later, the Gadsden Purchase) was another. The necessity for colonizing these regions assumed a high priority. Finally, the discovery of gold in California and its importance to the Union initiated serious discussion of a transcontinental railroad.

Surveys were authorized by Congress and Army engineers traced five alternative routes. Although a majority of legislators were in favor of building the railroad, agreement on a route could not be reached until the Civil War forced the withdrawal of the Southern bloc from the Congress. In 1862, a bill to construct the railroad was enacted. The new road was to extend from Council Bluffs, Iowa to Sacramento, California and two railroad companies, the Union Pacific and the Central Pacific were established, the former building west from Iowa (actually Omaha, Nebraska) and the latter working east from California. The companies were the recipients of government loans and land grants based on the number of miles of track laid. (See vignettes titled *"Railroad Land Grants"* and *"Within the 'Range of Our Sure and Easy Guardianship'."*)

The CP got underway first, but experienced difficult going as soon as it reached the Sierra mountains. As for the UP, not a single mile of UP track was laid before the Civil War ended. Then it made up for lost time along the flat valley of the Platte River until it encountered the Rocky Mountains. The Central Pacific had to import the necessary manufactured construction products and locomotives by sea around Cape Horn. Offsetting that disadvantage were their fine machine shops and skilled craftsmen at Sacramento and the proximity of forests to supply wood for ties and structures. The Union Pacific had no comparable shops at Omaha and wood was sometimes imported from as far away as Pennsylvania. Again, balanced against the snowy, bone-chilling climate in the Sierras, the UP encountered unbearably hot daytime temperatures that fell to below freezing at night in the desert east of Salt Lake City. Water had to be freighted in and water supply trains enjoyed the highest priority. Finally, unlike the CP, the Union Pacific also had to deal with hostile Indians.

The spur of mileage-based support and the desire to control certain locales, such as the coal-rich areas in Utah, spurred each company to build as quickly as possible, often in a shoddy or sub-standard fashion. For example, fewer crossties than usual were often laid on bare, unballasted ground and no provision for drainage was made. Another factor that contributed to speedy construction was the rivalry that grew between the two roads. The CP used mostly Chinese immigrants; the UP, Irish laborers. This rivalry culminated in a $10,000. wager proposed by the president of the Union Pacific Railroad, the winnings to go to the road that could lay ten miles of track in one day. The CP accepted the challenge but, shrewdly, delayed fulfillment until less than twenty miles separated the rival tracklayers. Then their construction superintendent, who had made meticulous preparations for the task, turned his workers loose. They achieved their goal and with less than ten miles to be laid before the rails met, the UP crew could not better the record that was set. Davidson wrote that upon completion, "By some patriotic accident of geography, America's newest railroad line was exactly 1,776 miles long." A trip from New York to San Francisco had been reduced from a three month long sea voyage to eight days.

All things considered, the remarkable achievement that was the building of the first transcontinental railroad was due more to logistics than to technological innovation. Probably the most well-known of the construction managers was General John Casement. He applied military organizational techniques and discipline to the work and assembled construction trains fitted out with specialized cars carrying a smithy, bunks, kitchens, tools, and supplies. A further fortunate circumstance that helped him were the numbers of young, healthy, able-bodied men available as a consequence of the end of the Civil War.

Those who built the road—the Irish and the Chinese, among others—were, as stated by S. DeWitt Bloodgood, a speaker at the convention of Pacific railroad corporators in 1862, "...men, who have been inured to fatigue, and the toils of the pick axe and the spade...(and have) the qualities of endurance and resolution." Thus, the highest praise should be reserved for the men who, despite all of the problems and hardships, built the "great and shining road." These men, in Robert Louis Stevenson's words, "...pigtailed Chinese... side by side with border ruffians and broken men from Europe, talking together in a mixed dialect mostly oaths," were the real heroes of the feat of spanning the continent with iron rails.

Taming the Missouri River

Although he was best known as an aviation pioneer, the greater part of Octave Chanute's (Scott #C93 and #C94) career was involved with railroading. He was one of the premier civil engineers of the 19th century although he had no formal training in the discipline. He was first employed by the Hudson River Railroad, learning his trade under the great John Jervis, and then worked for several western railroads, becoming Chief Engineer of the Chicago and Alton Railroad in 1863. One of his notable achievements was the planning and direction of the construction of the first bridge across the Missouri River at Kansas City, Missouri, which was completed in 1869.

Scott #C93-94   ©1979 USPS

Perhaps the greatest challenge facing the builders of the Kansas City Bridge was the behavior of the Missouri River at "the Grecian bend" of the river west of the city. Here, where the bridge was to be built, surveys determined that the river was capricious and the bed of the channel kept shifting and its depth varied continually. For example, it's depth increased by 20 feet in a single two-month period. Five hundred feet of one bank of the river was swept away in five days and pier piles were undermined almost as quickly as they were driven. One challenge lay in establishing piers for the bridge under these conditions. Caissons were built so that piers could be built within them but even they were affected by the scouring action of the water and shortly, one of them was undermined and fell over.

Chanute attacked the problem and produced an ingenious solution. He erected a falsework (similar to scaffolding, but much stronger) from a rock base and lowered a bottomless caisson from above by means of huge screws attached to the falsework. After this caisson was seated, the water was pumped out and construction of the pier proceeded. Ultimately, the piles were dispensed with and this pier was founded on bedrock.

The bridge superstructure was made of iron and wood and featured a drawspan which could be opened to allow unimpeded navigation along the river. The bridge was built to accommodate the Kansas City and Cameron branch of the Hannibal and St. Joseph Railway but six other railroads also utilized it. Construction of the bridge, specifically, the standard gauge of the track laid across it, compelled the Missouri Pacific Railroad, one of those using the bridge, to change from a broad gauge. Trains and vehicles traveled along its eighteen foot wide roadway (though not at the same time). Pedestrians used a four foot wide footpath.

A most interesting aside that is included in one technical analysis of the bridge and its construction describes the vista from the bridge. It mentions that "Opposite Kansas City there is nothing but a few shanties in the primitive forest, and it is rumored that they are to form the nucleus for a 'new Kansas City.'" Although Kansas City, Kansas, had its beginnings in the town of Wyandotte, the bridge unquestionably accelerated its enlargement to eventually include the "few shanties in the primitive forest."

By the time that Octave Chanute was engaged in this work he was a widely respected engineer and was known to his peers as "an affable and courteous gentleman." Upon completion of the Kansas City bridge, he undertook to build four railroads in Kansas and then entered a private consulting practice, specializing in the construction of iron railroad bridges.

In the waning years of his life, Chanute became interested in flight and conducted some of the earliest scientific experiments in gliding. The Wright brothers used his data to establish some of their tests; the rigging of their first glider was modeled after that of Chanute's biplane hang-glider. Octave Chanute died in 1910 and Chanute Air Force Base in Illinois was named for him.

Rack and Roll

The idea of using a rack and gear arrangement to insure positive traction was applied around 1812 when a colliery steam locomotive in England was so outfitted. The very first locomotive built in the United States, by John Stevens in 1825, was geared to mesh with a rack mounted along the guideway. Early in the development of American railroads, when a steep hill or range of mountains was encountered, one of the stratagems to surmount them was to build an inclined plane. There cars were literally pulled up the hill by an endless rope driven by a stationary engine. A novel locomotive was built by the Baldwin Works for the Madison and Indianapolis Railroad in 1847 that combined conventional adhesion characteristics with a rack/spur gear driving system that could be engaged over a critical portion of the road with a high grade.

Scott #2463   ©1995 USPS

For steep hill climbing, conventional adhesion locomotives were very limited. The rack concept was applied for surmounting steep hills in 1869 by Sylvester Marsh. Marsh built a rack railway in New Hampshire on the highest mountain east of the Rockies, Mount Washington. He had difficulty obtaining a charter from the state because was he was adjudged a crackpot and "at the time of the final passage of the bill, an amendment was offered to permit the construction of a railroad to the moon!" His argument that no public funds would be expended seems to have swayed the legislators who felt that if he chose to waste his money that was his right.

A cog wheel on the locomotive meshed with "rungs" of a ladder-like rack made of round bars riveted to iron sides. The rack extended for five miles up the mountain, where locomotive and car ran upon iron strap rails supported upon a wooden trestle. The first engine on the road, *Old Peppersass* (so called because, with its upright boiler, it resembled a peppersauce bottle), was built in Cambridge, Massachusetts. With *Old Peppersass* pushing a loaded car, the trip to the summit took 1 1/2 hours to climb the 3,600 foot vertical distance. The maximum, or limiting, grade was over 33 percent. Because the grade was so steep, Marsh provided for six different means to stop a train, including common mechanical friction brakes. Scott #2463 depicts the locomotive *The Cloud*, number 5 on the Mount Washington Cog Railway roster.

The track was inspected regularly using an inspection "locomotive" that was "merely a wooden sleigh with flanged runners sliding on the rails." This sled-like carrier, used on downhill runs only, was described by one person who saw the "experience of tobogganing down a grade 1 in 3 on this contrivance...a unique one." Another individual was closer to the mark when he suggested the device as "a practical realization...to stop railroad accidents by tying a couple of directors to each (inspection) locomotive."

Surveys were conducted later for a new track up Mount Washington. This plan, envisioning electric powered equipment, would have had the path of the road encircling the mountain three times in order to reduce the grade. It was never developed.

Two decades after the Mount Washington Railway was completed, the Manitou and Pike's Peak Railway was finished in Colorado. The rack construction was similar in both cases but the latter road used two side-by-side racks where the teeth on one rack were opposed to the spaces between teeth on the adjacent rack.

The track of the Pike's Peak line extended over 9 1/3 miles to reach the 14,100 foot high summit. The locomotives used at Pike's Peak were built by Baldwin and, like their Mount Washington sisters, their boilers were mounted at an angle to their frames so that when the machine was traversing the incline, the boiler water level was more nearly horizontal.

Interestingly, over a century later, these two roads still operate...although with more modern equipment.

U.S. Grant: Crédit Mobilier and Other Railroad Affairs

Ulysses S. Grant's (Scott #2217i) involvement with railroads was mostly peripheral but two significant railroad events occurred during his first administration—the Transcontinental Railroad was completed and the Crédit Mobilier scandal erupted.

Scott #2217i   *©1986 USPS*

The Pacific Railroad project was so ambitious that there were questions in the minds of private investors whether it could be completed before 1876, when the government could exercise confiscation rights. As a result, financing was difficult to obtain. George Train conceived the idea of organizing a construction company, the Crédit Mobilier, with the responsibility of building the Union Pacific Railroad. Investor interest was heightened because, by investing in the Crédit Mobilier rather than the railroad directly, investor liability was limited and return on investment would be obtained from construction company profits, a more immediate prospect. The device had been used before for railroad building. (The first of the construction companies probably was one established about 1848 to build the Erie Railway.)

Although Thomas Durant, the vice-president of the Union Pacific, embraced the idea, it was not long before illegalities began to be employed to personally enrich many of the major investors. For example, the road's chief engineer was asked to estimate the per mile cost from Omaha, which he fixed at $30,000. He was then asked to rework the numbers for lower grades and better roadbed, $50,000. in his estimation. "Contractor" Durant then raised the cost to $60,000. which he billed to "Vice-President" Durant, who ordered the line built to the lower standard.

Among the investors were the Ames brothers (who, with Durant, were owners of the Crédit Mobilier), dealers in construction tools and suppliers to the Union Pacific Railroad. After a while, Durant was replaced by Oliver Ames, who became president of the road while his brother Oakes assumed direction of the Crédit Mobilier. The Ames's evolved a scheme to take funds that Congress had intended as an endowment to the railroad and transferred them to the construction company and into their own pockets. Since Oakes Ames was a United States congressman, he had many friends in Congress who he made partners in his scheme by distributing shares in the Crédit Mobilier to them, far below their actual value. In his words, he passed them out, "Where it would do us the most good."

Scott #2218b   ©1986 USPS

During the presidential campaign of 1872, the affair was publicized by the *New York Sun* and caused the disgrace and ruin of several politicians, Ames among them. Ulysses S. Grant had the ill-fortune to be President while the financial manipulations were occurring and then, running for reelection when the sordid affair became public. Although he had never been involved in the fraud, his friendship with the many irreputable financiers and politicians (including his vice-president, Schuyler Colfax), aroused suspicion and he was tarred with the same brush. Some accused him of incompetence, if not dishonesty, yet he won reelection handily.

As a postscript in testament to his ethical conduct was his position in dealing with two other prominent railroad moguls. In the summer of 1869, Jay Gould and Jim Fisk, who at the time controlled the Erie Railway, attempted to corner the gold market. On at least one arranged social occasion they tried to persuade Grant to withhold any of the Treasury's gold supply from the open market and even attempted to bribe his secretary. Meanwhile, they continued to buy gold, thereby driving up the price. When Grant finally realized their objective, he ordered $4 million worth of Federal gold to be sold and prices immediately fell. Later, despite insinuations to the contrary by Gould and Fisk, a congressional committee, chaired by James Garfield (Scott #2218b), neither an ally or admirer of the President, cleared Grant of any prior knowledge or complicity in the scheme. Ironically, Garfield was to become another whose reputation was seriously compromised by the Crédit Mobilier scandal.

At a later time (1880) and needing money, Grant allied himself with Jay Gould and other railroad moguls when he was named president of the

Mexican Central Railroad. Grenville Dodge, of Pacific Railroad fame and a Gould associate, was made vice-president. Gould, Grant, Collis Huntington and others met and agreed to act together to build the Mexican Central and to develop other railroads in Mexico. The ex-president was chosen for the post because of his fame and stature, which were expected to help him promote the line. He was chiefly responsible for securing the necessary concessions for the road from the authorities at Mexico City, but his only return was a modest salary and he never received any profits from the undertaking, which eventually foundered and went bankrupt in 1884.

George Westinghouse and Jimmy Rodgers, Famous "Brake" Men

Brakes on early trains were rudimentary or non-existent. One method used for braking involved employing gangs of men to grab onto and stop a locomotive as it neared a station and was reversed by the driver. This stratagem, used on the New Castle and Frenchtown Railroad, worked no better than the one used on the Mohawk and Hudson, the placement of a heavy wedge between a rolling wheel and the truck frame or the leather straps placed across the Camden and Amboy's tracks. Admittedly, when trains ran slowly and traffic was light, good brakes were relatively unimportant. But, within a very short time, train speeds and traffic increased; the absence of signals on the single track lines also contributed to the danger.

Although 305 railway brake patents had been issued in the United States before 1870, including spring-actuated and "momentum" brakes, none provided a practical solution to the problem. Each car was fitted with its own brakes but these had to be manually applied. On a passenger train, the conductor was charged with that responsibility; he had to move from car to car, tightening the brake wheel mounted on the car platforms. Freight car brake wheel shafts were mounted to the right or to the left, in a variety of positions: extending above the roof of a box car; mounted on the end of a refrigerator car; protruding from the platform of a flat car; or at the lip of a gondola car. Non-uniformity of brake wheel location increased the possibility of error and compromised safety.

Through most of the nineteenth century (and into the twentieth), a brakeman was expected to race along the tops of freight cars, regardless of the weather, to set brakes on the individual cars in response to a whistled signal. Eventually, George Westinghouse's automatic air brake became a universal appliance that reduced, but did not completely eliminate, the dangers associated with the brakeman's job. In 1869, Westinghouse was granted a patent for a "straight air brake." Brake cylinders mounted below each car were connected to a compressed air reservoir at the locomotive. When the engineer turned a valve in the cab, air pressure throughout the line actuated the brake cylinders and moved brake shoes against the wheels. Although the system worked better than any used before, it had a serious flaw—it was not fail-safe. If the compressed air line was broken for any reason, the brakes would not engage.

After reworking his Atmospheric Brake (its official name), a patent was issued to Westinghouse in 1872 for an "automatic air brake" that embraced all of the features of modern air brakes. Auxiliary air reservoirs, isolated from the main air line by a diaphragm, brake cylinders, and a so-called "triple valve" were installed under each car. The brake cylinders were connected to brake shoes at the wheels by various rods and levers. With this system, the brakes were maintained in an "off" position by the pressure in the main air line. Releasing pressure from the main air line (or its rupture) would cause the brakes to be applied. This is a very simple explanation that disregards the actions occurring at the triple valve which caused the brakes to be applied and released and which permitted the rebuilding of air pressure after brake application.

At first it was a "hard sell" to convince railroad management and surprisingly, locomotive engineers, to apply the Westinghouse system. The former were reluctant to incur the substantial expense of air brake installation. The latter also had an economic basis to their objections. Despite their vulnerable location at the front of a ponderous machine, they felt that if they were to be asked to do a brakeman's job in addition to their own, they should receive additional compensation. It took public pressure (resulting from fatal railroad accidents) to force the issue and then, rather quickly (for railroad applications), air brakes, by Westinghouse and others, were installed. By 1890, over 20,000 engines and almost 110,000 cars were outfitted with train brakes. These numbers increased further after the federal Railroad Safety Appliance Act of 1893 made the use of automatic air brakes mandatory in interstate service.

Only a few years later, in 1897, James Charles Rodgers (Scott #1755) was born in Mississippi. Best known as a popular country music singer,

"Jimmie" Rodgers might have been the archetypal railroad brakeman, a "boomer," reckless, and happy-go-lucky. He began his railroad career at an early age as a waterboy for track maintenance crews;during luncheon breaks he listened to the laborers singing railroad ditties. From those sessions, he acquired an extensive repertoire of folk songs. From his early teens until he was almost thirty, he worked for different railroads, variously as a call boy, section hand, flag man, baggage-master, and brakeman. In Rodgers time, the latter was still a dangerous occupation.

Rodgers contracted tuberculosis when he was twenty-seven whereupon he decided to leave the railroad and indulge his real love and passion, singing and playing the guitar. Becoming well-known and established was difficult; he suffered many setbacks from the time he broadcast over radio in Asheville, North Carolina to when he finally reached stardom recording for the Victor Company. Rodgers specialized in southern folk songs; some were his compositions, some borrowed, and many had railroad themes: "Ben Dewberry's Final Run," "Hobo Bill's Last Ride," and "Waiting For a Train" among them. His trademarks were "his sentimental ballads which trail off into a mournful yodel." These prompted a second nickname, "America's Blue Yodeler."

Scott #1755   *©1978 USPS*

When he performed in person it was usually in railroad garb, playing the role of the "Singing Brakeman," a publicity persona created for him by his recording studio. This image is shown on the stamp honoring him and it may have been inspired by a publicity still taken to advertise a short movie he made in 1929. At the peak of his success, atop the list of Victor best-selling records, Rodgers succumbed to the disease that had attacked him and died in New York City before his 36th birthday.

John Henry, A Steel-Driving Man

The Allegheny Mountains in northern Virginia were like a wall that prevented east-west railroad construction in the state. The Louisa Railroad, an early Virginia railroad, began in 1837 but halted at the mountain range because the cost of tunneling through was beyond its means. To extend the Louisa and establish communication to the west, the Blue Ridge Railroad was organized and financed by the state. Four tunnels were proposed along its seventeen mile long right of way. Work on the Blue Ridge tunnel was begun in early 1850 and the chief engineer optimistically anticipated that it would be completed in four years. By the end of 1855, however, only the two shorter tunnels had been finished. The Blue Ridge tunnel and the other long tunnel were not "holed through" until 1858. But funds ran short and finishing of the tunnels had to be delayed for ten years until the railroads were reorganized as the Chesapeake and Ohio Railroad. The merged road had sufficient capital to fully complete these tunnels and build others. One of these other tunnels was the 1.25 mile long Big Bend Tunnel near Hilldale, West Virginia.

Scott #3085   ©1996 USPS

The Big Bend Tunnel, built between 1870 and 1873, was the locale of one of the most well-known of all railroad songs, the *Ballad of John Henry*. In this piece, a legendary worker named John Henry (Scott # 3085) was matched against a machine in a race to see which could drive steel the fastest. Steel driving refers to the drilling of holes in rock to accept powder charges; men hammered on cold chisels until the steam drill was invented. According to the tale, when a steam drill was brought to the work site, Henry refused to yield to the machine and he challenged the operators to a drilling duel. In the song, John Henry, hammering at a drill with a ten pound hammer in each hand, won his race against a steam drill...

> "The man who owned the ol' steam drill,
> Thought it was mighty fine,
> But John Henry drove fourteen feet,
> And the steam drill only nine."

but was said to have died from the effort.

Air-powered rock drills had been invented many years earlier. In fact, there is a connection to early railroading in the fact that Richard

Trevithick, who was acknowledged to be the inventor of the steam loco-motive, devised a rotary air drill as early as 1813. But the first patent for a (steam-driven) rock drill was granted to J. J. Couch in 1849. Improvements to that invention were made by Joseph Fowle who later patented his own drill design. Fowle's design provided the basis for all subsequent rock drills.

For a time, when the Hoosac Tunnel was under construction in Massachusetts, its chief engineer was Herman Haupt of Civil War fame. Haupt developed a smaller and better version of the earlier Couch and Fowle drills that were used in the Hoosac headings. Later, after Haupt left, a Hoosac engineer was sent to Europe to investigate construction methods at the Mt. Cenis Tunnel. There, he found drilling machines run by compressed air, rather than steam, in use there. At home, that engineer recommended air-driven drills and a nearby resident, Charles Burleigh, bought a license to use Fowles' patent. After adding some features, Burleigh's machines were applied to the Hoosac bore in 1866.

The stamp depicts John Henry hefting a heavy sledge hammer while a steam locomotive climbs a grade in the background. Henry, the subject of the stamp and hero of the song was a real person, an African-American whose feat and antecedents were often misidentified. The best evidence said that he was a six foot tall, 200 pound laborer from North Carolina, a light-hearted banjo and card player. When the steam drill was brought to the tunnel, it was operated by one of the five drilling crews then at work. As the song describes, Henry drove two seven foot deep holes while the steam drill, which got caught in the seam, could only manage a nine foot deep hole. What is in question is John Henry's fate. Although most agree that he did not die from the drilling effort, it is unclear whether he left tunneling work or was killed in a later explosion.

Eads Mississippi River Bridge

Nine stamps comprised the Trans-Mississippi series. Scott #293 (not illustrated here), a $2 stamp representing the Mississippi River Bridge built by James Eads, originally would have been issued as a two cent stamp but after proofs were displayed it was agreed that the "Farming in the West" scene was more typical of the Great Plains and should be used on a more widely used 2 cent stamp. The Spanish-American War also played a part in a decision regarding this series. It was originally intended that they would be printed in two colors, but because the Bureau of Engraving and Printing was swamped with orders for revenue stamps (needed for special wartime taxes) and lacked the immediate resources, they had to be printed in single colors. The image of the Eads bridge was copied from an admission ticket to the Republican National Convention, which was held at St. Louis in June 1896. In 1998, 100 years later, the Trans-Mississippi series was reissued using the original dies but in two colors as originally intended. Furthermore, in the bi-color reissue, the Eads bridge stamp (Scott # 3209b) carried a two cent denomination, again as originally planned. Scott #3209b is shown here.

Scott #3209b   ©1998 USPS

The Mississippi River formed a barrier to rail traffic at St. Louis until the Eads bridge was erected. James Eads was chosen to be the chief engineer of the project principally because of his prior experience in diving operations on the river. Contrary to the proposals advanced by other bridge companies, Eads insisted on founding the bridge piers on bedrock. Masonry piers were begun in 1869: the west abutment within a huge, water-tight cofferdam (a method perfected by Roman engineers in the 2nd century B.C.) and the east side, where the river was deeper, within a compressed air caisson. The caisson technique was new to the United States, having been first used in France the previous year. Laborers had to work on that pier in a high-pressure air environment, necessary to exclude the river from the workings.

Once the working level neared seventy feet below the surface, some of the workers exhibited symptoms that were named "Grecian bends," a manifestation of "caisson disease." As they progressed even deeper, the laborers sickened and collapsed more frequently with some becoming paralyzed or dying. Although the link between the high pressure and the disease was obvious, its remediation was not. Some men applied "Abolition Oil" to their bodies and wore,

> "galvanic bands or armor, alternate scales of zinc and silver...around the wrists, arms, ankles, and waist, and also under the soles of the feet...(Presumably) sufficient moisture and acidity

were supplied by the perspiration to establish galvanic action in the armor...(and seemed to)...give remarkable immunity from these attacks."

Although the disease and its remedies were not understood for many more years, Eads mitigated the problem by keeping men at work in the high pressure environment for shorter periods and by avoiding sharp changes in pressure as the men ended their shifts.

For the superstructure of the bridge, Eads selected an arch design. The arches were built up from long, rust-resistant steel tubes. Each tube was raised from a supply barge and fastened to a similar tube that had been placed before. The free ends of the tubes (before they were joined to the subsequent member) were held by cables hung from towers on the shoreline or on a close-by pier. Erection progressed simultaneously from both piers of the bridge and the supporting cables had to be adjusted continuously to accommodate length changes due to thermal expansion and contraction.

When it came time to close the gap between the approaching structures at each side by inserting the central part of the arch, Eads discovered that the final members would not fit. He had intentionally made them longer than the intervening space so that, once they were in place, the structure would be stressed in compression, a condition that would increase its strength. His only miscalculation was due to the weather; he had believed that he could place the final segment on a cool day when the parts would be somewhat contracted, but the temperature remained hot. Working against a penalty deadline, he was compelled to find another solution. He packed the existing girders with ice, sixty tons in all, and used adjustable length tubes for the final closure. This worked and the bridge was completed.

To test the bridge before use, two trains, each pulled by seven locomotives, were run across on adjacent tracks. This 500 ton load produced deflections that corroborated the calculated values. A final test involved leading an elephant across the span. Though only a small fraction of the weight of the two trains, it was the common wisdom of the time that an elephant would not walk on an unsound structure. The animal crossed without pause. The Eads bridge, the missing link in America's central east-west rail system, was formally opened on Independence Day, 1874.

At the time that the original engraving was made for the 1898 issue, street cars traversed the upper deck of the Eads bridge with railroad trains crossing on the lower deck. At the present time, light rail vehicles use the lower deck tracks.

Eddy and His Clocks

Wilson Eddy became an apprentice machinist at the age of nineteen. Eight years later, he was appointed to foreman in the Western (Massachusetts) Railroad's shops at Springfield and in 1850, he was promoted to be Master Mechanic. In 1851 in this capacity, he designed and built his first engine, the 4-2-2 *Addison Gilmore*. Built at the Western Railroad's shops at Springfield, Massachusetts, it displayed many improvements over contemporary designs. Its horizontal cylinders, along with a straight boiler, provided an attractive profile. A traction increaser which "in case of a heavy train, or bad state of the rail" would redistribute some of the engine weight to the driving wheels was also provided. The *Gilmore*, in appearance and in some features, stood between earlier engines with their inclined cylinders and various outlines and those that came later. Eddy designed the locomotive to be speedy—she had large diameter drivers—and she was. In a race against five other passenger engines on the Boston and Lowell Railroad, the *Addison Gilmore* won with an average speed of almost 44 miles per hour. Curiously, another locomotive named *Addison Gilmore* was a contestant in the same race.

In the '70s and '80s, Eddy designed engines for the Boston and Albany Railroad that maintained their schedules so reliably that they came to be called "Eddy Clocks." Number 242, pictured on Scott #2845, is an Eddy Clock. The Clocks had a distinctive outline, a prominent feature exemplified by a safety valve mounted on a tall, slender structure reminiscent of a lighthouse or, in the eyes of some observers, upward aimed cannons. They were good engines but they did have a shortcomings: their fireboxes were firmly attached to the frame. Thermal expansion of the firebox and boiler structure was substantial and could not be wholly accommodated at the cylinder saddle and leakage was the result.

Eddy's locomotives departed from the popular "wagon top" type that provided additional steam space above the firebox. A wagon top boiler had a conical transition section between the firebox and the back of the straight portion of the boiler. Eddy, on the other hand, favored large diameter, straight boilers. He made a number of other important contributions to American locomotive design, including the perforated dry pipe, which was needed to offset the limited steam storage of his straight, domeless boiler design. This idea was adopted nearly one hundred years later for a domeless 4-8-4 engine built for the New York Central Railroad.

All of the Boston and Albany's Eddy Clocks (except one) were sold to a speculator in 1889. He planned to sell them to another railroad but the deal fell through and he scrapped the entire lot. The surviving Eddy Clock may have been saved because it had played a prominent part in a drama that occurred in 1872, the "Great Boston Fire." The fire was so dangerous and widespread that a call went out to neighboring communities for assistance. A company of firemen and their steam engine-driven fire apparatus were dispatched from Worcester, Massachusetts. The Eddy Clock at the head end of the special train carried them to Boston in 47 minutes, an outstanding time. Thirteen people and 776 buildings were lost in that fire, which caused $500 million in damage (calculated in today's dollars).

That last Eddy Clock became the heating plant for the Worcester, Massachusetts railroad station and was eventually given to Purdue University.

Scott #2845   ©1994 USPS

RAILROAD MATURITY
(1875-1900)

Workin' on the Railroad

Scott #1898   ©1983 USPS

Scott #1898 was one of the Transportation series of 1981-1995. It depicts the lowliest, yet a highly essential, piece of railroad rolling stock—a hand (or section) car. The earliest records of hand cars date from the 1830s, including a wooden wheeled one built for the Boston and Lowell Railroad that was belt-driven and used a hand crank. In 1831, a hand car brought Henry Clay (Scott #1846) and his wife from New Orleans on the Pontchartrain Railroad. Six men stood on the car and moved it by pushing against the ground with poles.

Early on, handcars were highly individualistic, built by each railroad to satisfy its needs. Some were gear driven; some, belt driven. A unique design, called a "lever," was a carriage-like apparatus, driven by a seated operator who pulled, to and fro, a handle attached to an operating lever at each side of the car, working much like the treadle on an old-fashioned foot-powered sewing machine. One lever, nicknamed *Old Grimes*, was used in front of trains passing through the streets of Philadelphia to warn pedestrians and street traffic of their approach.

The wind-powered car, which had been tried on the Baltimore and Ohio Railroad in the 1820s, enjoyed a revival in the sail hand cars employed on the Kansas Pacific Railroad in the 1870s. A steam engine-powered car that could carry six persons at 30 miles per hour for up to 40 miles was introduced in 1876. Not this car, or a similar one, the Ionia steam inspection car, ever caught on. Later, though, companies specializing in handcar construction began to appear and prosper and the apparatus was more or less standardized into the familiar form requiring see-saw operation of dual handlebars.

George Sheffield worked seven miles away from his home in Three Rivers, Michigan, an appreciable walk. He devised a three-wheeled rail "scooter" in the late 1870s to assuage the commute. Barreling along on the Michigan Central Railroad's tracks one evening, he discovered a broken track and stopped the evening train by signaling it with his lantern. Although he prevented a potential disaster, the railroad officials became aware of his trespassing. At first, some were inclined to prosecute him but wisdom prevailed and, instead, he was asked to reproduce his scooter design for use on the road.

The Sheffield Company grew and a few years later (1882) marketed a conventional section car and then worked toward reducing its weight. Weight was a problem with cars made of iron and wood; they might exceed 400 pounds and required two or more men to lift them on and off the track and the expenditure of more energy to propel them. Other manufacturers also introduced lightweight cars and one, made almost wholly of an aluminum alloy, was built by the St. Louis Aluminum Casting Company in 1899. Weighing about 150 pounds, it could attain 35 mile per hour speeds.

Other companies entered the handcar arena but the Sheffield Company remained the dominant player until replaced at a later time by the Buda Company. In 1896, coincident with automobile development, Sheffield demonstrated a gasoline-engine-driven section car. That same year, the Daimler Motor Company converted an automobile to railroad use by replacing its wheels with flanged ones. Operated by familiar motor car controls, it had two bench seats and a two horsepower gasoline engine. Despite the introduction of engine-powered handcars, the manually operated apparatus continued to be used for many years and representative samples of these machines can still be found in use on some present-day railroads.

Thomas Edison: The Electric Locomotive and the "Movies"

Scott #945 shows a likeness of the prolific inventor Thomas Alva Edison. Copied from a photograph made in 1919, it commemorated the 100th anniversary of his birth. A design that integrates a cogwheel, uplifted wings and a lightning flash—symbols of power, flight and electricity, are shown in the lower left hand corner of the stamp.

Scott #945

Although Edison had no more than a few months of formal schooling, his mother, Nancy, who had taught school in Canada, furnished his early education. Yet what he learned was what he wanted to learn. He could not spell well but had a vivid imagination and expressed ideas or numbers using abstract examples. When young Tom was ten, Nancy discovered her son's interest and aptitude for science. From that time, he devoted his energies toward scientific experiments and knowledge.

Perhaps best known for his work in electric lighting and sound recording, his inventions covered a wide gamut of devices. His earliest railroad connection was as a news butcher on the Grand Trunk Railway, but his serious contribution to railroading involved electric locomotives. Although the first electric locomotive was invented in 1837, ten years before his birth, they were not practical machines until the latter part of the 19th century. Edison's first venture into the field was in 1880 when he built a 12 horsepower engine and ran it around a one-third mile long track that he had constructed at Menlo Park, New Jersey. This machine was powered by a lighting dynamo that drove the wheels through a friction drive that was controlled by the operator. Electric current was collected from the running rails. This, the first full size electric locomotive made in the United States, was about six feet long and four feet wide. At its debut on May 13, 1880, a crowd gathered and at least 20 people clambered aboard the open trailing car and locomotive. While its outbound trip was successful, its return trip suffered a friction transmission failure and its passengers had to push the engine back to the starting point.

Within three weeks, the inventor had corrected the drive problems and provided a demonstration to his financial backers. This time, all went well until the engine derailed while negotiating a curve at 40 miles per hour. Despite this mishap, one of his backers, Henry Villard, who was president of the Northern Pacific Railroad (NP), contracted with Edison to furnish two electric locomotives that would be capable of pulling a twelve ton load at 60 miles per hour. Villard proposed to electrify a fifty mile stretch of NP track but economic setbacks prevented him from doing so.

Edison also ran into problems; patent litigation brought by Stephen Field led to an ultimate settlement and merger of the two interests as the Electric Railway Company of America, organized in 1883. A fifteen horsepower, geared electric locomotive named *The Judge* was built and demonstrated at the Chicago Railway Exposition in the same year; however, by that time, Edison's interest in electric railways had

Scott #3182c ©*1998 USPS*

waned. He stated, "I had too many other things to attend to..." Sprague, an outstanding innovator and competitor in the field, later wrote that "Edison was perhaps nearer the verge of great electric railway possibilities than any other American."

In the late 1880s, Edison's interest turned to motion pictures. He pioneered the Kinetoscope, a "peep show" type of box with which a single viewer could watch a time-limited presentation. He also had constructed a primitive sound stage, called the "Black Maria," for the production of kinetoscope shows. Meanwhile, others were working on an advance in the art using projected images but Edison was not persuaded that this was the way to go. Finally, when the advantages of projected images became apparent, he was asked to participate in the manufacture and further refinement of the technology. That he did, although in the role of entrepreneur, not inventor.

During the decade of the 90s, railroading—which had always, since its beginnings, captured the public's fascination—was the subject of numerous books, ballads, and dramatic plays. During this period, there were six or more plays with a railroad theme playing in theaters around the country. The plot of these invariably centered around a heroic railroader who was intent on (choose one): 1) preserving a heroine's honor; 2) saving the payroll from robbery; 3) defending a train against attack; or 4) preventing a wreck. Most ingenious stage effects were created, almost all involving a puffing, smoke-producing locomotive. Among these plays was *The Great Train Robbery*, staged in 1896, wherein the side of the mail car was shattered in a simulated dynamite explosion. One evening, Thomas Edison (who was in the audience) was so impressed that he later adapted this play for a motion picture.

Edison's film company continued to use the Black Maria for the production of projected films and in 1903, one of his cameramen produced a film, *The Life of an American Fireman*, that told a story. Until that time, Edison's productions were short presentations of boxing matches, comedic dances, and the like. *The American Fireman* film was followed by the classic, *The Great Train Robbery*. The latter film, directed by Edwin S. Porter and starring Justus Barnes, was the first Western and one of the most famous movies ever made. It was filmed in the freight yards of the Delaware, Lackawanna and Western Railroad at Paterson, New Jersey and is memorialized on Scott #3182c. From this beginning, an enormous industry developed but unfortunately, through the colossal blunder of not seeking European patent protection on his moving picture inventions, Edison was compelled to engage in protracted legal battles to assert his position. Eventually, in a manner reminiscent of his electric locomotive development, the lawsuits were settled by compromise and merger.

Ely's Locomotive #10

Theodore N. Ely was born in 1846 and graduated from Rensselaer Polytechnic Institute as a civil engineer. Following short stints at other jobs, he entered Pennsylvania Railroad service in 1868 and was rapidly advanced until, in 1893, he became Chief of Motive Power for the entire

Scott #2846   *©1994 USPS*

road. In the 1870s he was affiliated with the Philadelphia and Erie Railroad Division, based at the company's complex at Altoona, Pennsylvania. At that time, the Pennsylvania Railroad was engaged in direct competition with the Philadelphia and Reading Railroad for the Philadelphia-New York passenger traffic. A strong, speedy locomotive was needed to haul its trains on this run and the road turned to Ely to provide it. Ely's creation was the K class locomotive, whose design was based on the earlier class C machines. However, he soon realized that this first K class machine was not a good steamer and it was relegated to local passenger service.

Now, the original need for a new engine still existed, so Ely set about designing a new locomotive from the ground up. Although the same class designation "K" applied to it, in appearance it was entirely different from its predecessor. To attain the required speeds, it was outfitted with large, 78 inch diameter drivers and had large cylinders meant to operate from a boiler pressure of 140 pounds per square inch. The first of the new, anthracite burning engines, shown on Scott #2846, was constructed in 1881. It was assigned road number 10 and its weight was 93,000 pounds.

All told, eighteen class K machines were used between Philadelphia and New York and they typically pulled a five car train, including a combination car, a parlor car, and three coaches. Such a train, when empty, weighed about 130 tons and its locomotive could pull it easily, maintaining an average speed of almost 50 miles per hour between the two cities The class K engines, which incorporated the most advanced technology, were satisfactory on the New York Division run where speed was valued over strength. But these two attributes were highly interdependent. By using large diameter drivers, the starting tractive effort was compromised. Too, the steaming capacity, adequate at speed, was insufficient to produce a higher tractive force at the start. These flaws led to the development of the next generation of locomotive at Altoona, the class "P". With a better distribution of its weight and smaller diameter drivers, but operating at the same boiler pressure, the P class overcame the K class shortcomings and soon replaced the latter on the New York Division.

In general, speed became an important issue for railroads about this time. The air brake had been invented and, for the first time, the means to stop fast-running, heavy trains was available. For the next few decades, speed was critical to the publicity and marketing departments of numerous large railroads. Two of the best known (and probably best publicized), the Pennsylvania and the New York Central, competed intensively on their New York-Chicago run. Their competition, exacerbated by the anticipated increase in traffic to the World's Columbian Exposition, drove the Central to build its Paladin (Engine #999) in secrecy for fear that the Pennsylvania would attempt to build a speedier locomotive.

Blockade!

Scott #863

The Samuel Clemens stamp (Scott #863) in the American authors series provides an opportunity to discuss the railroads' problems with snow and its removal. Clemens (or Mark Twain, as he was better known), wrote a short story titled *Cannibalism in the Cars* that described the consequences of a train being held fast in a snow drift. Twain relates the story of a Congressman and his associates who are traveling through the midwest when, during the night, their train is stalled by the deep snow. Additionally, the efforts of the locomotive to force its way through the drift have caused a rod to break. The night passes into day; day after day the storm continues until finally, on the seventh day of the blockade and ravenously hungry, a passenger suggests that one of the party be sacrificed to furnish meals for the others. The tale goes on to relate the parliamentary proceedings conducted to identify the victims and the gastronomical deficiencies exhibited by one or another of the passengers. Although not in the same humorous vein as most of his writings, Twain provides a "twist" at the end of the story that mitigates its macabre theme.

However, Twain's tale was not as far fetched as it seemed. In Canada, where heavy snowfalls could be expected, it was common practice to leave supplies at close intervals along the line. And in the United States, many areas experienced blizzards. For instance, when the Central Pacific Railroad (CP) was under construction through the Sierra range, the winter of 1866-67 yielded a total snowfall of 40 feet, with never less than 18 feet on the ground. After the road was built, it was not uncommon to encounter "blockades," where the passage of trains was impossible for many days; the CP had the distinction of experiencing the longest blockade ever, when the San Francisco-Portland stretch was impassable for 64 days!

Obviously, in the early days of railroading, snow removal enjoyed a high priority; unfortunately, the equipment available to do the job did not measure up. On the Camden and Amboy Railroad in the early 1830s, men were positioned on the front of the locomotive where they held shovels against the track as the train moved slowly forward. It was not uncommon for a fellow to be tossed off his perch when the shovel caught on a track joint. Similarly, "a broom made of hickory splints" replaced shovels to sweep the rails on the Lexington and Ohio Railroad.

Before long, pilot plows comprised of an iron wedge and mounted on the front of the locomotive were put into use and eventually the "bucker" plows made their appearance. Charles Lowbaert's bucker plow, which established the pattern for all bucker plows that followed, was patented in 1840 and involved an iron sheet "descending to the rails of the road." A triangular assembly was welded onto the sheet so the snow was thrown to the sides of the car. The plow was designed to be pushed into the snow by a locomotive. Often several locomotives (sometimes as many as 14) were needed to overcome the deep drifts.

Linda Guilford wrote of a blockade that her train encountered near Batavia, New York, in 1879. There, seven locomotives were installed as pushers and, in her words, "the pushing and backing of the engines made a din unequalled since the blacksmithy of the Cyclops. By some hocus pocus the seven engines were made to pull together. After three hours toil - there was a tremendous jerk, a forward movement of a few moments and we were abreast of the station."

This brute force method was only moderately effective. In deep, heavily packed snow or ice, sterner measures were needed. The drift had to be "trenched," which involved the cutting and removal of ice and snow—block by block—and then backing up the plow (sometimes as far as two or three miles) to attain a speed of 60 to 70 miles per hour before crashing into the drift. The toll on men and equipment was extreme as the process was repeated until the blockade was cleared. One inventor's solution was the "Torpedo Snow Plow", which fired an explosive projectile into the drift. Although claimed to be "efficient in the heaviest packs and deepest drifts," it did not enjoy great popularity.

The ultimate weapon for the fight, the rotary snow plow, was developed near the end of the nineteenth century. Rotary plows had been proposed as early as 1865, when Willard Ball was granted a patent on the device but never exploited it commercially. The first practical rotary snow plow was patented by Orange Jull, a Canadian mill owner. Jull licensed the patent to John and Edward Leslie, who built a working model. After conducting successful tests on the Canadian Pacific Railway, the Leslies contracted with the Cooke Locomotive and Machine Company of Paterson, New Jersey to produce more plows. Further testing confirmed the effectiveness of the "Leslie Rotary," as it was called; by the end of 1888 there were about 50 employed in the United States. The Rotary had a self-contained boiler and steam engine to drive the snow wheel. A cab, the snow wheel and its drive were mounted ahead of the engine. The wheel was surrounded by a "carrying fan", whose function was to increase the velocity of the snow so that it could be thrown outward forcefully from the discharge chute. The wheel carried cutting knives, which could be reversed for cutting from either the right or the left.

Orange Jull became angry over the fact that his name was not included in subsequent patents and publicity and reentered the scene with a rotary snow plow, operating on a different principle. By the time his machine was ready for sale, the Leslie Rotary owned the marketplace and Jull sold only eleven plows all told.

Finally, Mark Twain's account of life in a blockaded car is at variance with a description that was included in the book, *Romance and Humor of the Rail*. There it was told that,

> "The conductor announced that the dining car had provisions for two days, and that headquarters would soon discover the trouble and send 'a working train to their assistance. The gentlemen could amuse themselves around the warm fires in the smoking and express cars, and the ladies could have sole possession of the sleeping and dining cars.'"

The latter anecdote portrays a more pleasant experience and provides a better ending to this story of the lifting of snow blockades.

#999: The Speed Queen and the Empire State Express

Scott #2847, issued in 1994, honors William Buchanan's magnificent locomotive, #999. Scott #295, issued much earlier in 1901, commemorates the famous train, the *Empire State Express*. Contrary to some accounts, Scott #295 was issued as one of the Pan-American Exposition issue, not the Columbian Exposition series. The engraver used a New York Central and Hudson River Railroad publicity photo as his source and the stamp shows the *Empire State Express* running at 60 miles per

101

hour. On the stamp, the locomotive is not the famous #999 but rather, engine #938, an I-class engine with 78 inch diameter drivers. #938 was of the class that replaced the earlier high-speed machine.

Scott #295

In the early days of railroading, travelers were astonished and concerned about the high rate of speed, 15 or 20 miles per hour, attained by trains. Many observers believed that the speed caused numerous maladies and that,

> "Travel in carriages drawn by a locomotive ought to be forbidden in the interest of public health. The rapid movement cannot fail to produce among the passengers the mental affection known as *delerium furiotum*."

Yet, 50 years later, the traveling public demanded and received high speed service on many routes. In the interim, there were records set, usually for publicity purposes, but safety considerations precluded normal operations at high speed. One notable run during the interim period was made by the *Antelope*, a locomotive on the Boston and Maine Railroad. In 1848, this machine pulled an abbreviated train from Boston to Lawrence, Massachusetts and maintained a speed of 60 miles per hour. The reporters who were invited to ride on that train,

> "were in no shape to write their copy until they had been treated at the nearest sample room by the populace and most of the gilt and red lacquer was blistered off the *Antelope*."

By the 1890s, locomotives were breaking speed records regularly, attaining speeds in excess of 100 miles per hour over short distances. By this time, improvements in track, signals, and especially—Westinghouse's air brakes—had made faster schedules possible and practical.

Two great rivals in the '90s were the Pennsylvania and the New York Central and Hudson River Railroads. They ran from New York City to Chicago along different routes but in approximately the same time, 24 hours. When the Columbian Exposition opened in Chicago, the two roads competed for the increased traffic occasioned by the fair by advertising premier, fast trains. As an aside, these runs were unprofitable in dollars but, measured in terms of favorable publicity, more than paid for themselves.

Goodwill and complimentary publicity for the New York Central was foremost in the mind of George H. Daniels, a man who has been called "the P. T. Barnum of the railroad industry." It was he who conceived the idea of a crack train, the *Empire State Express*, whose service was inaugurated in 1891. (A decade later he recommended *Twentieth Century Limited* service.) Although the *Empire State Express* became well-known as a fast train, Daniels proposed the development of a new engine to make the train even faster. Shattered speed records would provide an enormous publicity coup.

Consequently, the New York Central management tasked their Superintendent of Motive Power, William Buchanan (or Buchannan), to build the new engine. In 1893, he constructed Engine #999, an American type, 4-4-0 locomotive. Since a widely-used rule of thumb equated the driving wheel diameter to an acceptable running speed in terms of miles per hour, 999's 86 inch diameter drivers were intended to carry the locomotive at record-breaking speeds. The machine was built secretly at the Central's shops to prevent the Pennsylvania Railroad from gaining an advantage by quickly outshopping a faster machine.

Scott #2847   ©1994 USPS

#999 was placed at the head end of the four car *Empire State Express*, where, racing down a small hill between Batavia, New York and Buffalo on May 10, 1893, it attained a speed in excess of 100 miles per hour. (A speed of 112.5 miles per hour (over a measured mile) was claimed during that run but was probably inaccurate since the train only had reached a

103

maximum 102.8 miles per hour the night before. The road itself disclaimed the higher speed.) After the record-breaking run, Daniels had #999 withdrawn from service and then prepared to be an exhibit at the World's Columbian Exposition in Chicago. Thus, he extracted every last bit of publicity from the exploits of the machine and the train that it pulled. At the conclusion of the fair, #999 returned to service, sometimes at the head of the *Empire State Express*.

So much demand was generated by the *Empire State Express'* speed capabilities that more cars had to be added to accommodate the passengers. But #999 was a speed queen and could not handle the longer and heavier trains. She was rebuilt with smaller drivers and ignominiously assigned to milk train service. The *Empire State Express* train survived and, in 1900, was scheduled to travel between New York City and Buffalo at a speed averaging 53 miles per hour.

#999, in her last configuration, was donated to the Museum of Science and Industry in Chicago in 1962. From 1892 until the 1950s, she was the star of many toy train layouts because toy manufacturers adopted her as a symbol of modernity and speed and *their* publicity agents built upon the legend. She was depicted on the binding of one book in a famous series of children's railroad books, *Ralph of the Railroad,* and she has also been the subject of stamps of other countries.

THE GOLDEN YEARS
OF RAILROADING
(1900-1930)

Railroad Station Transfer

The first automobile depicted on a United States stamp was an electric cab that was used by the Baltimore and Ohio Railroad around the turn of the century. The image on the stamp (Scott #296) was copied from a publicity photo that was printed in a monthly publication of the railroad in early 1900.

Scott #296

The railroad initiated a service for their passengers in April 1900 by carrying them and their luggage to and from the B&O station in Washington, D.C. to various destinations within a certain area. A passenger desiring to avail him or herself of the service was required to notify the conductor of the train some distance before reaching the terminal so that arrangements could be made by telegraph. Upon detraining, the cab would be waiting and would bring the patron to a hotel or residence within a reasonable distance. The fee for this service was fifty cents per person plus twenty-five cents for each trunk. Hand baggage was carried free.

The automobiles, called "Electro-mobiles," were closed cabs with deeply cushioned seats, electric lights for reading and a clock for the convenience of the occupant. The service was so popular that similar arrangements were made at other cities: New York, Philadelphia, and Chicago. Interestingly, different models of electric cars were used in the various cities. A hansom cab, with the driver seated behind and above the passengers, was used in New York and Philadelphia; a brougham was used in Washington and Chicago.

Innovative as this service was, especially in its early application of electric motor vehicles, transfer services had been operating for many years at various railroad centers. In Chicago, where many railroads converged on a half-dozen different terminals, it was as though an unbridged river existed that prevented through travel from east to west. It was imperative to have the means to carry passengers requiring connections at different terminals.

As early as 1853, Frank Parmalee established a transfer service using horse-drawn omnibuses. When railroad passengers bought their tickets, they were also given coupons good for the transfer. The coupon went to Parmalee who, in turn, redeemed them at the appropriate railroad office. Because he was an agent of the railroads, Parmalee was subject to their instructions and demands. They dictated how many vehicles he must provide and when he must provide them. They too set the transfer fee. Over the years, Parmalee's company passed to various owners and by 1930, it was owned by Morris Markin, who also owned the Checker Cab Manufacturing Company.

The railroads at Chicago had no problem with Markin during the Depression and the World War II period. Following the war, however, Markin organized another transfer company, one that would bring airline travelers to and from Midway Field. The collective railroad management, represented by their committee, the Western Passenger Association, strenuously objected to the transfer company serving "two masters" and to the rate increases that Markin requested. The debate and conflict continued for over a decade; eventually, the Parmalee Company lost the Chicago transfer business.

"The Story of a Brave Engineer"

The designers of this stamp (Scott# 993) selected "Casey" Jones, framed by a locomotive tire which sits on a rail and crossties, to represent all railroad engineers of America. A steam locomotive is pictured at the left and a diesel locomotive at the right. A semaphore signal is visible above the diesel engine.

John Luther Jones was born in southeastern Missouri on March 14, 1864. His family moved to Cayce, Kentucky when he was thirteen years old and his nickname "Casey" derived from this fact. Jones began his railroad career on the Mobile and Ohio Railroad as a telegrapher and then became a fireman. Hearing that the ranks of trainmen on the Illinois Central Railroad (IC) had been decimated by a yellow fever epidemic, Casey Jones applied to work on it. He was hired and just two years later, not yet 26 years old, became an engineer.

Scott #993

For the next ten years, Casey worked over several routes along the IC, including some service pulling special shuttles that brought fairgoers from Chicago to the Columbian Exposition grounds in the early 1890s. Part of the Illinois Central exhibit at the fair was a 2-8-0 Consolidation locomotive, Number 638, and Casey became determined to make it his to drive. When the Exposition ended, Casey somehow acquired the credentials that directed officials to deliver the locomotive to his care for transfer to his home terminal in Mississippi.

For seven years, Number 638 was Casey's machine and he personalized it with a six-chime calliope whistle whose wail began with a crescendo and died with a whisper. Despite his love for this engine, when he was offered an opportunity to become a passenger train engineer, a position with greater status and pay, he accepted. The promotion necessitated a move to Memphis and for several months he drove freight engines to familiarize himself with his new route. During the evening of April 29, 1900, Jones was assigned to bring the incoming *Cannonball Express* into the Memphis station.

The engineer who was to take the *Cannonball* back south that evening reported in ill, and Casey was requested to pilot it to New Orleans. Leaving Memphis's Poplar Street Station 95 minutes late, he was determined to reach his destination on schedule. Directing his fireman to give him a full head of steam to, in the balladeer's words, "see de drivers roll,"

Jones recovered one hour during the 100 mile run to Grenada. After another 50 miles he was nearly on schedule. In the early morning of April 30, 1900, rolling at 70 miles an hour, he came around a curve near Vaughan, Mississippi and was confronted by a danger signal, a red lantern swung by a trainman from a freight train that partially blocked the track. Casey applied the brakes, threw the engine into reverse and shouted to his fireman to jump. Sim Webb, the fireman, did just that but Casey stayed with his locomotive and slammed into the rear end of the freight train. The locomotive smashed through four freight cars. Casey—mortally wounded by a bolt or splinter that pierced his throat—died, but Webb lived, as did all of the *Cannonball*'s passengers. As an aside, Webb was awarded $5.00 by the railroad in compensation for the "body bruises" he sustained by jumping from the engine.

An investigation conducted by the railroad placed all of the blame for the accident upon Jones. Webb testified that he heard the warning torpedoes, explosive devices detonated to warn of danger, and saw the flagman ahead. It may be that Jones was "short-flagged," a situation where the flagman of the freight train was not sufficiently far from his train to allow Jones to stop in time. Also, Jones was known to be a risk-taker: his record included nine suspensions for various rule infractions and safety violations during the ten years before the accident. In any event, the official accident report stated unequivocally that "Engineer Jones...was alone responsible for the accident."

"Casey Jones, he died at the throttle, With the whistle in his hand." These lines were included in the tale of that fateful journey that was first popularized in a ballad written by Wallace Saunders, an engine-wiper who knew Jones. Chanted by fellow workers, it was heard by a professional song writer who made several changes, set it to music and had it published.

Come all you rounders that want to hear
The story of a brave engineer
Casey Jones was the rounder's name,
On a big eight wheeler, boys, he won his fame.

The song ends where Jones "took his farewell trip to the promised land." Jones' life was also memorialized in countless books, a biography, a motion picture, and the stamp shown here.

Casey Jones worked on the Illinois Central Railroad which operated streamlined trains, including one of the first to be delivered. The IC received a five car streamliner in March 1936 and named it the *Green Diamond*. This train was assigned to the Chicago-St. Louis run. Many more streamliners (including *City of Miami, Panama Limited,* and *City of New Orleans*) followed on other routes. However, portrayed on this stamp is a *Rocket* streamliner of the Chicago, Rock Island and Pacific Railroad.

The original *Rocket* was a steam locomotive, the first on the Chicago and Rock Island Railroad. Its first trip in 1852 was between Chicago and Joliet, Illinois. Almost a century later, in 1937, the Chicago, Rock Island and Pacific Railroad purchased six streamlined cars from the Budd Company and 1,200 hp model TA diesel locomotives from Electro-Motive Company to haul them. The trains were semi-articulated and assigned to medium and long distance service. The *Peoria Rocket*, the longest-lived of all of the Rocket streamliners (*Peoria Rocket* service ended in 1979), made two round trips daily between Chicago and Peoria. The others were the *Des Moines Rocket* (Chicago-Des Moines); the *Texas Rocket* (Houston-Ft. Worth), the *Denver Rocket* (Kansas City-Denver), and two trainsets were assigned to the *Kansas City Rocket* (Minneapolis-Kansas City).

The Rockets were so well-accepted by the traveling public that the Rock Island added others to various runs, among them the *Choctaw Rocket,* the *Zephyr Rocket,* and the *Rocky Mountain Rocket.* Interestingly, the *Golden Rocket,* intended for Chicago-Los Angeles service in partnership with the Southern Pacific Railroad (SP), was never used in that service because the SP reneged on the agreement between the roads.

Mules Along the "Big Ditch"

Several stamps depicting the Panama Canal show electric "mules" at work. Scott #398 is a scene of a ship being towed through Pedro Miguel lock. This stamp was issued in 1913, the year before the canal was opened to commerce. Another stamp, issued by the Canal Zone (Scott #CZ165), shows a ship being towed by a mule. Scott #3183f, which was issued in 1998 as one of the "Celebrate the Century Series - 1910s," shows the *Ancon*, officially the first ship to transit the canal, moving through the

Miraflores lock. (Actually, the first ocean-going ship to pass through the Canal was the *Cristobal,* which made the passage on August 3, 1914. The Canal was formally opened on August 15th when the Ancon passed through that day.)

The mules, very powerful locomotives, were used to tow ships through the various locks of the canal. Their name derived from the animals traditionally used to tow boats through canals for hundreds of years. Negotiating a lock could be a tricky operation and extremely difficult for a large ship to accomplish under its own power. Ship control at low speed was minimal due to the propulsion systems in use at the time. Capricious currents established by lock gate movement and the introduction or removal of water from the lock added to the problem. The mules were needed to control the operation from the stable vantage point at the top of the locks.

Four mules were assigned to bring an average size ship through a lock, two pulling the ship and two aft that steadied the ship and, through the use of taut cables, kept it from smashing into the sides of the lock. They ran on tracks laid atop the lock walls at a speed of about two miles per hour, and they had to climb 45 degree inclines between the lower and upper levels of the locks.

Scott #398

The locomotives (and, in fact, the towing scheme itself) were designed by Edward Schildhauer, a young, civilian engineer (recall that the Canal was built under Army supervision). Built by the General Electric Company (GE), the first order was for forty machines, each costing $13,000. Each mule was slightly longer than thirty feet and weighed forty-three tons. They could be operated from cabs at either end so that turning the locomotive was unnecessary.

Key to the towing operation was a large windlass built on the mule. The windlass carried eight hundred feet of cable that could be payed out or rewound as necessary. This feature, powered separately, allowed a fine measure of control of the motion of a ship. Even when the locomotive was stationary, line tension could be maintained and up to 25,000 pounds of holding force could be applied to the ship from each side. An unusual characteristic of the windlass was that it was not built directly on the mule. Instead, each locomotive was divided into three parts with the central windlass section joined to the tractors (the front and rear parts) by a drawbar and supported by arms resting on the tractor wheels.

Scott #3183f   ©1998 USPS

Author David McCullough points out that the successful performance of these machines was essential to the fledgling General Electric Company. With the eyes of the world on the Panama Canal project, GE recognized it could not afford any unfavorable publicity that would flow from less than satisfactory functioning of its products. Yet, small, powerful locomotives had been built and used for more than two decades. Some of the initial prototypes had low profiles suitable for operation in a limited headroom mine environment. One of the first in the United States was used in a colliery at Scranton, Pennsylvania in 1889 and the Thomson-Houston Company was building squat, "terrapin back" locomotives in 1891.

The GE engines performed admirably and justified the choice of electricity as their motive power. One must remember that electric locomotion was in an early stage and it might have been safer politically to use small industrial steam locomotives where the performance characteristics were known thoroughly and the possibility of failure much less. However, Schildhauer considered the potential advantages of electricity: a high degree of precise control; motors that provided a high starting torque and the ability to deliver high horsepower in an overload mode; no smoke or ash generation at the site (the electric power plant was hydro-powered); and elimination of an explosion hazard.

The opening of the Canal did not enjoy the world-wide publicity that it deserved because as it was overshadowed by a coincident event of wider impact and interest—the beginning of World War I. The building of the Panama Canal was one of those occasions where government-industry cooperation excelled. In terms of project scope, difficulty and numbers of workers involved, it compared to conducting a small war, but the Army management of the large civilian workforce was accomplished without

111

the usual inefficiencies and waste that accompany a similar operation in wartime. This was done in large part because of the capability and determination of the project leaders (a stamp, Scott #856 honors Theodore Roosevelt and George Goethals and commemorates the Canal's 25th Anniversary) and competent, dedicated engineers like Schildhauer.

In this book about railroads and stamps, it is appropriate to add a post script to this vignette about the Panama Canal. After the French had abandoned their efforts to dig the canal, one of the first steps taken by the United States was to create a commission to select a route across the narrow neck of Central America. In 1900, the Isthmian Canal Commission recommended that an American canal be built across Nicaragua. However, Philippe Bunau-Varilla, the former Acting Director General of the French canal company, was determined to site the canal in Panama and continue along the line that the French had started. (If the French holdings could be sold to the United States, rather than be abandoned, the original stockholders would benefit.)

A contemporary Nicaraguan stamp showed a train of the Panama Railroad but, more importantly, included an image of a volcano. Bunau-Varilla used the stamp in his lobbying efforts with influential American congressmen and executives as evidence that active volcanoes, which would impede progress and operations, existed in Nicaragua; he affirmed that there were none in Panama. The stamp was a decisive element in the acceptance of his position and the canal was completed through the French holdings.

From Tinplate to Golden Perfection

Four different toy train images are represented on United States stamps. Scott #1415 displays an Ives Company number 19-5 trackless clockwork locomotive made of tin and cast iron. This toy was modeled after the 2-2-0 locomotive *Grand Duke* and dates from 1880. Scott #2712 portrays a cast iron pull toy, a 2-2-0 locomotive and tender. Scott #3184d, an illustration from the front cover of the 1929 Lionel train catalog, shows Joe Adda, Jr. of Hunterdon County, N.J. playing with his Lionel electric train. (Junior was the son of the original artist. In 1998, at age 75, Adda reportedly was still a model railroader.) Finally, the locomotive *Jupiter* (Scott #3627) is one of four different images of antique toys shown on a block of first class denomination stamps. The *Jupiter* toy was made of cast iron and stamped tinplated steel and intended to copy its prototype, which was one of the locomotives that celebrated the completion of the transcontinental railway (see vignette titled *"Walter McQueen – From Old Puff to Jupiter."*

From a railroading point of view these are particularly appropriate subjects because toy trains were made almost as early as the pioneer trains themselves. Modeled out of wood, homemade trains were carved by many fathers as presents for their children, to be pushed or pulled across the

Scott #1415

Scott #3627   ©2002 USPS

floor, accompanied by suitable "choo-choo" noises. Like their prototypes, miniature trains matured into detailed scale models that faithfully reproduced every rivet and curve of the original. From providing toys exclusively for children, the industry has grown to embrace adult enthusiasts who operate model railroad layouts that equal some real-life railroads and might have made some earlier railroad executives jealous.

Apart from the homemade models and those that the pioneer locomotive inventors built, the earliest commercially made toy trains were produced in the 1840s and were made of tin-plated metal or wood. Many wooden versions had lithographed paper, showing the cab (with crew members), wheels, and valve gear, glued to the substrate. As mentioned, the earliest and crudest of these were intended to be pushed or pulled by hand. Very soon, though, friction drives were incorporated which, when the wheels were pushed against the floor, would store sufficient energy in a flywheel to power the device for a few yards. From there, it was not long before clockwork motors were driving the small copies of some railroad's locomotive. The ability to travel under their own power led to the production of trains with flanged wheels and track on which to run them.

The next advance in motive power involved a more direct imitation of the "big boys." Miniature steam engines, fueled by alcohol, were developed. Finally, electricity was applied to mass-produced model trains a few years after the originals appeared on the scene. (One of the first electric locomotives was a model built by Thomas Davenport in 1835. In 1883,

Scott #2712 ©*1992 USPS*

the Novelty Company produced the first electric trains for sale but the Ives Company was the first to produce electric trains (in 1910) that were widely accepted and close facsimiles of the real thing.)

In the latter part of the 19th century, many beautiful models were made by the manufacturers of real locomotives. Builder's agents traveled the world over with beautifully crafted models that demonstrated their principal's capabilities. Often these were the first representations of locomotives that potential customers had ever seen. Also, superbly crafted locomotive and railroad car models were made for museums. Probably the first of these was built by Matthias Baldwin in 1830 for Charles Peale, who operated a museum in Philadelphia. This small steam locomotive could pull two cars, each seating four passengers. From this small beginning, Baldwin went on to create what was probably the greatest locomotive manufactory in the world.

Up until the turn of the century, most toy train manufacturers paid little attention to accuracy of scale and there was no standardization of track gauge. At about that time (1900), some European manufacturers established gauge sizes, which they designated #1 (45 millimeters between the rails), #2 (54 mm.), #3 (2.25 inches), and #4 (3 inches). When Ives introduced its new electric trains in the U. S., it built them smaller, to a track gauge of 1.25 inches. Since this was smaller than #1 gauge, Ives designated their new gauge, "0." Thus, what is now commonly referred to as "oh" gauge is really "zero" gauge. The new gauge became very popular, both for toy trains and for the burgeoning scale model product meant for adult aficionados.

For a few years in the 20s and 30s, Lionel and American Flyer, two giants (along with Ives) of the American toy train industry, produced "standard" gauge (2.125 inches) trains, but these were displaced by the more popular O gauge. Then, as miniaturization techniques improved, HO gauge (essentially Half-O gauge) was offered and, because of its ability to pack more layout into a much smaller space, eventually dominated the field. Then, even smaller gauges were established and Lilliputian models built to these scales were available. A retrogression of sorts has occurred more recently with the popularization of larger (than O gauge) gauge European train sets.

Scott #3184d   ©1998 USPS

Speaking of larger gauges, there is a class of model trains that is significantly bigger than the toy models. These are mainly used in outdoor settings or gardens and most of them are fired with oil that produces live steam in the locomotive boiler. Such scale models require infinite patience to build and, unlike the amusement park variety, they are smaller but unusually realistic in appearance and operation. (There is a record of a garden railway at the court of France's King Louis XIV at Marly-le-Roi before 1714 where the cars were propelled by servants.)

The stamps that depict toy trains provide insight into the creation and development of two new industries: toy train manufacturing and model railroading. The toy train industry has diminished in popularity because of the many other innovations and distractions available to young people. Yet, although the average boy no longer anticipates finding a train set under the Christmas tree, he is still fascinated by watching a miniature train negotiating a model layout at public shows arranged by model railroad clubs. It is here that the concept lives on. Building upon the toy industry, some manufacturers produce super-detailed, brass train models that are not toys, but meant for display. Also available are accurate scale models meant for operation and parts that can be used to build cars and locomotives "from scratch." Regardless of the avenue followed and, as with the toy train sets before them, these products can provide hours of pleasure and satisfaction for a railroad lover of any age.

RETREAT AND RENAISSANCE
(1930-1950)

1930s: Streamlining Brings a New Look

The private automobile and the Great Depression dealt a shattering blow to railroad passenger travel. Only essential travel was undertaken; people had little disposable income and many of those who did owned autos which they preferred to use for short journeys. To change this picture, the railroads adopted an innovation that projected a new image of safe, comfortable, and speedy travel—the streamliner.

Isolated instances of streamlining had been applied to some railroad equipment since the nineteenth century but, except for a very few instances, had never been applied to an entire train. One of those exceptions was the *Windsplitter*, a train designed by Frederick Adams and built in the Baltimore and Ohio Railroad shops in 1900. Although that train reached high speeds during its tests, the concept was not carried further. The 1930s provided a fertile environment that was exemplified by the 1933-34 World's Fair held in Chicago. Streamlining furnished a forward-looking image, one of speed and technological accomplishment. It was seen by some railroad managers as the solution to the railroad's passenger decline. Yet, image was not enough; a technological breakthrough—air conditioning—added a necessary ingredient to functional streamlining. Until train air conditioning became practical, railroad car streamlining would have been a mere facade. Only when it became possible to operate a train at high speed without opening any windows or ventilators did streamlining become meaningful in terms of reducing air drag and power requirements at speed.

Another point was that there were no satisfactory diesel engines available for application to high speed, over-the-road locomotives in the early 1930s. Diesel engines had been applied to slow switching engines but the first practical engine for high speed locomotive use was a gasoline engine produced by the Winston Engine Company, a subsidiary of General Motors Corporation. Consequently, some railroad managements gambled on the new diesel technology, but others remained committed to steam power to haul their new flyers.

Two early streamlined trains were the *Railplane*, which was designed by an engineer trained as an aircraft designer and built by the Pullman Company, and the *Silver Slipper*, a train built by the Budd Manufacturing Company. The former never advanced beyond the demonstration phase and the latter, while used on the Texas and Pacific Railroad, never achieved recognition on a national scale.

The first successful streamliner to take to the tracks in the United States was the *M10000*. (Later, as more of the same kinds of trains were added to the Union Pacific Railroad (UP) roster, the trains were designated by city names and the *M10000* was renamed *City of Salina*.) The *M10000* was delivered to the UP in February 1934. This offering was a trainset consisting of three cars: the first was a power car containing cab, engine, a Railway Post Office (RPO), and baggage compartment; the second car seated 60 people; and the last had seats for 56 people and a kitchen and buffet counter. The trainset was articulated, each car sharing a truck with its neighboring car.

The cars were made of aluminum and the train was powered by a gasoline-fueled, spark ignition engine made by the Winton Engine Company. The road chose a gasoline engine because it represented a proven technology and was the most quickly available power source. The use of aluminum by its builder, Pullman-Standard, yielded a train with a total weight of 124 tons, about the same as one steel Pullman car.

The next streamlined train to be delivered, in April 1934, was the *Burlington Zephyr* (Zephyrus was the Greek god of the west wind). Interestingly, the name was chosen by Ralph Budd, president of the Burlington road at the time. Budd believed the train to be the last word in passenger rail service and, as such, he thought that the last word in the dictionary might make an appropriate title. Alas, the last word in his dictionary was *zymurgy*, a totally obscure and incongruent word relating to fermentation. He turned to an associate who referred to **his** dictionary where the last word was *zyzzle*, meaning "to sputter," an even worse choice. Budd then recalled the passage from Chaucer's *Canterbury Tales* dealing with Zephyrus and he had found his name. This stainless steel train was diesel-electric powered and, as with the *M10000*, consisted of three cars articulated in a similar manner. The interior of the cars was designed by Paul Phillipe Cret, a noted Philadelphia architect. Indirect lighting complimented the golden brown seats and gray and light green walls.

It was difficult to join stainless steel seamlessly, so the fabrication of the *Zephyr's* cars required a new and novel fabrication technique, shot welding, that had been developed by its builder, the Budd Company. After delivery, the train's owner, the Chicago, Burlington and Quincy Railroad, soon discovered that operating costs for the unit were halved, compared to conventional steam-powered equipment. On its first run, from Denver to Chicago, it ran non-stop over 1,015 miles in less than 14 hours. No train before had ever operated more than 775 miles non-stop. The Burlington's crack *Aristocrat* took 27 hours to make the trip but the *Zephyr* covered the route in a bit more than 13 hours. The original *Zephyr* is now on public display at the Museum of Science and Industry in Chicago.

Both trains were enthusiastically accepted by the traveling public and economical to operate. Those rewarding results insured that other streamliners would be built and they were. Additional copies, with more cars in the trainset, of the first two trains were ordered; later, other railroads joined in with offerings of their own. Of special interest is the fact that in 1934, the New York, New Haven and Hartford Railroad purchased an articulated trainset, the *Comet*, from the Goodyear-Zeppelin Company. The latter was a joint adventure formed after the crash of the airship *Akron* , whose disaster presaged a decline in airship production.

Other early streamliners included the Baltimore and Ohio's *Royal Blue*, the Gulf, Mobile and Northern's *Rebel*, and the Milwaukee Road's *Hiawatha*.

Hiawatha Train

The *Hiawatha*, which entered regular service in May 1935, differed from its earlier cousins, the *M10000* and the *Zephyrs*, by being built in the Milwaukee Road's own shops and employing a steam locomotive at its head end, rather than an internal combustion power plant. The locomotive for this train was a 4-4-2 Atlantic type, built by the American

Locomotive Works and shrouded to present a streamlined appearance. The locomotive's paint scheme of orange, maroon, and gray matched that of the four cars following. In addition to the locomotive, the train consisted of three coaches, a dining car, a parlor car, and a "beaver tail" observation car. During trials, the train achieved a speed of 112.5 miles per hour, exceeding the swiftness of its legendary namesake, who was memorialized by Longfellow's (Scott # 864) lines:

Swift of foot was Hiawatha:
He could shoot an arrow from him,
And run forward with such fleetness,
That the arrow fell behind him!

Scott #3336   *©1999 USPS*

The Chicago, Milwaukee, St. Paul & Pacific Railroad recognized that articulation, that feature of the earlier streamliners that shared trucks between cars, was a handicap that reduced the flexibility of the trainset. Each car of the *Hiawatha* rode on two, 4-wheel trucks and could be added to or removed from the consist as traffic or maintenance dictated. The train regularly made its run from Chicago to St. Paul in six and one-half hours...better than a mile per minute average speed. The train was so successful that additional *Hiawathas* were added to numerous Milwaukee Road routes.

The *Hiawatha* depicted on the stamp, Scott #3336, is of 1939 vintage which employed a streamlined 4-6-4 Hudson type steam locomotive at its head end with upgraded rolling stock following it. Otto Kuhler was commissioned to provide the design. In 1947, the *Hiawatha* name was added to the Milwaukee Road's premier train to the Pacific Northwest, the *Olympian*. Diesel and electric locomotives shared the responsibility of pulling the *Olympian Hiawatha* over parts of the route. *Hiawathas* were still on Amtrak's schedules in the 1990s, plying some of the original routes.

Congressional Limited Train

Raymond Loewy was employed by the Pennsylvania Railroad in early 1934 to refine the design of the GG-1, an electric locomotive that the road had chosen to be its principal passenger motive power on its electrified routes. Working with several rail equipment contractors, he was investigating the possibility of "unit trains" to be used in the New York-Washington corridor and an articulated streamliner for New York-Chicago service. (The debut of the Union Pacific's *M10000* was the impetus for the latter project.) However, the success of their principal competitor's *Mercury* and then, the announcement of the imminent upgrading of the *Twentieth Century Limited*, caused the abandonment of Loewy's assignments. Now the Pennsylvania Railroad proposed joining with the New York Central in building the equipment for two streamlined trains, the *Twentieth Century Limited* and the *Broadway Limited*.

Scott #3334   ©1999 USPS

Although the road continued to streamline other trains, including the *Spirit of St. Louis*, the *Jeffersonian*, the *Trail Blazer* and others, its *Congressional Limited* did not share these modernizations. *Congressional* service began on the Pennsylvania Railroad in 1885, competing against the B&O's *Royal Blue* between Washington, D. C. and Jersey City, New Jersey. In the 19th century, its cars were painted olive green with cream color between the windows. Through the years, it continued to be a premier train on the New York-Washington route.

Drawn by one of 58 new GG-1s, its cars were given a fresh new look in 1935, but the train was never streamlined until 1952. In fact, the train depicted on the stamp (Scott #3334) is shown before new, streamlined cars were assigned. The GG-1 locomotive, number 4935, in now on permanent display at the Railroad Museum of Pennsylvania. In addition to its unique and pleasing appearance, (which was made even more elegant by finishing touches, like the "cat's whiskers" pin stripes, added by Loewy), the GG-1 was a capable and speedy machine. Where the *Congressional Limited* operated on a four hour and forty minute schedule before their assignment, the GG-1s reduced that time to three and one-half hours to cover the 226 miles...almost 75 miles per hour average! A GG-1 could accelerate from zero to 100 miles per hour in just over sixty seconds and could reach a top speed of 128 miles per hour.

The *Congressional* operated over first class roadbed and rails along the much traveled New York-Washington corridor so the speeds that it attained were quite within prudent limits for safe operation. Yet it was not immune to accident. In fact, the worst rail accident in 25 years involved an advance section of the *Congressional Limited* at Philadelphia, Pennsylvania. Rounding a curve at the relatively low speed of 45 miles per hour, the seventh car of the train lurched, then rose off the tracks. Six cars following smashed into each other and 79 people died in the wreck. This disaster occurred during wartime, in September 1943, and the Federal Bureau of Investigation was summoned to establish whether sabotage was the cause. However, it was ascertained quickly that a "hot box" destroyed a truck journal on the seventh car and that, in turn, caused its axle to break.

When the *Congressional* was streamlined, Budd built the cars and the railroad looked no farther than its own GG-1 locomotives, painted Tuscan red, for the motive power. Although the cars had stainless steel exteriors, the road's trademark Tuscan red color was retained on the letterboards. A colonial theme prevailed within and the cars were named after prominent colonial personages. Most of the cars were reclining seat coaches, but dining, parlor-observation, and drawing room cars were also part of the consist.

Super Chief Train

In the West, the Atchison, Topeka & Santa Fe Railroad had operated a crack train called the *Chief* since the 1920s. To compete with the Union Pacific Railroad between Los Angeles and Chicago, the Santa Fe inaugurated *Super Chief* service in May 1936. Although billed as one of the road's premier trains, the *Super Chief* was not streamlined. Modern, heavyweight Pullman cars were hauled over the route at an average speed of 56 miles per hour by an Electro-Motive Corporation (EMC) boxcab diesel locomotive that delivered 1,800 horsepower. The boxcab engines were the first diesels made by EMC. Of the initial lot of five machines, two were to be used as demonstrators, the other three destined for customers, including two which were delivered to the Santa Fe. For the first time on land, Los Angeles could be reached from Chicago in less than 40 hours on a regular basis. (The Union Pacific Railroad matched this feat one day later when its *City of Los Angeles* entered service.)

When the Santa Fe entered the streamlining sweepstakes, it selected an E1 type Diesel engine from EMC and lightweight stainless steel cars from the Budd Company. Each car of the train was decorated uniquely with rare woods and Native American paintings and tapestries. The train carried observation/lounge "Pleasure Dome" cars with glass cupolas for sightseeing built into their roofs. Outside, the gleaming stainless steel cars were unadorned but the locomotive received a distinctive, "warbonnet," paint scheme in red, yellow, black, and silver (Scott #3337). The color scheme was devised by EMC designer, Leland Knickerbocker and was applied by the Santa Fe to many of its other locomotives. The first of eleven of the E1 engines was delivered in May 1937 when the *Super Chief* entered regular service.

Scott #3337   ©1999 USPS

The E1 was an entirely new design for a road locomotive. Other diesel locomotives had located the cab right up front, but EMC engineers felt that location was too vulnerable for the crew in the event of a high speed crash. Instead, the cab was moved back somewhat and the nose, rather than being blunt, was gracefully sloped, rounded, and reinforced to deflect objects on the track. In this respect, it performed the same function as the pilot on its ancestor, the steam locomotive. Although the engineer had an excellent view from his high perch, his position, removed somewhat away from the front, shielded his vision from the tracks immediately in front of the locomotive. Thus, he was protected from "train nystagmus," an involuntary oscillation of the eyeball caused by watching the rapid passing of the crossties at high speed, which was believed to induce hypnosis.

Additional cars were ordered from Budd, yet because the road had decided against articulation, it was possible to mix these cars with their regular heavyweight cars as needed. By 1938, the Santa Fe had more streamlined cars on its roster than any other railroad in the country.

Daylight Train

As early as 1906, the Southern Pacific Railroad (Espee) was promoting the coast line route between Los Angeles and San Francisco as the most beautiful train ride in the world. They ran fast, modern trains along this line culminating in the establishment, in April 1922, of a non-stop express called the *Daylight Limited*. Named to promote its daylight journey along the Pacific Ocean, it soon proved to be enormously popular and its schedule was increased from two days per week to daily service. Using conventional steam locomotives and heavyweight cars, it ran for 471 miles without stopping for passengers making it the longest non-stop passenger train in the world.

Improvements were made steadily through the 20s and the train's popularity increased until the Depression of the 1930s began. Then, small adjustments to schedule and equipment became necessary, yet Espee management decided to upgrade their passenger operations and naturally turned to the *Daylight* as the harbinger of a new image. They recruited Charles L. Eggelston, a talented designer, to produce a concept for the new train. Eggleston's first effort was totally unacceptable, looking like, in the words of the Espee's president, "a high speed trolley." Back at his drawing board, Eggelston, in association with Osker Kurlfinke, a well-known boiler and tender designer, and many other technical individuals from the railroad and from locomotive concerns, produced the soon-to-be-famous, modernized *Daylight*.

Scott #3333   ©1999 USPS

In March 1937, the Espee introduced its streamlined *Daylight* train (Scott #3333). The new, streamlined cars were built by Pullman-Standard but, because the shotwelding process that was essential to the joining of all stainless steel cars was protected by Budd Company patents, Pullman adopted a composite design. The cars were made principally of CorTen steel with stainless steel side panels. Their cost was about 25% lower than an equivalent Budd car but, unfortunately, water could penetrate the shell and rust eventually deteriorated the car bodies. It became necessary to rebuild the cars.

The class of the steam locomotives, 4-8-4 Northern types, used to haul the *Daylights*, were designated "Golden State" (GS). The first GS(-1) locomotives were delivered to the Southern Pacific Railroad in 1930 by the Baldwin Locomotive Works. When the streamlined *Daylight* trains entered service the road ordered six GS-2 models from the Lima Locomotive Works of essentially the same basic design as the original GS-1's, except that the latter were streamlined to complement the cars following. The streamlined engines, dramatic though they were, retained more than a hint of the steam locomotive beneath. Black and orange were their dominant colors with red accents; the smokebox front was painted silver. Railroad fans billed the *Daylight* as "the most beautiful train in the world" but it was practical also, reducing the inter-city time from 13 hours to less than 10.

In all, there were eight distinctly different Golden State models; models GS-2 through GS-5 were streamlined and all were built by Lima to meet increasing power and speed requirements imposed by the popularity of the *Daylights*. Models GS-6 through GS-8 were non-streamlined engines ordered by the Espee from various manufacturers to meet World War II demands in other than *Daylight* service.

The Espee was anxious to establish and maintain an excellent reputation for reliability and adherence to schedule on the *Daylight* route. For a time after *Coast Daylight* service was initiated, a standby streamlined locomotive was kept in readiness at San Luis Obispo, the halfway point of the run between San Francisco and Los Angeles. If either the northbound or southbound *Daylight* locomotive experienced a problem, the reserve locomotive could be substituted and the run could be completed with little delay.

The train was so popular and demand for seats so great that the Espee added a second *Daylight*, leaving later in the day. They were known as the *Morning Daylight* and the *Noon Daylight*. Later *Daylights* adopted diesel motive power.

Twentieth Century Limited Train

The New York Central Railroad had operated a crack express train called the *Twentieth Century Limited* between New York City and Chicago since 1902. That train shortened the scheduled time between those two cities to about 20 hours, eight hours less than the fastest trains before. When the *Century* service was inaugurated, the train was drawn by 2-6-2, Prairie type, locomotives. These were soon replaced by 4-6-0s built by the Brooks Locomotive Company. As new and better motive power was developed, it was quickly applied to this premier train. In the teens of the new century, Pacific type, 4-6-2, engines were installed at the head end and finally, the Central's famous Hudson type, 4-6-4 machines built by the American Locomotive Company, took over around 1927.

When the road's management realized that streamlining was an important, if not necessary, ingredient for success in attracting passengers, they looked to their premier train as a prime candidate for upgrading. (The Central had earlier upgraded a midwestern train, the *Mercury*, and discovered the economic advantages to be gained from streamlining.)

The 1938 *Century* (Scott #3335) consisted of room cars exclusively (except for Railway Post Office, dining and observation/lounge cars), some having a new configuration called "roomettes." Responsibility for the styling for the entire train was given to Henry Dreyfuss, one of the prominent industrial designers of the period. Dreyfuss delivered a product that many railroading authorities believe to be the ultimate in design, even to this day. His elegant creation was decorated mainly in blue and gray: light and dark gray with blue and aluminum highlights on the outside and gray, blue, tan, and rust colors within. An indication of its eminence is that the *Century* was pictured on two different United States stamps.

Scott #3335   ©1999 USPS

Beautiful though they were, the appearance of the cars alone would not have provided the enduring praise and honor given to this train. The outstanding element of Dreyfuss' design was his inspired treatment of the locomotive. The Central had decided to use a 4-6-4 Hudson type steam locomotive at the head end. The Hudson type locomotive originated with the New York Central Railroad and the first of them was delivered in 1927. The Central's fleet of 4-6-4 locomotives numbered 255 in total, acquired over a number of years. The Hudson type proliferated on the New York Central Railroad and was, arguably, the most eye-appealing steam locomotive type ever built. Its mechanical components were carefully positioned and they symbolized power, speed, and grace in the recognizable steam locomotive form.

In 1937, the American Locomotive Company began delivery of an order for 50 engines, designated class J-3a. The last 10 of these, delivered in 1938, were designated for application to the *Twentieth Century Limited* and were streamlined versions. Under Dreyfuss' direction, the familiar outline of the locomotive was covered strategically to convey the sem-

blance of streamlining while leaving impressive mechanical parts, like the cylinders and wheels, exposed. The result was a product (Scott 3185k) that delivered the best of both worlds: a modern streamlined appearance that still revealed massive mechanical elements to the steam aficionado. The most recognizable characteristic was the rounded, bulbous nose bisected by a crescent-shaped fin that was reminiscent of the crest on an ancient Roman soldier's helmet. As an measure of Dreyfuss' genius, the streamlining shrouds added only 5,500 pounds to the weight of the locomotive.

Able though they were, the J-3s were used only for a few years but during that time, in 1943, one of them experienced difficulties with a feedwater pump during its run south from Buffalo. Its relief crew at Syracuse declined to switch engines and continued the journey to New York City. About 22 miles east of Syracuse, running at 70 miles per hour, her boiler exploded for lack of water. The cab crew died, 29 others were injured, and eleven cars derailed and blocked the four main line tracks. The locomotive was destroyed and then there were nine.

During World War II, the road applied some conventional (non-streamlined) 4-8-2 Mohawk type locomotives to the *Twentieth Century Limited* and then, beginning in 1945, assigned Electro-Motive Division E7 diesel locomotives to haul the train. As the diesels assumed this responsibility, the Dreyfuss locomotives were withdrawn and, between 1945 and 1947, were sent back to the shops to have their shrouds removed, whereupon they continued to be used in general service.

To reduce fueling delays between New York and Chicago, a new tender was designed for the *Twentieth Century Limited* in 1943. This tender was exceptionally large, almost as long as the locomotive itself, and enabled the run to be made with only one stop for fuel. (For steam locomotives, one of the serious handicaps to fast schedules was the necessity to stop fairly frequently to refuel and add water to its tender. The latter problem had been solved earlier when track pans were installed at strategically-spaced intervals. These were wooden or iron troughs, hundreds of feet long, located between and below the rails. This watering system was invented by an Englishman, John Ramsbottom, and first applied in the United States on the New York Central and Hudson River Railroad at Montrose, New York, in 1870. Traveling at speed and equipped with a "jerk water" scoop on its tender, a locomotive could scoop up hundreds of gallons of water without stopping. Numerous improvements were made to the system before the end of the century and, although pans required considerable attention, including the chipping of accumulated ice in the winter and keeping them clear of rocks and debris, mineral deposits, and even fish and turtles, the New York Central, along with many other railroads, continued to used track pans on their steam powered routes. Coal refueling was more difficult.)

Aboard the train, numerous personal services, evocative of those amenities supplied on the original *Twentieth Century Limited*, a barber and secretary, were available. One could shower in the private room situated near the barber shop and radio-telephone service (beginning in 1947) was available. As an extra fare train, it was patronized mostly by businessmen, stars of the entertainment world, and other well-to-do personages.

The Central's great competitor on the New York-Chicago run was the Pennsylvania Railroad, whose first streamlined *Broadway Limiteds* left, not coincidentally, the same terminal cities at the same time. The first two of these new, grand trains, the *Century* and the *Broadway*, left Chicago and New York at the same time on June 15, 1938. The departure of the Chicago-bound *Century* was memorialized by short speeches by passengers James Cagney, the actor, Ford Frick, the president of the National Baseball League, and F. E. Williamson, president of the New York Central Railroad. Their remarks were broadcast by the Columbia Broadcasting Company. Alas, on its last run, in December 1967, the westbound *Century* arrived nine hours late, delayed by a freight train wreck at Conneaut, Ohio, then detoured over Norfolk and Western tracks. Although occasioned by conditions beyond its control, this incident resulted in a humiliating ending to the illustrious record of the *Twentieth Century Limited.*

Interestingly, although competition always was a factor between the two roads, the order for the cars that would comprise the *Century* and those of the *Broadway Limited* was placed with Pullman Standard at the same time. This enabled the builder to achieve economies of scale in its production of the equipment and a consequent lower cost to both railroads. It also resulted in a sameness in car design and features. However, the *Broadway Limited* was given its own personality by Raymond Loewy, another renowned industrial designer.

In addition to those mentioned (and their descendants), there were many streamlined trains operating throughout the United States in the pre- and post-World War II years, some operating over regional routes, others over long distances. Many of these famous trains adopted their names from earlier renowned trains.

In the former category were the Reading's *Crusader*, the Lackawanna's *Phoebe Snow*, the Central of Georgia's *Nancy Hanks* II (named after an earlier *Nancy Hanks* train which honored a famous racehorse), and the Rock Island's *Rockets*.

Long haul trains included the *Sunset Limited* of the Southern Pacific Railroad, the Great Northern's *Empire Builder*, the Atlantic Coast Lines *Champion*, the Southern's *Southerner*, and the Seaboard Air Line's *Silver Comet*. These latter trains used Pennsylvania Railroad tracks to reach New York City.

The *California Zephyr* was a collaborative effort between the Chicago, Burlington & Quincy, the Denver, Rio Grande & Western, and the Western Pacific Railroads.

World War II severely curtailed the production of new railroad equipment; streamlined passenger cars did not merit a high priority. At the war's conclusion, however, the necessity for upgrading and augmenting railroad passenger fleets brought in floods of orders to the major builders. Unfortunately, it was to be a short-lived renaissance because within two decades, rail passenger business had passed in large measure to the highways and the airways.

The Diesel Takes Over

In addition to the recognizable diesel locomotives pictured on Scott #s 993, 1006, and 1573 (all discussed previously), three other stamps portray diesel locomotives. In two of these instances (Scott #947, U. S. Postage Stamp Centenary, and 1511, ZIP Code), the engines are included with a number of other transport means—horses, ships, trucks, and airplanes—that have been used to move the mails. It should be noted that before the Postal service was organized by Benjamin Franklin in 1753, the mails in this country were inefficient and unreliable. Franklin, unpaid for eight years, contributed his own money to establish 24 hour service, new routes, and the distribution of newspapers. The third stamp (Scott #987) carries a design intended to describe the form of the top half of a coin. Issued to commemorate the American Bankers Association, founded in 1875 to "promote the general welfare and usefulness of banks," it pictures a scene that suggests typical recipients of banking services: the home; farm; factory; and the transportation industry, the latter represented by a diesel railcar. Note that in the following discussion the terms "diesel locomotive" and "diesel-electric locomotive" are used interchangeably. Although diesel-mechanical and diesel-hydraulic locomotives have been built, the overwhelming majority of units use a diesel engine as the prime mover to drive a generator that produces electricity, which is used by electric motors at the axles to propel the machine.

Scott #947

The first application of diesel engines to railroad motive power in the United States was for a railcar built by the Southern Pacific Railroad in 1905 which performed poorly. The first successful diesel locomotive was built in Germany and used on Swiss railways in 1913. Back in America, the General Electric Company (GE) collaborated with the American Locomotive Company (ALCO) and Ingersoll-Rand (I-R) in the development of a diesel-electric locomotive. A successful switcher was demonstrated and used on the Central Railroad of New Jersey in 1925. However, the move to supplant steam power was not accomplished quickly.

Scott #1511

First, it was a number of years before a diesel road engine became available and, second, the Great Depression delayed all but the most essential improvements and innovations. As discussed earlier, streamlining was adopted in the mid-1930s to increase railroad passenger business and, at that point, it was natural to look to the diesel locomotive to complete the streamlined effect. Of course, the business-oriented railroad executives were quick to recognize the other advantages that the diesel engine provided over steam engines. Longer runs between fueling (without need for constant water replenishment), higher thermal efficiencies (and reduced fuel costs), and relative cleanliness were among its attributes. Axle loadings were low and the drive wheels did not pound and damage the rails. Many operating tasks, such as oiling, could be automated and the engines could develop maximum power at any speed. The diesel was less affected by ambient temperature changes and parts standardization allowed more rapid servicing, quicker turnaround times, and greater availability.

General Motors Corporation entered the diesel locomotive field in 1930 when it acquired Electro-Motive Company (EMC), a manufacturer of gas-electric railcars and the Winton Engine Company, EMC's engine supplier. The first of the company's diesel locomotive offerings, a switching engine, was marketed in 1935. 1939 saw the introduction of the first mass-produced road freight engine, EMC's model FT and, in 1941, EMC and Winton were merged into the parent company and became the Electro-Motive Division (EMD) of GM. During World War II, EMD built diesel locomotives (it sold over 1,000 FT units) and diesel engines for Navy ships. Because new locomotive development was prohibited during the war years, EMD emerged from wartime service as the preeminent American diesel locomotive manufacturer. By 1951, it had produced 10,000 units.

After their first offering, ALCO continued their partnership with I-R but in 1929 they acquired an engine company of their own. They did continue to rely upon GE for the electrical content of their engines. In the mid-1950s, GE started their own locomotive division and became a direct competitor of ALCO. ALCO left the field in December 1969, when it ceased production of all new locomotives. GE continues to make diesel-electric locomotives in competition with EMD. Although the latter dominated the field before 1980, General Electric gradually increased its market share and became the principal producer of diesel-electric locomotives by the 1990s.

131

The Baldwin Locomotive Works began erecting diesel-electric locomotives in 1939; however, the third major locomotive manufacturer, the Lima Locomotive Works, delayed its entry until 1949 when it merged with enginemaker Hamilton. Shortly thereafter (1950), the combined company, Lima-Hamilton, merged with Baldwin, but their (Lima-Hamilton's) line of diesels was discontinued. Just as GE and ALCO, neighbors in Schenectady, New York, collaborated, so did Baldwin and Westinghouse Corporation, both Pennsylvania concerns. Baldwin left the locomotive market in 1956.

Scott #987

There were numerous other builders of diesel locomotives ranging from Fairbanks-Morse to the Heisler Locomotive Works. The latter, which built only one diesel locomotive, was the same company that built geared steam locomotives beginning in the late 1800s. A few diesel-electric locomotives were also built in the shops of three or four railways.

Unquestionably, the diesel locomotive revolutionized and provided immeasurable benefits to railroading but, in so doing, and in Maury Klein's words, "it swept away a rich, century-old way of life." One of the consequences of its acceptance had nothing to do with its technical attributes, but rather with labor requirements. The longest and heaviest trains could be handled by the simple addition of "booster" units without increasing the crew requirements. The possibilities for automating various tasks led to the elimination of oilers and wipers and, most important of all, the layoff of firemen. The latter did not happen immediately; the brotherhoods fought the issue tooth and nail from 1937 to 1963. In that year, the Supreme Court upheld the railroad's position and permitted them to change the work rules that required a firemen (sometimes two) on diesel locomotives.

Diesel locomotives have remained the major type of motive power since the demise of the steam locomotive, a transition that began in earnest after World War II. Except on a few electrified routes in scattered parts of the country, the words "diesel" and "locomotive" are now synonymous in railroad usage in the United States. There is no question regarding the superiority of diesel locomotives but most would agree that in appearance it is a pale substitute for the old steam engine. Although it is a model of efficiency and sophisticated ability, it does not convey the same sense of harnessed power—most of its moving parts are shrouded—and it emits no staccato blasts and blowoff of steam. The old iron horse has been relegated to museum status but, thankfully, many of those museums are operating tourist lines where children (and even some grown-ups) can still see a steam locomotive in action.

IS THERE LIGHT AT THE END OF THE TUNNEL?

(1950-Present)

Various authorities define the first half of the twentieth century as the "Golden Age of Railroading." That age is better delimited by the years between 1900 and 1930. During most of that period inter-city travel was mainly by train. The railroad's only competitor for passengers was the motor bus; highways and automobiles were insufficiently developed to provide a realistic alternative. Insofar as freight was concerned, the railroad reigned supreme for long distance movement.

There was nothing golden for the railroads during the Depression years of the 30s and the 1940s saw an artificially stimulated increase in traffic due to World War II and the shortage of available, new automobiles in the five years following. After that shortage was overcome, travelers adopted the auto for medium length trips. The airplane, which had undergone extraordinary development during the war, became a preferred means of transportation for longer journeys.

Beginning about 1945, railroads experienced a slow, steady decline in passenger traffic, a trend that accelerated in the 50s, helped by the construction of the interstate highway system. Railroads recorded 25.3 billion passenger-miles in 1941, a figure that climbed to 86.3 billion passenger-miles in 1945. A scant four years later, that number had dropped to 32.2 billion passenger-miles and it continued its slide without interruption.
The railroads, finding themselves in a "Catch-22" situation, fought a losing fight. Although they recognized the need to rehabilitate their rights of way and replace their fleets with modern equipment, low profits (or outright losses) prevented them from doing so. In the alternative, they offered regular announcements of "trains of tomorrow" while many of the popular magazines served up impractical solutions, such as long-distance monorail systems and the promise of train speeds to match airplanes.

Even the few practical, well-accepted innovations, like "Vista-dome" cars, were unable to halt the steep decline to the point where only a few, highly traveled "corridors" —where significant numbers of passengers are carried—remain. Granted, there is a (much reduced) inter-city network, but understandably, service is infrequent and much slower than air travel.

Yet technical innovations continued to be proposed. Baldwin and Westinghouse built a steam-electric locomotive in 1947 that was delivered to the Chesapeake and Ohio Railway; the Pennsylvania Railroad had a steam turbine engine. New lightweight cars proliferated and, in later years, cars that "leaned" into curves, so that high speeds could be maintained, were adopted. Even more advanced schemes, such as magnetic levitation, were seriously being considered to increase train speed. Yet none of these developments, alone or in total, were able to stem the passenger exodus.

As passenger loads diminished, perishable freight became the next casualty; many of those commodities were lost to the airplane and motor truck, despite the adoption of "piggy-backing" which provided door-to-door movement. Bulk freight was the only bright spot for the railroads but even there, pipe lines appropriated some of that business. Again, the railroads were innovative; unit trains and huge unloading machines permitted rapid turnaround times and sped coal and ore to their destination in record times.

It may be that the railroads will triumph yet because of their unquestionable superiority in the energy conservation and environmental arenas. There are a few encouraging signs on the horizon. Commuter railroads still prosper (although requiring subsidies in many cases). Interurban cars, now called "light rail," are staging a comeback. These include the notable Tijuana trolley, running between San Diego and Tijuana, Mexico, and a light rail line between Camden and Trenton in the most densely populated state, New Jersey. A new, high speed, extra-fare train, the *Acela*, has been introduced on the Northeast Corridor line between Boston and Washington, D.C. There are optimists and, yes, some realists, who are willing to give the old iron horse another chance. Railroading may be ill and suffering but it is not yet dead.

Balanced On One Rail

A monorail is a railroad upon which trains are either suspended from or straddle a single supporting rail or beam. Although the concept is over

175 years old (the first monorail was built in England in 1821 to carry materials), it is being promoted today as a modern system that has great potential for solving people moving problems.

Scott #1196 portrays the 550 foot high "Space Needle" at the 1962 Seattle World's Fair, encircled by a high speed monorail track and train. The monorail was built especially to connect downtown Seattle with the outlying World's Fair site and it offered the first municipal monorail service in the United States.

As early as 1874, the "Prismoid One Rail Railroad" was promoted as an inexpensive and safer kind of track. In this system, a train was supported on wheels mounted 90° apart from each other and they rolled along an inverted V-shaped track. A few years later, the Meigs Elevated Railway was demonstrated. Here, an iron girder with lower "bearing rails" was mounted on posts and the train wheels, angularly separated, rolled against it. Although these, and other monorail proposals, were novel and practical concepts that fired the public imagination, they were never adopted by the railroad fraternity.

Scott #1196

The first passenger monorails were built at the end of the 19th century and one of these, the "Unicycle Railway," was applied in Brooklyn, New York in 1890. Boynton's monorail used a steam locomotive with in-line wheels built by the Portland Company in Maine. The locomotive and cars ran on a single rail and were prevented from falling over by an overhead steadying structure. Boynton tested the idea on a stretch of abandoned standard gauge railroad, using only one of the two rails for the trials. It worked well enough to serve as the prototype for another application in the west. The scheme was later refined to use electric motive power and another, two mile long, demonstration track was built in 1894 on Long Island for Boynton's "Bicycle Electric Railway." The motor car, which carried 24 passengers, was streamlined in anticipation of 100 mile per hour speeds. Trailing cars were to carry up to 50 people each. The planned railroad never did get off the ground.

Probably the most famous of the early monorails was the one erected at Wuppertal in Germany and inaugurated in 1901. The 9.3 mile long Wuppertal installation, where the car hangs from an upper rail, is still in daily use. Modern suspended monorails use a "split-rail," essentially two rails that are closely spaced. Some systems that use an overhead rail are gyroscopically stabilized.

The Alweg monorail (named for Axel L. Wenner-Gren) employs cars that straddle a concrete beamway which serves as a structural member and the running surface for the rubber-tired cars. Stability is provided by guide wheels that bear on the sides of the beam. Since 1950, about a dozen Alweg (or similar) systems have been built worldwide, including two of the most famous ever, those at the Disney parks in the United States. The Disneyland line in California (the first practical monorail to be built in this country) was 2.5 miles long when built in the late 1950s while the Disney World installation, built in 1971, traverses 14 miles of beamways.

At this time, most monorails are short systems, circling amusement parks or moving people from parking lots to terminals at airports (Tampa and Newark) but there are a number of current proposals for longer, mass transit systems. One of the monorail's advantages is that it can be built as an elevated system using a minimum of ground level real estate in densely trafficked urban areas. Construction costs are about one-quarter those of conventional underground railways (some advocates put the cost at 10% of the cost to build a subway). But critics complain about the unsightliness of the above ground structure and low speeds and the fact that switching of cars is not as easily accomplished as on a conventional railroad.

Monorail systems are under consideration in a number of U. S. cities but as yet there are no major new installations. Las Vegas has opened the first section of a projected city-wide system and Jacksonville has recently installed a small-scale downtown monorail. Denver and Indianapolis are exploring the technology. The Seattle monorail, which survived a massive earthquake in early 2001, is an Alweg design and uses the only Alweg-built trains that are still in operation. The mile long line is operated by a private corporation that pays the city for the concession. A voter referendum held in 1997 approved an extension for a 40 mile long system which is now in the planning stage.

LABOR AND LEGISLATION

Railroads, Labor, and the Law: Strikes, Regulation, and Administration

Railroad employees were organized early on in the labor movement into so-called "Brotherhoods." The Brotherhoods were part labor union, part fraternal organization, and part insurance company and the first of them, the Brotherhood of Locomotive Engineers (which was called initially the Brotherhood of the Footboard), was founded in 1863. This group was followed shortly by brotherhoods confined to railway

Scott #824

conductors (1868), railway firemen (1873), and trainmen (1883). As unions, they adopted the position that their members were of a superior class insofar as labor was concerned. They were slow to strike and maintained close and effective relationships with railroad management. As a result, their members enjoyed a respected status, high wages, and a strong seniority system that protected their jobs and assured promotion into increasingly responsible and better paying jobs. As fraternal groups, they maintained "lodges" where business was conducted and social activities were held. A railroader was entitled to a fine funeral, arranged by the organization, and his widow could expect monetary and emotional support from the deceased's "brothers" and their families. The benevolent aspect of the brotherhood's activities was a strong factor in the loyalty of its members. Some important events in the railroad labor and legislative picture involved many personages illustrated on American postage stamps, some of which are presented below.

In 1877, the railroad scene erupted in violence in what was probably the first widespread labor unrest in the country. **Rutherford B. Hayes** (Scott #824) was president when the "Great Railway Strikes of 1877" exploded at Martinsburg, West Virginia. Several large eastern railroads had colluded on rates and then announced reductions in wages. The railroads continued to effect "economies," some in petty ways. For example, the Lake Shore and Michigan Central railroad, a New York Central affiliate, charged its train crews for the return trip to their starting point. In one egregious case, they paid an engineer 16 cents for making one run and then charged 25 cents to return him home!

Other roads followed the lead of the eastern roads and a strike was begun against the Baltimore and Ohio Railroad. The state militia was sympathetic to the strikers but ineffective at curbing the strike and Hayes ordered Federal troops to the scene. The troops fired on the crowd and killed ten people; their action precipitated rebellion over a wider region, with the worst unrest occurring at Pittsburgh, Pennsylvania. In the course of the insurrection at Pittsburgh, more than 100 locomotives and 2,000 cars were destroyed and many railroad structures were burned. Twenty four people were killed, thousands were hurt, damages exceeded $5 million, and it took more than 10,000 soldiers to end the strike.

One of the consequences of the 1877 railroad disputes (and the earlier actions of the Molly Maguires in the Pennsylvania coal fields) was the emergence of the Knights of Labor, an organization that had heretofore operated mostly in secret. The Knights attracted workers from all industries and occupations into their union and precipitated a number of strikes against western railroads in 1884-85 until Jay Gould agreed to end his opposition to their organizing efforts. The Knights enjoyed a string of successes but then went into decline in the late 1880s when they failed to prevail against the Texas and Pacific Railroad, which had abrogated an earlier agreement. (Another, perhaps more telling, blow was the loss of public acceptance after the Haymarket riots of 1886.)

Because of the Brotherhoods disinclination to strike and "cozy" position with management, a more radical leader, Eugene Debs, who was secretary of the Brotherhood of Locomotive Fireman, lost patience and organized his own, more militant, competing organization, the American Railway Union (ARU) in 1893. The ARU drew its members from the ranks of other railroad employees, shop men, track and yard laborers, and station workers. It was a powerful force, potentially capable of exerting enormous influence, yet was short-lived and "lost" its first major battle when its members supported the Pullman strike of 1894.

Grover Cleveland, the 22nd and 24th President of the United States (Scott #827), alienated several disparate groups because of positions that he advocated. Like Rutherford Hayes before him, he lost the support of

139

one of these, organized labor, by siding against the strikers at the Pullman works in 1894. The strike was occasioned by a cut in wages, unaccompanied by any reduction in rents or staples at Pullman's stores in his model city (see "Palaces on Wheels" vignette). Eugene Debs, leader of the American Railway Union attempted to convince Pullman to submit the dispute to arbitration, but failed. Against Debs' advice,

Scott #827

union members nationwide struck against any railroad that carried Pullman cars. Again, despite contrary advice from the Governor of Illinois, Cleveland—through his Attorney-General, Richard Olney—secured an injunction against the strikers and dispatched Federal troops to Pullman, Illinois to break the bitter strike. The president remarked, "If it takes the entire Army and Navy of the United States to deliver a postal card to Chicago, that card will be delivered." In the ensuing riots, 12 died, Debs was arrested, and the strike was quelled. After the strike was broken, the various railroads fired those who walked out and adopted a stratagem to prevent their re-hire by other roads. They required a "service letter," a recommendation from their previous employer that certified that they were not involved in the Pullman action. The fraternity of railroad "boomers" quickly found ways to circumvent the blacklist, the most common of which was to buy faked service letters from railroad clerk counterfeiters.

Scott #988

It may be that **Samuel Gompers** (Scott #988) contribution to railroad history lies not in what he did, but rather in what he did not do. In his own words, keeping the American Federation of Labor (AFL) detached from the Pullman dispute in 1894, "was the biggest service that could have been performed to maintain the integrity of the Railroad Brotherhoods." He remained aloof despite entreaties for help by Eugene Debs and other labor factors as the AFL was not affiliated with them and also because Debs' organization had recruited many members from the ranks of the long-standing railroad operating brotherhoods. Gompers saw Debs' defeat as a victory for the brotherhoods, for whom he entertained the hope of inclusion into the AFL. At a later time, Gompers made inquiries into the legality of incidents surrounding the Railroad Shopmen's strike but chose not to involve himself in that conflict.

Scott #1039

One of the most important and far-reaching pieces of legislation enacted in the United States was the Sherman Anti-Trust Act. An injunction under the Act had been applied against the Pullman strikers in 1894. Although it became law in 1890,but before **Theodore Roosevelt's** (Scott #1039) election to the presidency, Roosevelt—called TR by many— wielded the Act as a weapon and established a reputation as a "trustbuster." The pinnacle of his success in this arena occurred during his first term and involved the Northern Securities case.

Around the turn of the century (1901), the Union Pacific's Harriman and the Great Northern's Jim Hill both sought to bring their tracks into Chicago. Through stock accumulation, Hill bought control of the Chicago, Burlington and Quincy Railroad which entered the city. For his part, to keep from being excluded from the city, Harriman tried to buy sufficient Northern Pacific Railroad (which also reached into Chicago) shares to gain control. Interestingly, the Northern Pacific was owned by Jim Hill at the time, so Harriman's action became very personal to Hill. With the two giants competing against each other, the value of Northern Pacific stock soared ten-fold within a few days. This precipitated a financial panic as margin buyers had to dump other stocks to cover their positions. At this point, J. P. Morgan entered the scene. Morgan, who preferred order in the market, mediated a solution and oversaw the establishment of the Northern Securities Company.

Control of the Great Northern, the Northern Pacific, and the Burlington roads was vested in the Northern Securities Company and Harriman was made a member of the board. Thus, it dominated the Chicago railroad market and, as important, affected the market in the securities of the involved railroads. The incorporation reprised the public outcry against trusts, and against Northern Securities in particular. Several states intended to fight the company in court but Roosevelt acted swiftly and

141

preempted them. He commanded his attorney general to sue for the company's dissolution. The legal battle ensued for two years and eventually ended at the Supreme Court. Contrary to expectation, the Court upheld a lower court decision and closed down Northern Securities. One of the associate justices, **Oliver Wendell Holmes, Jr.** (Scott #1288), had been appointed to the Court by Roosevelt in 1902. Seen to be "liberal," an

Scott #1288

attitude thought to be "anti-trust," he surprised observers by joining the dissenting minority. Holmes' action precipitated TR's wrath; the president, feeling betrayed by his appointee, thundered, "I could carve a better judge out of a banana." Holmes, however, felt strongly about his position and its correctness under the Constitution as evidenced by a rather long written dissent. He did admit that "it broke up our incipient friendship."

During his second term, TR turned his attention to the railroads and spoke against rate fixing and other abuses perpetuated by them (perpetuated, in large part, because the consolidations during the latter decades of the 19th century furthered near-monopolistic powers). He attempted to provide the Interstate Commerce Commission (ICC) with greater power to set rates and for valuing railroad property. His proposal, modified somewhat, passed the House but was bitterly debated in the Senate. (This could be explained by the fact that railroad reform was popular with the public and the House of Representatives was an elected body more attuned to the public's will. At that time, before the 17th amendment to the Constitution was ratified, some senators were elected and some appointed by their state legislatures, depending upon the governing state law. Not being a wholly elected body many of the senators were influenced by railroad interests.) In the end, the Senate did pass an amended version which strengthened the ICC considerably.

Despite Roosevelt's vigorous application of anti-trust legislation, many inequities remained. An English journalist summed up the situation in 1910 thus: "(the United States is) an enormously rich country overrun by a horde of robber barons, and very inadequately policed by the central government."

Scott #1202

Sam Rayburn (Scott #1202) was raised in the agrarian state of Texas, at a time when politicians were railing against the abuses by railroads. As a young state legislator, he sought—and won— a position on the Common Carriers Committee in order to influence railroad legislation. But it was as a United States representative in the Wilson administration that he drafted more important and farther-reaching legislation affecting railroads. The "Rayburn Bill," introduced in 1914, charged the Interstate Commerce Commission with the responsibility for approving all issues of railroad stocks and bonds before they were sold to the public, and it also restricted an individual from serving on more than one railroad board, an attack on interlocking directorates. The House passed the bill and the Senate amended it slightly. However, events conspired to deny its passage. Louis Brandeis, a confidant of President Wilson, had reservations and Wilson himself saw a need to court business leaders and to be seen as less antagonistic by modifying his strong antitrust position. Finally, World War One began and affected the stock market and railroad business adversely. Despite intense personal promotion, which continued until 1917, Rayburn could not get the bill voted into law.

Charles Evans Hughes (Scott #1195) was a governor of the state of New York, a justice (and Chief Justice) of the Supreme Court, and a presidential candidate. In each of these roles, he affected railroad legislation. As governor, he proposed legislation that paralleled the national Interstate Commerce Commission Act by establishing a commission that oversaw railroad operations within the state. This commission was granted broader authority to regulate rates and to provide for the safety of employees and public; unlike the national body, it could act upon its own initiative. While a member of the Supreme Court, he wrote opinions

Scott #1195

involving rate setting which extended federal authority over railroads while protecting states rights in the area. These were complex issues in which he rendered impartial and clear judgments. When he was a presidential contender, running against Woodrow Wilson, he criticized Wilson for yielding to demands made by the railroad brotherhoods in order to avoid a strike. After the brotherhoods refused to arbitrate their quarrel with the railroads as he requested, Wilson asked Congress for the passage of a law which acceded to the demands of the unions. Hughes (and many others) believed that this was an abandonment of principle and denounced the president. Though it typified Hughes' high moral standards, his arguments were lost in the grater issues involving war and general prosperity.

As the year 1917 drew to a close, President **Woodrow Wilson** (Scott #1040) took over the operation of the nation's railroads. This singular, dramatic act was in response to the extraordinarily poor performance demonstrated by the railroad managements as wartime traffic increased. As materiel flowed into the eastern ports, freight cars choked the yards. Rather than moving the empties west to receive more goods, an unprofitable

Scott #1040

movement, the cars sat unused. Then, the Railroad War Board was established by the railroads themselves to provide direction for their operation. But each railroad, protecting its own business, routed trains in roundabout (but profitable to their own company) trips. The Board awarded priority status in profusion—at one time 85% of all trains ran under a "top" priority. By November 1917, over 200,000 cars sat idle in eastern yards and Wilson acted. Within a few months after assumption of the railroads, the United States Railroad Administration (USRA) established coordination measures that eliminated the congestion. The USRA ran the nation's railroads for the next 26 months. It enjoyed the freedom to disregard the many state rules and regulations and to increase wages so that labor, which had fled to the wartime manufacturing industries, returned. On the other hand, critics complained that equipment, rolling stock, and tracks were allowed to deteriorate and that the labor concessions reduced productivity by as much as 30 percent. Government losses during its management averaged nearly 2 million dollars a day! Whether the drastic expropriation was justified is still questioned but there is no doubt that it kept the trains and their loads moving.

Scott #684

In the same year that the Esch-Cummins Transportation Act of 1920 was passed, railroad management returned to the owners. The Act established a Railroad Labor Board to help mediate labor disputes and also directed the Interstate Commerce Commission to consolidate the nation's railroads, yet maintain competition. Some of the provisions from Sam Rayburn's earlier bill were incorporated into the Esch-Cummins Act. It was hoped that such action would improve the financial health of the railroads and, over the next three years, a plan was generated that would have brought the roads into nineteen separate systems. As presidents, **Warren G. Harding** (Scott #684) and **Calvin Coolidge** (Scott #2219b) both endorsed the plan, but it never was approved by the legislative branch. Coolidge was faulted for failing to implement the ICC plan because he did not push it vigorously. He believed his endorsement was sufficient support; his critics blamed his "lack of vision." Coolidge was less sanguine concerning the Labor Board and was pleased that the Watson-Parker Act of 1926 advocated collective bargaining and included "cooling-off" measures that prevented work stoppages.

During Warren G. Harding's administration, **Herbert Hoover** (Scott #1269) became Secretary of Commerce, a post that he continued to occupy into Calvin Coolidge's administration. In 1922, nearly 400,000 railroad shop men went on strike nationwide. The catalysts for this strike were the establishment of a labor-sympathetic Department of Labor in 1913 and the government operation of the railroads during World War I. The United States Railroad Administration, during the labor shortages of the war years, freely permitted union organizers to recruit members and union membership in the rail

Scott #2219b   ©1986 USPS

trades (as opposed to the operating brother-hoods) increased dramatically. When the owners recovered their property after the war, wage cuts and sub-contracting of shop services were the trigger that precipitated the strike. It was a bitter, vicious strike with considerable violence reported and elements of it dragged on for two years. The Railroad Labor Board, established two years earlier, failed to mediate the dispute, despite the personal intervention of Harding, Hoover, and Hooper, chairman of the Board. Next, Attorney General Harry Daugherty obtained a sweeping restraining order against the strikers, an action that was con-

Scott 1269

demned by Hoover. Harding supported his Attorney General but instructed him to apply the injunction with restraint. Ultimately, settlements were achieved piecemeal; union leaders settled with some roads, but left workers at other locations to continue their strikes, essentially unsupported. The bitter fruits of the strike included the defeat suffered by labor, the halting of management attempts to reduce wages further, reconsideration of the mechanisms in place to settle strikes, and the loss of power suffered by the Railway Labor Board, which was shown to be completely ineffectual. As an aside, William Allen White (Scott #960), editor of the *Emporia Gazette*, demonstrated his support of the strikers on cards displayed in his office windows. Threatened with arrest, Allen removed the cards but wrote a stinging editorial in defense of free speech.

Both before and after his presidency, Calvin Coolidge was involved with railroads. As a Massachusetts state senator, he supported the New Haven Railroad's proposal to build a trolley system in his district. He shepherded the bill through the Senate and it was passed by the House. The Governor vetoed the bill but the veto was overridden by the General Court. Senator Coolidge went on to chair the railroad committee where he generally acted sympathetically to the interests of the railroads. In 1932, Coolidge was appointed to the National Transportation Committee, a group charged with recommending changes in the transportation industry. The group's final report proposed a greatly expanded and strengthened ICC. But Coolidge, who died before the work was completed, went even further. He suggested a high level transportation department, anticipating the current cabinet-level Department of Transportation, that would regulate all modes of interstate transportation.

In 1892, the People's Party of America (Populists) convened in Omaha and, among other things, espoused government ownership of railroads. This position was born in the Granger movement (see vignette, "*National Grange*") and by the time **George W. Norris** (Scott #1184) was elected to Congress, many states and the Federal government were involved in regulation of railroad rates and safety practices. Norris was an agrarian who believed in public ownership of railroads because, in his words, whoever "controls transportation wields enormous power for good or ill over the lives of his fellow creatures." At first, Norris attempted to tighten control through the Interstate Commerce Commission but was rebuffed in the Senate. In 1924, he introduced a bill establishing a government corporation that would be empowered to build and operate railroads (and dams and coal mines) throughout the United States and operate them at cost. The bill was defeated and Norris never again advanced this position regarding transportation. He did continue to argue for public ownership of electricity production, especially hydro power and he was instrumental in the establishment of the Tennessee Valley Authority. One of the dams in that complex was named for him.

Scott #1184

When **Franklin D. Roosevelt** (Scott #1950) entered office in 1932, his administration became involved with the railroads almost immediately. The Great Depression had affected the railroads severely; roads totaling over 40,000 miles were in receivership or being reorganized. Business declined and essential maintenance was suspended for the most part, a situation that reverberated into the steel and coal industries. FDR's "New Deal" policies redefined the role and functions of the Interstate

Commerce Commission and granted it additional powers concerning failing railroads. Within the first 100 days of his inauguration, the Railroad Coordination Act, intended to encourage railroad self-reorganization, was passed. The Railroad Retirement Act of 1934 facilitated the pensioning of veteran employees but was declared unconstitutional the following year. (It was reenacted in 1937 in a court-acceptable form.) But the

Scott #1950   ©1982 USPS

problems were too deep and too widespread to provide quick and ready solutions and it was not until World War II began that a general economic recovery extended to the railroads.

During World War II (in 1943), the government's 1918 action of taking over the railroads was reprised, although the cause compelling the action was different. In the more recent instance, a strike threat loomed and Roosevelt, through his Secretary of Labor, Frances Perkins (Scott # 1821), exercised his wartime executive powers to effect the takeover. The government's administrative tenure, though it was short, enabled the railroads to keep operating in the national interest.

George Meany (Scott #2848) was a powerful labor leader who was an officer in the American Federation of Labor (AFL) from 1939 to 1955, and then, the Congress of Industrial Organizations (CIO) from 1955 to 1979. Since the railroad brotherhoods were independent organizations,

Meany had no direct involvement in railroad issues. However, one of the unions that was in the province of his responsibility was the Transport Workers Union (TWU), an affiliate that organized the New York City subway system. Financial support for the TWU was provided by the Communist Party but, after the union left the AFL and joined the CIO, it renounced its Communist sponsorship. This relatively small but strong union brought the city to a near-standstill through a sit-down action in 1937. When the AFL and CIO merged in 1955, Meany was elected president of

Scott #2848   ©1994 USPS

the combined organization. Meany also worked closely with A. Philip Randolph, the head of the Brotherhood of Sleeping Car Porters (see vignette, *"Palaces on Wheels"*) on outreach and other programs intended to increase the representation of minorities in the union movement.

Harlan F. Stone (Scott # 965) a Supreme Court justice, believed that the Railroad Retirement Act, which required the railroads to retire older workers, was "a bad one." In a close decision, the Act was found to be

Scott #965

unconstitutional; the majority opinion stated, in part, that "Congressional effort to compel railroads to pension off older workers must fail for want of any relation between the pensioning system and the efficiency or safety of the national rail network." In 1945, when he was Chief Justice, the State of Georgia asked the Court to adjudicate a dispute in which they claimed the state was subjected to discriminatory freight rates. Although Stone believed that a remedy should be sought from a lower federal court, he opened the door to hearing the case which, over his negative vote, was settled in favor of the state. Later, he interpreted the Railway Labor Act to "protect equally the members of the craft" in a case of racial discrimination brought by an African-American fireman. The Railway Labor Act demanded that individuals bargain with railroad management only through their union. Yet, the Brotherhood of Locomotive Firemen and Enginemen prohibited Negro membership. Bester Steel, the fireman, was caught between the two requirements. His argument, which had been dismissed by the Alabama Supreme Court, found favor with Stone.

Harry S. Truman (Scott #1499) was faced with making momentous decisions from the instant he assumed the presidency. The most famous and far-reaching of these was his decision to drop the atomic bomb on Japan. But, with the war won quickly thereafter (almost certainly a result of Truman's action), he was faced with domestic issues that had been festering during the war years. In 1946, the United Auto Workers and the United Mine Workers struck their industries and then came a call to strike by two influential Railroad Brotherhoods. There had never been a nationwide rail stoppage and the effects were disastrous...the media reported passengers stranded at remote wayside stops, produce and other perishables rotting, panic buying, and other equally ruinous conse-

149

quences. But negotiations and Truman's resolute stand, threatening to have the army take over the railroads and to draft railroad workers into the army unless the strike ended immediately, was effective. The strike was settled as he was disclosing his plans in a speech to the press. This was just as well because the constitutionality of those plans was questionable and, although the House of Representatives passed a bill to draft the railroad strikers, the Senate demurred and the proposed legislation was defeated in that chamber.

Scott #1499

During the 1960s, railroads sought revision of the outdated work rules which cost hundreds of million of dollars of additional expense. Among these "featherbedding" practices which the roads wanted to eliminate were the necessity to retain firemen on diesel locomotives and extra trainmen who really were not needed. The Supreme Court ruled (1963) that the railroads could change work rules; the same decision noted that the unions could strike in protest. A strike called soon thereafter was prohibited by Congress until an arbitration board could review the issues but in April 1964, the unions struck the Illinois Central Railroad. Immediately, other railroads announced the installation of new work rules and the unions threatened a nationwide strike. **Lyndon Johnson's** (Scott #1503) Secretary of Labor intervened but

Scott #1503

to no avail. At this point, the president himself stepped into the role of chief labor negotiator. Johnson thereby exposed himself to embarrassment if his efforts failed but relied upon his personal prestige and powers of persuasion to effect a compromise. After substantial negotiation, he was successful and, in typical fashion, praised both management and labor for their acquiescence.

In conclusion, it should be mentioned that the railroad brotherhoods were courted by Gompers and his American Federation of Labor (AFL) but remained independent well into the 20th century. Then, as railroads and their associated labor declined in size and importance, the operating brotherhoods eventually merged into the United Transportation Union, an affiliate of the AFL-CIO. Only the Brotherhood of Locomotive Engineers remained apart.

MASS TRANSIT BY RAIL

Going Out on the Town - from Horses to Horsepower

Local, intracity public transportation may have originated in Paris in 1819 but less than ten years later (1827) scheduled stagecoach service was introduced in New York City. Within a few years, hundreds of omnibuses (Scott #1897) were operating in New York, Philadelphia, and Boston. At about the same time as the omnibus arrived on the scene, railroads began to be built in the United States. Many of the earliest railroads began service with horse-drawn cars because it was realized that, all other things being equal, an omnibus on rails would experience lower frictional forces and consequently could haul a greater load with the same expenditure of power. Thus, it is not surprising that horse-cars, distinguished from omnibuses by the fact that they ran on rails, rather quickly proliferated on the streets of American cities.

The horse-car was the sole means of mass public transportation in most cities for most of the 19th century. Its first serious competitor, the cable car, appeared in the 1870s but the latter's application was limited because its first cost was so much larger. Great powerhouses, needed to drive huge drums and enormous lengths of wire rope, were essential. Then too, the range of the cable car was bounded by certain physical factors: cable weight and strength and thermal expansion effects. Complex mechanisms were required at the car to grip the cable and considerable adroitness and experience was required to manipulate the controls. Cable cars were particularly applicable in hilly locales where steep grades were all but impossible for horses to climb with any load. The most appropriate and spectacular installation was the first, in hilly San Francisco. Yet others followed, even in some generally flat areas, where traffic levels justified the high initial investment. Elevated railroads also began to be built in American cities in the 1870s (the first New York "el" was opened in 1878) and these, at first, relied upon steam locomotives to pull trains of cars.

Steam "dummies," locomotives that were totally enclosed to convey the appearance of an ordinary horse-car, were used extensively but never fully satisfied the demands of frequent stops and rapid acceleration. A number of other means of propulsion, some more fanciful than practical, for street railway cars were proposed or offered about this time including: a human-powered car; cars propelled by springs; a "soda-motor" that utilized the reaction between water and caustic soda to evaporate boiler water, gas-driven or compressed air engines, and various other fireless locomotives. But a definitive solution was near at hand.

Werner von Siemens, a pioneer in the field who had demonstrated electric propulsion in 1879, established a one and one-half mile long electric railway in Germany in 1881, the first commercial electric railway in the world. In the United States many inventors were actively pursuing practical electric propulsion systems. Moses Farmer had built the first electric train capable of carrying people in 1847 but it was not until 1880, when Thomas Edison demonstrated a tiny experimental locomotive, that electricity began to realize its promise to provide clean motive power. Development intensified and many other important practitioners, Stephen Field, Leo Daft, John C. Henry, Charles van Depoele, and,

Scott #2060 ©1983 USPS

arguably, the most important contributor of all, Frank Sprague, were active during this period. One result was the trolley car.

In 1884, Edward M. Bentley and Walter H. Knight electrified two miles of the East Cleveland Horse Railway Company—the first electric railroad for public use in the United States. The method of current transfer was significant. Conductors of electricity were placed in a conduit between the rails. The conduit, made of wood, was slotted on top so that a collector (called a "plow") mounted on the car could access and brush along the conductor. The Bentley-Knight Company attempted several other installations but then merged with the Thomson-Houston Company in 1889. The Bentley-Knight conduit concept was improved

153

and revived later in a notable application in Washington, D. C. Its use was necessary because Congress had forbidden the use of overhead trolley wires when they eliminated horsecars in the District.

There were some other short electric railway installations in the mid-1880s but the first all-electric street railway system in the United States was built at Montgomery, Alabama and opened in 1886. This system, built by Charles J. Van Depoele, used an overhead current collection scheme. At first, Van Depoele used a "troller," a small carriage that traveled along the two overhead wires and was connected to the car by a flexible cable. He refined this into a roller mounted on a rod that pressed upward against the overhead wire. Oliver Wendell Holmes, in his poem, *The Broomstick Train*, likened the apparatus to a witch's broomstick:

> Since then on many a car you'll see
> A broomstick plain as plain can be;
> On every stick there's a witch astride—-
> The string you see to her leg is tied.

To assuage the patrons' fears of the new force, electricity, the local newspaper, the Montgomery *Advertiser*, wrote, "There is more real danger...in a Texas mule's heels than in all the electric motor system." While not perfect, the Montgomery application was successful and within a few years, extended over 15 miles of track. One of its street cars is shown on Scott #2060.

Scott #2561   ©1991 USPS

In the nation's capital, horsecars were used extensively until Congress passed legislation that encouraged their replacement in the late 1880s. They were supplanted by short-lived cable cars: their life was abbreviated by a disastrous fire at the cable power plant in 1897. Rather than rebuild, the directors of the company decided to turn to electric trolley cars which had, by this time, proven themselves in numerous applications. An improved Bentley-Knight conduit method of current collection was applied. The District of Columbia trolley system is represented on Scott #2561. Although this stamp is titled "Pennsylvania Avenue, circa 1903," the scene is taken from a photograph that Middleton, in his book, The *Time of the Trolley*, stated was made in the mid-1890s. Some artistic license was taken...the trees are shorter, the street somewhat less crowded...but the resemblance of the stamp to the photograph is unmistakable. The last trolley car ran in Washington, D.C. on January 27, 1962.

Before 1890 other installations, many upgrades of horse-car lines, were completed and by the turn of the century, the acceptance of electric traction was widespread. In 1890, 1,262 miles of street railway track were electrified but by 1902, electric trolley cars ran on 22,000 miles of track in this country! That phenomenal increase could be attributed in large measure to the work of Frank J. Sprague. This prolific inventor worked for a time for Thomas Edison, but finding Edison unreceptive to his ideas on electric traction, left to form his own company. His first improvements involved motor mounting using a cantilevered motor suspension that allowed motors to be geared directly to wheel axles, thereby eliminating the cumbersome arrangement of belts and chains previously used. His big break came in 1887 with the fulfillment of a contract for the construction of an electrified street railway for the city of Richmond, Virginia. Although he experienced many difficulties and setbacks and lost money, the system was a technical success and Sprague's reputation in the field was enhanced immeasurably.

In 1897, Sprague demonstrated multiple unit (MU) operation where one controller in a lead car could successfully regulate the operation of motors on cars following in train. Single motor cars were limited in passenger capacity and locomotive motive power degraded as the train was lengthened but the MU system, regardless of the length of the train, performed with the same power and acceleration characteristics as a single car. Thus, train length could be a variable, dependent only upon need, without affecting schedule. These, and many other innovations, rank Sprague as one of the most important electric traction pioneers.

Coincidentally, while trolleys were beginning to zip along the surface, a new competitor appeared. Subways had been promoted for many years,

155

both here and abroad, and there were steam locomotive-powered subways in operation in London as early as 1863. The advent of electric propulsion added a new and critical dimension because now underground operation was feasible without the attendant risk of asphyxia. The first subway in the United States using electric power was built in Boston in 1897 and, by 1904, an electrified New York City subway was in operation.

Trolleys continued to coexist with subways through most of the first half of the 20th century but before 1920 another competitor appeared, one that was to sound the death knell for the ubiquitous trolley car. An enterprising entrepreneur in Los Angeles recognized that his automobile might be used to carry paying passengers and, in 1914, he began to do just that. By the end of the year, more than 700 "jitneys" were operating in that western city and the idea had spread elsewhere in the country. The logical progression was to larger vehicles—buses—to carry passengers and it was not long before their advantages were recognized. Unlike trolley cars, buses required no huge investments for power plants; lighter vehicles, their first cost was less, and they were flexible, that is, their route was not restricted to the streets with tracks, and they could be rerouted as need dictated. At a later time, an attempt was made to exploit some of the economies achieved by producing power at a central location through the introduction of the trolley bus—a vehicle that was more bus than trolley car and whose propulsive force was electricity derived from overhead trolley wires. Although there are still some trolley lines in operation, notably in Europe, most left the scene after World War II, victims of the more versatile bus. (Incidentally, speaking of World War II, one of the most memorable and widely published photographs of the celebrations ending that war was the one showing a sailor kissing a young lady at New York's Times Square. This image, taken by Alfred Eisenstaedt, a famous photographer of the period, was reproduced on Scott #2981i (not shown) and has a peripheral connection to railroading through the inclusion of streetcar tracks in the scene.)

One class of trolley neither covered on any United States postage stamp nor elsewhere in this book is the interurban. At one time, interurban cars were used extensively to provide rapid transportation between nearby towns. Although their routes usually originated and terminated within municipal boundaries, the fact remained that they were not intra-city vehicles. Unlike their city cousins, they used larger and heavier cars that were intended to run at relatively high speeds over private rights of way with limited stops. The first interurban service began in the 1890s and the concept grew until it was possible to travel from New York City to Chicago on interurban lines exclusively (although not without numerous changes of equipment). Like the city trolley, their numbers began to decline after World War I, also victims of the motor bus, but a renaissance of this mode of operation, known as "light rail," is in progress.

The history of urban mass transportation on rails is told on a number of other United States postage stamps which are described in the following vignettes.

Horsecars, First to Last, 1832-1926

Many of the earliest railroads began service with horse-drawn cars and one of these, the Baltimore and Ohio Railroad's *Pioneer*, a horse-drawn car on rails (Scott #1006) made its first trip on December 22, 1829. A distinction must be made between these and local horse-cars. The *Pioneer* and others like it were the early motive power on what were, and were always intended to be, extensive, inter-city railroads. Local horse-cars, truly omnibuses on rails, were intended for intra-city service.

Scott #2059 ©1983 USPS

Surprisingly, in New York City, there was no regularly scheduled, local public transportation service until 1827. In that year, the first omnibus, a modified stage coach called the *Accommodation*, entered service. Being an omnibus, it did not use rails and it was not until five years later that John Mason, a merchant and banker, and some associates secured a charter to organize the New York and Harlem Railroad Company. The company was authorized to build a "single or double railroad" from 23rd Street north to the Harlem River along Fourth Avenue.

Since the area through which the railroad would pass was quite rural and because Mason was aware of the remarkable performance of the early railroads, steam locomotives might have been employed from the start. However, before construction began, the company was allowed to extend its rails farther downtown, into the more densely populated streets below 23rd Street. Obviously, steam power could not be used to propel vehicles or trains in this region. Apart from the noise and pollutants emanating from a steam engine, it was not the proper power source for the stop and go traffic on the often crowded city streets. Horses would provide the motive power.

Scott #2061 ©1983 USPS

Construction began downtown while two cars were ordered from John Stephenson, a notable omnibus builder. The cars followed the English stage coach outline but were lower, for easier access, and much larger, with three compartments and upholstered seats. Each compartment held ten persons and 30 more people could be accommodated on the roof. These cars were not much different than cars being employed on the steam railroads, many of which, according to John White, used "swell-sided car(s) for railway service." Stephenson patented his design and used it as the basis for many subsequent cars.

Service on the line began in 1832 with a celebratory demonstration of the equipment (Scott #2059). Two cars were filled, the leading car with city officials driven by a veteran driver, the second with company officials under the care of a local hackman. To show how safe the railroad was, its vice president arranged to display a signal to the drivers to bring the trotting horses to a quick stop. When the signal was given, the first driver responded quickly and, with the help of a mechanical brake, stopped his car within a few feet. The second, less experienced driver forgot about the brake and relied solely upon his reins and repeated shouts of "Whoa!"

Without mechanical braking, it was impossible for the horses to bring the car to a stop and it crashed into the car ahead; this was the first street car accident in the United States. Two years later, the road was four miles long and the procurement of additional cars permitted operation with a 15 minute headway.

The New York and Harlem Railroad turned to steam locomotives to haul its trains in 1837, operating from an "uptown" terminal between 26th and 27th Streets. Horse-cars continued to be used south of that point. However, the steam locomotives were such a nuisance to residents that, in 1858, the City Council was persuaded to ban them south of 42nd Street, a fact that was instrumental in the decision to build the New York City terminus of the New York Central and Hudson River Railroad at 42nd Street. The New York and Harlem Railroad was merged with the Hudson River road in 1873.

Strangely, except for New Orleans (see the vignette in this book titled "A Streetcar Named Desire"), horsecars were not introduced into other American cities until the 1850s, when they made an appearance in Brooklyn, Boston, Philadelphia, and other cities. Horsecar companies had difficulty operating during the Civil War when the federal government confiscated their horses to pull artillery pieces and to outfit mounted troops. Hard on the heels of that problem was the "Great Epizootic" of 1872, an influenza-like epidemic among horses in New York, Baltimore, and elsewhere. Within a few weeks many thousands of horses died or were destroyed (about 18,000 in New York City alone). To maintain service, gangs of laborers, mostly new immigrants, were pressed into service to pull the horsecars. But the companies recovered and prospered in the 1880s when, country-wide, there were more than 100,000 animals employed to haul 18,000 cars over 3,000 miles of street railway tracks.

The fact that horse-car companies were prosperous did not necessarily mean that their patrons were thrilled with their service. Their cars were slow, crowded, and often dirty. A passage from a poem titled *Street Car Salad*, published in *Harper's Magazine* in 1867, expresses a prevalent contemporary perception of horsecar travel,"

> "Packed together unwashed bodies
> Bathed in fumes of whisky toddies;
> Tobacco, garlic, cheese, and beer
> Perfume the heated atmosphere."

Beginning in the 1890s, horsecars began to decline in numbers and popularity as other local transportation systems (particularly electric street car and cable railways) were developed. The last horsecar line in the United States operated in Sulphur Rock, Arkansas (Scott #2061) and used "bobtail" cars. (There is some confusion between the illustration and the description on the stamp. A bobtail car was one without a rear platform yet the stamp clearly shows a platform.) The line shut down in 1926.

Climbing Halfway to the Stars Via Cable Cars

The cable street railway was invented by Andrew Hallidie. The first installation was completed and began operation on the Clay Street hill in San Francisco in 1873. Hallidie was the owner of a wire rope company in that city and had observed a tragic accident involving a car drawn by four horses on one of the many steep hills. The horses were injured so badly they had to be destroyed. Casting about for a better way to negotiate the grades, he developed a cable railway system.

Scott #1442

The system required the construction of a "power house" where giant sheaves were driven by steam engines. A long length (11,000 feet) of wire rope passed over the sheaves and was then routed out of the power house and into troughs located between the car tracks but below the street surface. The troughs were open at the top so that a "grip" mounted on the cable car could engage the cable. The cable was continuous and, while running, a number of cars could be attached and carried along with it. Stopping was simply a matter of disengaging from the cable (and holding the car stationary by a hand-operated brake). Originally, service was provided by cars running in pairs, a grip car and a passenger car but later the gripman was moved into the car with the patrons.

USA 20
Cable Car 1880s

Scott #2263   ©1988 USPS

The Clay Street Hill Railroad Company was so successful that other horse-car lines in the city began to convert their systems to cable operation. Each line was organized as a different entity and in some cases, horse-cars shared the tracks until the system was completely converted. An umbrella organization, the Traction Railway Company of San Francisco controlled all of the individual lines.

Now, other cities, near and far, hilly and flat, began to adopt cable systems. Chicago developed an extensive system and cable cars appeared in Los Angeles, Denver, and Seattle in the West, at Cincinnati, St. Louis, and Kansas City in the Midwest, and at Philadelphia, and Washington, D.C. in the East. They carried passengers over the newly constructed Brooklyn Bridge. But, although they exhibited some advantages as compared to horse-cars, even on level terrain such as cleaner operation and much lower operating expenses, cable systems were really best suited to hilly locales where other means were unable to provide safe and adequate service. Cable systems also demonstrated some serious disadvantages: high initial costs; all cars on the line were operated from one cable, cable failure meant that all service was interrupted until the cable was repaired; the weight of the cable was enormous and much power was utilized just to move its great mass; gripmen on the cars had to be nimble and experienced to work the controls properly and to prevent damage to the subterranean fixtures; in snowy climates, snow and ice could constrict the grip slot, slowing or stopping operation.

Around the turn of the century, cable car operations began to diminish as cities turned to electric trolley lines. By 1902, cable car mileage in the country was half of what it was in 1890 and one of the last to be abandoned was in Chicago where the last trip was made in July 1906. Only one cable car line remains—appropriately at San Francisco, where it all started. Much in demand as a tourist attraction, the little cars which "climb halfway to the stars" still serve many residents of that hilly city.

Scott #1442, issued in 1971 as one of a block of four "Historic Preservation" stamps, shows cable car #506 on Hyde Street in San

Francisco in 1894. Scott #2263, a cable car topping an incline in 1880, was issued as one of 16 stamps in the 1987-1988 "Transportation" series.

Underground Railways

Subways are depicted only peripherally on one United States postage stamp, Scott #3187j. This stamp was issued to commemorate the meetings between the New York Yankees and the Brooklyn Dodgers in the World Series of baseball between 1949 and 1956. During this time, the two teams played each other in five "Subway Series," so-called because fans could travel from one rival's ball park to the other by subway. Not

Scott #3187j   *©1998 USPS*

for more than forty years (October 2000) would New Yorkers be able to reach both World Series venues for the price of a subway token. The subway association lies in the representation of a New York City subway token on the stamp. (Incidentally, the name "Dodgers," attached to the team, described pedestrians who dodged trolley cars on the Brooklyn streets.)

The first underground railway for mass transit was built in London and completed in 1863. Its major problem, as with most long tunnels, was inadequate ventilation to remove the smoke generated by the steam locomotives. One writer remarked, "The fumes were left to be consumed by the passengers." In the United States, a long tunnel was built in Baltimore to bring long-distance railroad trains into the city center in 1874. Ventilation remained a problem until practical and powerful electric-powered locomotives became available in the decade before 1900. The first mass transit, electrified trolley subway was built at Boston in 1897.

The New York City subway system had its beginnings in the promotions of Alfred Beach. Beach was the co-owner and editor of *Scientific American* who became interested in pneumatic propulsion of rail cars. Building upon English experience, in 1867 he demonstrated a passenger-carrying car that was pushed through a six foot diameter tube by fan-generated air pressure. Buoyed by the success of his demonstration, Beach proposed a more extensive underground system but was thwarted by politicians who were promoting an elevated railroad alternative.

Beach thereupon proceeded to build his tunnel surreptitiously below the city's streets. He excavated a tunnel of about eight feet in diameter almost 22 feet below some of the busiest real estate in the city of New York; digging under existing buildings, without affecting the integrity of their foundations and without opening any streets. He maintained the proper tunnel alignment by driving a rod from the tunnel to the surface during each night and taking measurements from it at the street level. By making adjustments to a tunneling shield that he had devised, he was able to change the tunnel's direction. The resultant tunnel was opened in 1870 and a grandly appointed car carried passengers about 300 feet, speedily and comfortably, pushed by air generated by a fan named the "Western Tornado." Despite the success of this demonstration, a larger subway would require a better propulsion method and Beach recommended steam locomotives for a longer system. Attempts to lengthen the tracks were at first opposed by the Tweed political interests and then failed for lack of funds. That first New York City subway was eventually sealed, lost from sight and memory until a fire destroyed a building above it in December 1898. Workers removing the rubble unintentionally broke into the tunnel and found it, the waiting room, car, and tunneling shield still in place and in good condition.

The present New York City subway system, begun in 1900 and opened in 1904, is one of the most extensive in the world; in the 1990s, it operated over 230 route miles (various authorities offer different mileage). The first lines were built by the Interborough Rapid Transit Company and extended through three city boroughs. In the north, the subway connected with the New York and Putnam Railroad and at the south, to the Long Island Railroad terminal in Brooklyn. Extensions snaked out into the borough of Queens and parallel lines were established along the length of Manhattan Island. Before World War II, the entire system was essentially completed and furnished cheap, dependable service to the entire city, with the exception of Staten Island. A few acquisitions since that time have extended the routes.

Because of the unusual distribution, depth-wise, of soft earth, the first New York subway was built at a depth of 15 to 20 feet below the surface. The hard Manhattan schist was about 20 feet below the surface at the lower end of the island. Proceeding north, it dropped to 160 feet below the surface until mid-town where it rose again to within 16 feet of the ground level. Thus, to avoid drilling through the hard, granite-like material, the subway was bored mostly through soft soil. (The uneven distribution of the solid bedrock is the reason for the distinctive above-ground profile of New York City: tall buildings at midtown and at its lower tip, with shorter buildings, whose foundations do not reach bedrock, between.)

For a transportation system that carries about 3.5 million passenger each day (down from a past average of 4.5 million and a one day record of nearly 9 million), the New York City subway can boast of an excellent operating safety record. Its worst accident—one that has never since been approached in magnitude—occurred in 1918 when a virtually untrained motorman lost control of his train at Malbone Street in Brooklyn. The train derailed and about 100 riders died. To erase the memory of that tragedy, Malbone Street was renamed "Empire Boulevard."

The subway has been an important element in numerous books, songs, and motion pictures and, in addition to the anticipated recounting of baby births and lost children, robberies and homicides, many other strange and unusual incidents have occurred underground. There are tales of voodoo sacrifices conducted in the tunnels, of exotic and mutated creatures at large, of a scientific experiment to establish that most rocks are radioactive and, in a happy vein, the pleasure of a ride with a singing conductor, a balladeer who entertained his patrons on their journey. Perhaps the most unexpected involved a well-intentioned but fully predictable top-secret test conducted by the U. S. Army in 1967. About twenty men and women descended upon the subway to ride the cars and drop small bulbs containing a chemical upon the tracks. The point of the experiment was to determine the vulnerability of the subway system to a gas attack. The verdict was that "the subway could not be safeguarded." Of course, once known, the episode provided a field day for journalists. The wry comment of one, Russell Baker, was that,

> "It apparently has not occurred to the CIA that New York subway riders have a natural immunity to lethal gases and diseases...Every subway rider knows he is marinated in anthrax from the moment he steps underground. Do we worry about it? Of course not. Those who were going to die of it did so after the first few subway rides. The rest of us are immune."

Obviously, not much had changed since that long-gone London observer complained about inadequate ventilation in 1863.

Antecedents of the Toonerville Trolley

The stars of the *Toonerville Trolley* cartoons were the trolley itself, the "Skipper," and a cast of characters including Aunt Eppie, Mr. Bang, and Mickey "Himself" McGuire. This long-running cartoon series was drawn by Fontaine Fox and was first published in 1910 (or 1908). Fox was a frequent passenger on Louisville, Kentucky trolleys, some of which were converted from horse cars. Many of the cars were so dilapidated that the city of Louisville insisted that it was their equipment that provided the inspiration for the comic strip. Another source reported that Fox was impressed by a "friendly old bearded motorman who ran a rundown trolley in Pelham, New York." Fox ran into this character when he traveled to visit a fellow cartoonist's home. Upon returning to his hometown, the Pelham operation reminded him of the Brook Street route in Louisville. He melded the two lines in his imagination into the *Toonerville Trolley* and the Skipper, its conductor-motorman. In addition to its very obvious relationship to railroading, there are two specific similarities with early railroading that were prototypical of the *Toonerville Trolley*.

Scott #3000g   ©1995 USPS

First, an early passenger car of the Erie and Kalamazoo Railroad (E&K), a predecessor of the Michigan Southern Railroad, had much the same general appearance as the Trolley. Known as the "Pleasure Car," the E&K car had the same general outline, short in length but tall in height, with a gracefully curved roof line. Even the gothic-like arch windows were somewhat similar. The difference was that it's entrance door was on the side of the car rather than at the ends. An old illustration titled, "The Old Erie and Kalamazoo Flyer," shows this 4-wheeled car attached to an antique 4-2-0 locomotive with a huge smokestack and "haystack" boiler.

Second, as depicted on the stamp Scott #3000g, the preferred method of stopping the *Toonerville Trolley* was to toss an anchor overboard.

Stopping was certain and effective, albeit abrupt. Early railroads tried many poorly considered or ridiculous schemes for braking a railroad train but eventually adopted air brakes as the solution to the problem (see the vignette in this book titled "George Westinghouse and Jimmy Rodgers, famous 'brake' men"). Yet, even after air brakes had already come into use, a nautical remedy was suggested in the pages of the *Railroad Gazette* in the late 1880s for stopping a train in an emergency. There it was proposed,

> "To have an anchor to drop from the rear end of the train and engage with the ties...(so that)...a train might easily be brought to a stop within 15 or 20 feet from an ordinary passenger speed, if something did not give way."

It is almost as though the writer was anticipating Fox's inspired creation.

Little known today is the fact that there was a real-life *Toonerville Trolley* that was built by the Betzwood Film Company in Pennsylvania for the express purpose of translating the cartoons to the silver screen. A photograph of this car is shown in Andrew Young's book with a contingent of men aboard. The group was responsible for arranging exhibits at the American Electric Railroad Association's convention in 1923 and their purpose was to dramatize the progress made in streetcar equipment in recent years by comparing the *Toonerville Trolley* to the modern equipment on the convention's floor.

The *Toonerville Trolley* was decrepit and shabby yet, as Rowsome says, projected "a feeling so warm and friendly that cheery derision was its natural manifestation." That same feeling was never transferred to busses when they replaced trolleys. The complaints may have remained but the derision was no longer cheery!

A Streetcar Named Desire

When a new fleet of cars was acquired in New Orleans, Louisiana in the 1920s, one of them became, arguably, the most widely known streetcar in the world, made famous by Tennessee Williams' play, *A Streetcar Named Desire*. The play opens with Blanche DuBois' arrival at the Kowalski flat announcing that she had been told "to take the street-car named Desire, and then transfer to one called Cemeteries..." The play premiered in New

York in December 1947 and won the 1948 Pulitzer prize for drama. Blanche was played by Jessica Tandy and a young Marlon Brando made his mark as Stanley Kowalski.

Scott #2062 represents a streetcar of the St. Charles line, a model identical to the Desire car. Two other stamps are related to the play: the first, Scott # 3002, shown here, portrays Tennessee Williams with a streetcar in the background and the other, Scott # 3186n (not shown) depicts the poster advertising the play.

Scott #2062   *©1983 USPS*

New Orleans was the second city in the United States to inaugurate horse-drawn street car service. There (in late 1834 or in 1835, depending upon the source), the New Orleans & Carrollton Railway was organized to carry passengers from Canal Street to the suburb of Carrollton, 4 1/2 miles away, where an elegant resort hotel commanded a magnificent view of the Mississippi River. Ever innovative, local entrepreneurs promoted "cutting edge" technologies for their transportation system. At one time or another, a "walking-beam car," propelled by human power through the action of walking beams mounted on its roof, and an ammonia gas-driven car, using ammonia gas instead of steam as the working fluid in a conventional steam engine, were tested. But, as in most other cities, electric street cars became the preferred means of propulsion.

Although by the mid-1920s,when the heyday (1917-1923) of the street car was coming to an end and they were being replaced by motor buses or trolley buses, the city of New Orleans still chose to modernize its streetcar fleet. Many new cars of the latest model were purchased from several manufacturers. Ten of the new cars were built by the St. Louis Car Company. These cars proved to be rugged and durable and some continue to be used to this day. The St. Charles cars that still operate are the remaining vestiges of what was an extensive system of streetcars in the city. Although continuing to provide effective local transportation, they are maintained principally as a tourist attraction, much in the same manner as the cable railway in San Francisco. As in other American cities, New Orleans experienced a decline in streetcar ridership as its more flexible internal combustion engine competitors, the bus and auto, increased in popularity.

Scott #3002   *©1995 USPS*

Finally, as a "last gasp" measure to forestall the demise of the streetcar, an entirely new design was developed with funds provided by the Electric Railway President's Conference Committee (PCC), an industry group founded in 1929. The first car was built by the St. Louis Car Company and testing was begun in 1933. Its performance—acceleration, comfort, and silent operation—was outstanding. Shortly, afterwards, orders began to arrive from various operators; demand remained brisk and, helped by the war, sales remained high through most of the 1940s. However, technical qualities aside, the car could not compete with the bus to revive streetcar operations. Street car companies gradually died throughout the country.

The streetcar named Desire operated last in 1951. It was replaced by a bus named Desire but plans are afoot to reintroduce some street car lines in New Orleans. One of these, planned to run along Rampart Street, will have a stop at Desire Street. It is certain, that even if it is not officially so named, it will become the streetcar named *Desire*—again.

POST SCRIPT:
A FEW OTHER STAMPS

There are a number of other United States stamps whose subjects involve a casual relationship to railroading and have not been discussed at length in this book. A number of presidents (in addition to those mentioned in various vignettes) had incidental connections to railroading. During railroading's pioneer age, there was a fascination with this new technology that prompted authors to write about trains. Several stamps carrying the likenesses of poets and authors who mentioned railroads in their works are shown on United States stamps. Then there was an artist, a jurist, and a radio commentator who enjoyed an even more unsubstantial association with railroads. In the brief paragraphs below, the reader may find some of the railroad connections to be tenuous and inconsequential but it is my purpose to include any connections to railroading, no matter how slight, associated with people, places, and events commemorated on United States postage stamps. The related stamps are not illustrated.

Louisa May Alcott's (Scott #862) biographer, Martha Saxton, describes several train trips that Alcott took. One in particular, when young Louisa was 11 years old, occurred when her family returned to Concord aboard a train of the newly-built Fitchburg Railroad. They rode on "stiff narrow benches facing one another in the cars, which looked like coaches on platforms. At either end of the cars small stoves overheated the ends of the vehicle and left the center ice cold. The roof was usually a canvas platform and there was no ventilation. Tallow candles provided a flickering light and the passengers emerged covered with dust, cramped and cold." This representation is accurate save for the description of the roof. Unlike English railroads, on which third and fourth class passengers were carried in roofless cars until the Gladstone Act was enacted in 1844, American roads provided wooden roofs for their passenger cars. Those roofs were often permanently covered by canvas to make them rainproof.

Most biographies about **Clara Barton** (Scott #967) make much ado about her role in caring for the wounded brought to Washington D.C. from the field at the Battle of Bull Run, but this was but a fragment of her efforts to ameliorate the pain and suffering of Civil War soldiers, Union and Confederate alike. Her more important, greater contribution involved her work with the Union army at the front. Trains played a major role in her ministrations and she wrote several vivid pictures that illustrated their importance. In letters to friends and relatives, Clara spoke of accompanying cars loaded with medical supplies in "coaches (that) were not elegant or commodious; they had no windows, no seats, no platforms, no steps, a slide door on the side..;" they were box cars. Again, she described the aftermath of the Battle of Chantilly: "train after train of cars was rushing on for the wounded," yet "the weaker portion must be past recovery before reaching the hospitals of Washington." And, despite prompt attention, Clara noted "If immediately placed upon the trains and not detained, at least twenty four hours must elapse before they could be in the hospital." Many expired on the way. Out of such experience and possibly through suggestions made by Barton, the Sanitary Commission developed "hospital cars." These special cars were fitted with stretchers slung as bunks along the sides of the car. A doctor or nurse, who occupied a small office built at the end of the car, attended the patients. These cars went far toward reducing the terrible death toll. Toward the end of the Civil War, Barton was appointed Superintendent of the Department of Nurses for the Army of the James and some years later (in 1881) she went on to establish, almost single-handedly, the American Red Cross.

Stephen Vincent Benét, Scott #3221, wrote a short story titled, *O'Halloran's Luck*. The tale was about the men who built the transcontinental railroad and Tim O'Halloran, in particular. Tim, in his youth, was strong and solid, essential attributes for working with shovel and pick "as if the devil was driving behind." Although Benét provides a good explanation of the difficulties the pioneer builders faced and paints a word picture of the railroad scenes including "the fussy cough of the wood-burning locomotives," his story becomes a fantasy. O'Halloran, having drunk too much potheen, encounters a leprechaun on his way home. The sprite (O'Halloran's Luck) becomes his personal servant and then, although his mischievous ways make him a cross to bear, tells him of a construction problem that will be encountered shortly. O'Halloran brings the information to an engineer and convinces him to make ground tests. When O'Halloran's information proves correct, he is promoted. The leprechaun continues to offer advice, O'Halloran passes it on and is rapidly advanced. He returns to his love in Boston, not as he left—a laborer—but as a respected "railroad man." The story continues Tim's adventures and ends with him as president of the railroad who rides in a private car named, *The Leprechaun.*

Benét collaborated with his wife, Rosemary, to write *A Book of Americans.* This short volume is a collection of poems about famous (and infamous) persons associated with America. Among the pantheon of prominent historical characters in the book is Daniel Drew. Drew was, early in his career, a drover who (he claimed) originated the practice of watering his livestock just before entering the marketplace where they would be weighed. Later, as a notable financier and president of the Erie Railway, he conducted an equivalent practice but, instead, "watering financial stock" to increase the paper value of his railroad. The Benéts wrote that Drew,

> "With sleek Jay Gould and blithe Jim Fisk, Made other people's money fly And sucked the Erie Railroad dry. They foiled the laws, they bribed the courts, They watered stock, they squeezed the shorts."

Irving Berlin (Scott #3669), one of the most prolific of American songwriters, involved railroad associations in a few of his creations. He wrote a ragtime song in 1912 titled, *When the Midnight Choo-Choo Leaves for Alabam'* and another, *San Francisco Bound,* for the 1913 Broadway show, *All Aboard.* Berlin wrote the score for *Stop! Look! Listen!* a show produced in 1915. As with *All Aboard,* the title of the show was taken directly from phrases familiar to railroad fans, but that was the only railroad connection. In 1947, Berlin wrote a song, *Freedom Train,* which memorialized the train that toured over 37,000 miles from 1947 to 1949, carrying priceless documents of American heritage across the length and breadth of the country. The song was sung and recorded by Bing Crosby as well as the Andrews sisters, popular contemporary artists.

Nellie Bly/Elizabeth Cochrane (Scott #3665), was a strong, independent woman who defied custom to become a newspaper reporter in a profession which, up to that time (1885), had been male-dominated. She became famous through her crusading pieces involving divorce and marriage reform laws, the hazardous working conditions in factories, and unhealthy living conditions in the city slums. One of her most significant and dangerous assignments involved feigning insanity in order to be admitted to the notorious madhouse on Blackwell's Island. Her articles on this experience prompted significant changes for the care of mental patients.

She conceived of taking a trip around the world, emulating Jules Verne's character Phileas Fogg, but hoped to better his time of eighty days. Amid great publicity and fanfare, she embarked on this adventure. Mostly, she traveled by ship but some short European legs were taken by train. Upon her arrival in San Francisco, she boarded a reserved car, the *San Lorenzo*, for the trip home to New York. She did beat Fogg's record by eight days.

Nellie Bly covered the violent Pullman strike of 1894 and demonstrated her sympathy for the strikers in an article that decried sub-standard living conditions and other grievances. But, probably, her best known association with railroading had to do with the train that was named for her.

Her pen name, Nellie Bly, was conferred by her first editor who overheard another staff member humming the song "Nelly Bly," a popular tune written by Stephen Foster. The short, stylish, and easily remembered name was misspelled by a typesetter and she became known as Nellie Bly. At a later time, when a train on the Pennsylvania Railroad was named for her, it was in the same serendipitous vein as the original selection of her *nom de plume*.

The Pennsylvania and the Jersey Central Railroads competed for the Jersey shore traffic between New York and Atlantic City. On somewhat parallel routes, the run took about three hours on either road. The Central used a flyer named the *Blue Comet* and the Pennsylvania's train, unnamed at first, became the *Nellie Bly*. Unofficially, the name was adopted around 1915 when a small girl, fascinated by her trip across New Jersey, remarked to the conductor, "This is much like Nellie Bly and her trip around the world." In 1920, the railroad officially designated the train *Nellie Bly* on its timetables.

Railroads have figured in several of **Willa Cather's** (Scott #1487) stories. That might be expected of an author who grew up in Red Cloud, a prairie town in Nebraska whose most important distinction in the 1880s was that it was a division point on the Chicago, Burlington and Quincy Railroad. Although exposed to cultural experiences offered in that small town by friends and neighbors (classical literature and language studies) and touring theatrical companies, her early years were highly fashioned by the tales of the men who had brought the railroad to the west. As a consequence, a number of her stories are played out against a railroad background. For instance, *The Song of the Lark* tells of a railroad brakeman who dies in a train wreck. Another tale, *Tom Outland's Story*, is about railroad people in Pardee, New Mexico—a call boy, Blake, a boomer fireman, and others who discover a lost Indian village of cliff dwellings. Their adventures recounted, Tom, the call boy, finally realizes some important facts about faith and friendship. *The Affair at Grover Station*, a murder mystery, with touches of romance and supernatural occurrences, revolves around the disappearance of a station agent. *The Westbound Train*, a story in play form, narrates the confusion experienced by Mrs. Johnston when told by the agent at the Union Pacific Railroad station in Cheyenne that another woman has already picked up the pass sent on to her by her husband. The situation becomes muddier still and a denouement is precipitated by the unexpected, yet timely, arrival of Mr. Johnston.

It takes a long stretch to associate **George M. Cohan's** (Scott #1756) name with railroads but in one of his plays, *Get-Rich-Quick Wallingford*, he incorporated a visual effect that impressed audiences of the time (1910). Theater-goers enjoyed seeing an illuminated object, usually a train, moving slowly across the stage along the backdrop. In this play, Cohan displayed a distant lighted trolley car; that the audience enjoyed the device immensely was demonstrated by the thunderous applause at its appearance.

Emily Dickinson (Scott #1436), most of whose poetry was discovered after her death, spoke of her fascination with a locomotive in a poem written around 1862. She liked, "...to see it lap the Miles, And lick the Valleys up, And stop to feed itself at Tanks— And then—prodigious step..." until it finally stopped, "docile and omnipotent, At its own stable door."

W. E. B. DuBois (Scott #2617) related how, when he was a child, he had heard stories about a local African-American who had escaped to freedom via the "underground railway." At the time, DuBois had no idea what that term signified. In the late 18th century, Quakers were prominent in the establishment of an organized system to help slaves flee from captivity. The escape network grew and at about the same time (1830) that railroads were coming into being in America, the expression "underground railway" began to be applied to it. Presently, railroad jargon began to be used to describe various elements of the arrangement. Runaway slaves were "passengers" and they were escorted by "conductors." Safe houses became "stations" or "depots" that were owned by "stationmasters." The connection to railroading was oblique, limited to terms and expressions, although trains sometimes figured in the escapes. Doctor DuBois, a bright and talented individual, was educated at Fisk and Harvard Universities and the University of Berlin. He became a powerful advocate for black equality and spoke and wrote extensively for the movement to achieve that goal. He founded the Niagara Movement, the precursor to the National Association for the Advancement of Colored People. Because he believed in immediate, not gradual change, he became impatient with progress and, at the age of 93, joined the Communist Party, renounced his United States citizenship, and became a citizen of Ghana.

Dwight D. Eisenhower's (Scott #2513) minimal connection to railroading lay in the fact that his father, David, was, at one time, employed by the Missouri-Kansas-Texas (Katy) Railroad. After his general store in Hope, Kansas foundered, David Eisenhower obtained work as an engine wiper in Denison, Texas. In the late 1890s that dirty, tiring job demanded a 12-hour work day and paid only ten dollars a week. Although finances required that he leave his family behind for a time, he eventually returned to Kansas to work as a refrigeration machinery mechanic in a creamery. Thus it was that Dwight, who was two years old at the time, called Abilene his home.

Unlike much of **T. S. Eliot's** (Scott #2239) work, *Old Possum's Book of Practical Cats*, is a light-hearted exposition of cats and their different personas. The various poems comprising the volume were written in the 1930s for his godchildren. He names the various cats with "a name that you never will guess," one that only "the cat himself knows, and will never confess." One of them—Skimbleshanks, The Railway Cat—rides the Night Mail and oversees all functions aboard the cars: he patrols the aisles and maintains quiet; catches mice and makes sure the guard has attended each traveler properly; greets the stationmasters at various stops; helps the passengers to disembark. You may be certain that "You'll meet without fail on the Midnight Mail, The Cat of the Railway Train." *The Railway Train Cat* was written for Alison Tandy in 1938. Already well-known and a favorite of many, the popularity of the *Book of Practical Cats* was increased enormously by its adaptation to the successful and long-running musical stage play, *Cats*, by Andrew Lloyd Webber.

Ralph Waldo Emerson (Scott #861), in a lecture, *The Young American*, delivered to the Mercantile Library Association in Boston in 1844, discussed the new railroads which "annihilated" distance and "introduced a multitude of picturesque traits...tunneling of mountains, bridging of streams..." His observations might have been written in last night's newspaper as a criticism of the environmental damage done to "beautiful lakes until now the haunt of the wild duck..." Yet Emerson was accepting; he called "travelling on the railroad...dreamlike." His editor suggests that all his "doubts and pleasures are merged into a single paean of praise for American enterprise."

Trains are mentioned in a number of **William Faulkner's** (Scott #2350) stories, but only in an incidental manner. Yet, there is one tale, *Old Man*, that describes the adventures of a convict during a flood in the delta region of Mississippi. This man, using pulp novels as his guide, attempted a train robbery, was caught, convicted, and sentenced to 15 years in prison. Soon (in the story) there is a catastrophic flood in the area and a number of convicts are dispatched by train to help with rescue efforts. Our protagonist is caught up in the flood, adrift in a small skiff, and rescues a pregnant woman. Swept away with the woman aboard the skiff, his misadventures along the raging river continue for weeks. Interestingly, Faulkner introduces train images at several points in the story. The convict party embark in a passenger coach, "a single, open-ended wooden car coupled to the nose of a pushing switch engine." They hear the rushing of a small stream "sounding like a subway train passing far beneath the street" and they come upon a boat "resembling a train itself...(a)... motor launch to which was attached a string of skiffs and flat boats."

Edna Ferber (Scott #3432), wrote stories that combined strong female characters involved in a love interest against a background of mighty endeavors. One of her most famous novels, *Saratoga Trunk*, teams Clio Dulaine, a New Orleans temptress, and Clint Maroon, a Texas gambler. The pair invade Saratoga society: she to avenge the shabby treatment of her mother by marrying a wealthy man and he to race his horses at the famous track. Clio soon entices Bartholomew Van Steed, the millionaire owner of the Albany and Tuscarora Railroad, to court her. Van Steed, who, along with J. P. Morgan, is in a struggle with the Gould interests for control of the road, takes Clint as an ally. Maroon recruits a bunch of Texas cowboys to counter Jay Gould's harassing tactics and, in pitched battles along the line, save the railroad but at the cost of wounding Clint.

The final scenes recount Clio's realization that it is Clint Maroon whom she loves and will marry. The reader has been aware of this since the opening chapter which portrays Clio and Clint many years later. Clint has become successful as a railroad magnate, stemming from the ownership of shares in the Saratoga Trunk, a gift from a grateful Van Steed and J. P. Morgan. The book was made into a motion picture starring Gary Cooper and Ingrid Bergman.

F. Scott Fitzgerald's (Scott #3104) play, *The Vegetable*, is about a $3,000 a year railroad clerk who yearns to be a postman and then, intoxicated, dreams that he has been nominated as a presidential candidate. Other tales by Fitzgerald use train trips as incidental backgrounds for their plots and in one short piece he writes of "Engines puffing up and down for their afternoon exercise." However, included in a collection of Fitzgerald's short stories, *Taps at Reveille*, are two that are more closely involved with railroading. One, *The Night at Chancellorsville* describes a journey taken by 40 "camp followers." Two of these women are along because they have expectations that, business-wise, they will fare better among the soldiers of General Hooker's army than they would in the northern cities. Riding "in the car, smoky and full of bugs," an officer attempts to commandeer their car for wounded from the ongoing action. Further adventures include an attack on their train by Confederate soldiers before the tide of battle is turned and the "hookers" are returned to Washington.

The second story, *A Short Trip Home*, is concerned with Ellen, a young lady who becomes enamored with, perhaps bewitched by, a man she has met on a train while on a trip to her home in St. Paul. The stranger, "a hard looking customer," brawls with Joe Jelke, who is infatuated with Ellen and persuades her to entrain for Chicago with him. The narrator of the story, Eddie, follows, determined to protect Ellen. His encounter with the stranger on the train is volatile and ends with a ghostly encounter. Later, Eddie discovers that the stranger, a confidence man who preyed on young women, had died a year earlier. One reviewer interprets Eddie's vision as "that of the adolescent suddenly frightened by the glimpse of the great impersonal continent outside the frosted window panes of the Twentieth Century Limited." That interpretation may be correct but the identification of the train was not—the travelers were on a Burlington Route train.

Of **Robert Frost's** (Scott #1526) many poems, only a few make passing reference to railroads. One, *On the Heart's Beginning to Cloud the Mind*, has the author looking "Far into the lives of other folk" as he stands watching a passing train. In another, *The Figure in the Doorway*, as he eats in the dining car, he observes a man standing in a doorway who, "if so moved," could "uncurl a hand in greeting."

President **James Garfield** (Scott #2218b), who is mentioned in an earlier vignette, was wounded in July 1881 by an bullet fired by a disappointed office seeker at the railway station in Washington, D. C. After several weeks, the doctors attending him believed that he might recover more quickly if he were moved to Elberon on the New Jersey shore. Because the main line of the railroad that was to bring him from the capital was situated some distance from his oceanfront cottage, a small army of workers was conscripted to lay tracks directly to the cottage. That was done of the night of September 5th and Garfield was brought directly to the retreat. Unfortunately, the move did not help and the president died about two weeks later. The rapid construction that night was typical of the forces that railroads could bring to bear in other circumstances when catastrophe struck and destroyed track and essential structures.

Cary Grant (Scott #3692), starred in a movie whose script was originally titled, "The Man in Lincoln's Nose." The movie, directed by Alfred Hitchcock and released as *North by Northwest* was one of that master's most famous. One railroad angle lies in Grant's stowing away in Eva Marie Saint's compartment on the *Twentieth Century Limited* between New York and Chicago.

Almost everyone has seen *North by Northwest* but how many remember a much earlier (1937) Cary Grant film with a strong railroad association? That motion picture, *The Toast of New York*, had Grant playing Jim Fisk's partner Nick Boyd and begins with the two engaged in smuggling cotton through the Union blockade during the Civil War.

Fisk was a real person and the photoplay goes on to recount his (and his fictional partner Nick's) exploits involving the financial struggle with Cornelius Vanderbilt for the Erie Railway. Allied with Daniel Drew (see PS, Stephen Vincent Benét), Fisk and Jay Gould gained control of the railway. The two (Fisk and Gould) later attempted to corner the gold market (see vignette titled, "*U. S. Grant: Crédit Mobilier and Other*

*Rail*road *Affairs*") but were thwarted in this endeavor by President Grant. Fisk, a notorious figure, almost continually involved in various newsworthy escapades, died as he lived—in the public eye—murdered by a rival for a woman's affections.

The movie version of Fisk's later days had him falling in love with Josie Mansfield, an aspiring actress, who really loved Nick. Fisk is denounced at a Broadway show that he underwrote as a vehicle for Josie to star in and in retaliation, attempted to corner the market in gold. Nick, who also loved Josie, broke with Jim over this latest gambit. Although unsuccessful, Jim's foray into the gold market ruined many and he is confronted and shot by an angry mob. Before dying, Fisk conferred his approval of Nick and Josie's love. This version of Fisk's story was necessitated by restrictions imposed by the Hays office, watchdog of Hollywood morals at the time.

Horace Greeley (Scott #1177) founded the *New York Tribune* in 1841. During his long editorial reign, which encompassed the consideration and then the building of the transcontinental railroad and the financial scandals that followed, Greeley was its strong supporter. He was said to be "if anything, more anxious to span the continent with steel than (Stephen) Douglas." Long a "free soil" advocate, Greeley believed that the Pacific railroad "would stimulate industrialization, extend free soil, and unify the nation." Later, he railed against the corrupt schemes that had been applied to finance the road. His position was especially relevant because, earlier, his voice was raised against irregular financing methods. Exasperated, he had written "Can't we have a Pacific Railroad bill that don't stink of land-jobbing?"

Railroading was a popular theme in early motion pictures. In those directed by **D. W. Griffith** (Scott #1555), particularly, this was the case. His *Lonedale Operator*, a seven minute long variant of *The Great Train Robbery*, was made in 1911 and starred Blanche Sweet as a plucky telegraph operator who outwits holdup men who invade her railroad station. Griffith's *Arcadian Maid*, a railroad film which featured Mary Pickford, was made even earlier, in 1910. Another of the famous director's railroad-based movies was *The Block Signal*.

Benjamin Harrison's (Scott #2218e) contribution to railroading was to call upon Congress to enact legislation designed for "protection of the lives and limbs of those engaged in operating the great interstate freight lines of the country, especially the yard-men and brakemen." Arguably, the greatest contributor to railroad accidents was the link and pin coupler. To couple two railroad cars, a brakeman had to raise a dangling link attached to one car to mate with a pocket in the coupler of the second car and then drop a pin through a hole in the coupler to complete the connection. In 1890 alone, 369 brakemen were killed and 7,841 were maimed while effecting that operation. The Railroad Safety Appliance Act, calling for the widespread use of automatic couplers, was signed into law in 1893.

Moss Hart (Scott number not yet available), the celebrated playwright and director, wrote his first play at the age of 21. Perhaps it was the fact that Hart worked for a producer who promoted traveling road companies and whose most valuable tool was the *Railway Guide* that influenced him to incorporate a train into the plot. The play, a flop despite rewrites and a succession of new titles, began aboard the *Dublin Express* and involved an opera star who "kidnapped" a banker's daughter in order to win her heart. But it was his next play, written a few years later in collaboration with George S. Kaufman, that really launched his career. *Once in a Lifetime* was a burlesque of Hollywood and its first act involved an assorted group of actors on a train headed for Hollywood. This play also required revisions, the most significant of which involved changing the scene of act three to the same Pullman car in which the actors arrived, but now leaving Hollywood and carrying a disillusioned actress. After a poignant meeting with an acquaintance at a stop on the route and the arrival of news of her theatrical success, the actress from Wilkes-Barre returns in triumph. But it is 1930 and it appears that aviation pictures are the coming trend; the studio that May Daniels returns to is torn down to accommodate a fleet of aircraft. The ascendancy of the airplane, as expressed by Moss Hart, is an inverse parallel to the decline of railroads from that time forward...to some extent because of the same agent...airplanes.

In addition to penning the lines shown in the vignette titled *"Walter McQueen - from Old Puff to Jupiter,"* **Bret Harte** (Scott #2196) also composed *The Engineer's Signal,* a poem about the signal that Engineer Guild regularly whistled to his wife as he drove his train through Providence. To the woman waiting for it, "That whistle seemed to say: 'To my trust true, So love to you...And then one night, it was heard no more," but all those who missed its sound believed that Guild had forgotten to greet his wife that evening. Only one, Guild's wife, realized that it was silent because Guild's train was wrecked and her husband was dead.

The writer **Nathaniel Hawthorne** (Scott #2047) was interested in allegory and demonstrated that interest in his tale, *The Celestial Railroad*. This writing parodies John Bunyan's work, *The Pilgrim's Progress*, and describes a railroad journey from the City of Destruction (hell) to the Celestial City (heaven). Written in 1843, little more than a decade after the first railroad was built in the United States, it is interesting to the railroad historian that he (Hawthorne) should choose to employ the newly established medium as the means of conveyance for the trip. Even at this early date, Hawthorne recognized that the "iron road" provided the most comfortable and convenient way to travel. A vivid comparison is drawn between Bunyan's pilgrim plodding along under the burden of his load and the ease with which travel is accomplished by rail. The devil's minions are railroad employees and the journey parallels that taken by Bunyan's Christian but under much more "favorable circumstance...as compared with those of past pilgrims." Hawthorne's trip by train (which, by the way, is prohibited from entering the Celestial City, its railroad having been refused articles of incorporation by the Creator) equated the then popular theological shortcuts to heaven to an effortless train journey but one that did not necessarily lead man to salvation. At the end, the reader finds that Hawthorne has described a dream.

Ernest Hemingway (Scott #2418) a prolific writer, mentions railroad subjects in several of his short stories. In some, for example, *A Canary for One*, he employs railroad stations or cars as devices to emphasize a beginning or an ending of a relationship. Several chapters of an unfinished novel were published as short stories titled, *A Train Trip, and The Porter*. The first of these two tales is about a trip taken by a young boy with his father and an incident involving detectives and a murder suspect in their custody. As the trip continues, the sleeping car porter imparts some worldly advice to the boy.

Washington Irving, who is represented on Scott #859, had a brush with the new railroad being built from New York to Albany along the banks of the Hudson River. His mansion, *Sunnyside*, was located near Tarrytown, atop a wooded slope very close to the river. Although the tracks were built on filled land at water's edge, Irving's fears about noise and pollution from the trains were realized. He commented angrily that "if the Garden of

Eden were on earth, men would not hesitate to run a railroad through it." Unable to change the course of progress, he resigned himself to his new neighbor and, following a path of least resistance, moved his bedroom from the desirable river side of the house to the opposite.

Andrew Jackson, who became president in 1828, is represented on Scott #1286, 19 other U. S. stamps, and also on a stamp of the Confederacy. "Old Hickory" was the first president to mention railroads in a speech when he did so in a message to the Congress on December 6, 1831. He was also the first president to ride on a train. According to information provided by the Baltimore & Ohio Railroad (B&O), he adjourned a cabinet meeting to be among the spectators viewing the first train (pulled by the B &O's "grasshopper" locomotive *Atlantic)* to enter Washington. Despite his interest in railroads and his belief that internal improvements (roads, railways, etc.) were essential to the strength of the nation, Jackson has been accused of being unsympathetic to federal support for them. In his inaugural address, he declared, "Internal improvements...so far as they can be promoted by the constitutional acts of the Federal Government, are of high importance." It may be that he was opposed to federal expenditures on purely local programs. That position was espoused by **Martin Van Buren** (Scott # 813) Jackson's Secretary of State, who counseled him (Jackson) to veto legislation that would have authorized the federal government to buy stock of a proposed railroad between Marysville and Lexington, Kentucky.

One of the grasshopper class locomotives was named *Andrew Jackson* and this machine was still being used regularly by the road in switching service at Mount Clare in 1892. At that time it was withdrawn from service and rebuilt to be displayed at the World's Columbian Exposition as the *Atlantic*.

Andrew Johnson (Scott #822) congressman, senator, governor, and accidental president was no champion of railroads. In speeches made while he was serving in the Tennessee House of Representatives, he deplored the fact that railroads affected the business of drovers and inns and he usually voted against bills that favored them. Specifically, he failed to support the incorporation of the East Tennessee Railroad Company. Politically, this was an unpopular position because it was contrary to the desire of the electorate. His constituency deserted him when he ran for reelection in 1837. He rebounded and later won a seat in the United States Congress. In the 1840s, the railroad mania was in full flower and it was a foolish politician who opposed it. Johnson changed his position and now supported construction of the East Tennessee and Virginia Railroad. His about-face was to dog him through future campaigns and provide an issue for opponents to seize upon. As a United States senator, he attacked the transcontinental railroad bill as unconstitutional and later voted against the Pacific Railroad Act. Toward the end of his career, when he was president, railroads even figured in the charges proffered against him when his enemies sought to impeach him; he was accused of profiting from the "illegal disposal of railroads in Tennessee."

Scott Joplin's (Scott# 2044) father, Jiles, worked as a railroad laborer in Texarkana, Texas. His advice to his son was to forego his interest in music to seek a more lucrative and stable railroad job. Fortunately for musical art, young Scott Joplin disregarded his father's suggestion and became a ragtime composer. Ragtime is defined in the Random House Dictionary as "rhythm in which the accompaniment is strict two-four time and the melody...is in steady syncopation." Songs in this style became popular from the late 1890s and this popularity continued for 30 years or so. Joplin, almost unremembered until his classic, *The Entertainer*, was featured in the 1973 movie, *The Sting*, became known as the "King of Ragtime." One of his pieces, copyrighted in 1896, was the *Crush Collision March*. This lively tune celebrated the intentional destruction of two locomotives in a head-on collision on the Missouri-Kansas-Texas Railway. Such performances, while not common, usually were conducted as money-raising events but the incident described in the song was staged in 1896 by a railway official, aptly named William Crush, as a public relations gambit to heal an ongoing feud between railroaders and local farmers. The event attracted fifty thousand spectators and, although the train crews jumped clear, three onlookers were killed when the locomotive boilers exploded. Joplin's score emphasizes,

> "The noise of the trains while running at the rate of sixty miles per hour, Whistling for the crossing."

Dr. Percy Julian (Scott #2746) was a noted chemist who developed numerous pharmaceutical products among which was Compound-S, a cortisone-like compound that was applied to the treatment of arthritis. Julian's only relationship to railroading came through his father who was a railroad clerk in Montgomery, Alabama.

There was no significant relationship to trains in **Robert Kennedy's** (Scott #1770) short life. But in death he is, arguably, most remembered by the image of the special railway train in which he was carried from New York to Washington, D.C. for burial. A friend, William Walton, said, "His life, in a way, was all aboard that funeral train; all the phases: the people he had known...people who had gotten woven into his life." The trip, reminiscent of Lincoln's funeral trip, is well-documented by the book *American Journey*, a collection of interviews conducted by Jean Stein. Oral accounts of those aboard, including the crew, and also of many onlookers provide a compelling account. An especially sententious statement, "his people live along the railway tracks," was provided by John Kenneth Galbraith.

Composer **Jerome Kern** (Scott #2110) was one of the most acclaimed and famous authors of stage and screen music. His songs numbered in the hundreds and many of them were hits. Among them were the musical selections from a play called *Toot-Toot!* The action in this farce occurs on a train after Lt. Harry Mallory and his girlfriend decide to marry and hope to find a minister on the train. During their quest, they are beset by a bizarre troupe of dancers, a divorce-bound couple, a man seeking a romantic escapade, and not least, a train robbery. This show opened on Broadway in 1918. For the 1946 motion picture *Centennial Summer*, Kern wrote a railway-oriented tune named *Railroad Song*. Kern had died eight months before the movie's release.

Fiorello LaGuardia (Scott #1397) was mayor of New York City through most of the Great Depression and into the WWII years. During the 1930s, there were three great subway lines in the city: the municipally-owned IND (Independent Subway System); the IRT (Interborough Rapid Transit Company); and the BMT (Brooklyn-Manhattan Transit Corporation), the latter two privately owned. The IRT was the pioneer subway in New York City, having been built in the early years of the twentieth century. However, by the end of the 1930s, it was in receivership. The other systems were no better off: the IND lost nine cents per passenger ride and debt service committed by the city to the creditors of the other two roads was staggering. With this as background, LaGuardia pressed for unification of the three entities into a municipally-owned and-operated network. He believed this would produce economies of scale and that its debt could be renegotiated and lowered. Negotiations with the private firms began in 1934. Their stockholders favored consolidation and bargained for a selling price that would enable them to recoup some of their investment. But it was not until 1940, after some surface lines involving streetcars and buses were included in the mix, that a deal was finally arranged and the largest railroad merger in United States history to date was accomplished.

Railroads were better utilized by the North than by the South during the Civil War. The Union established the United States Military Railroads, which managed all captured railroads. The Confederacy, on the other hand, relied upon voluntary cooperation between its railroads. Then too, the rail network was far more mature in the north and all of the locomotive manufactures were there. Despite the imbalance, **Robert E. Lee** (Scott #2975b), an ex-Corps of Engineers officer in the Union Army while commander of the Confederate forces, employed railroads to his advantage at every opportunity. However, a more personal association with railroads occurred after the war. President of Washington College at the time, he agreed to accept the presidency of the Valley Railroad in Virginia, a road that was in the subscription phase. He was probably selected for that post because of his reputation and the consequent money-raising potential attached to his name. Unfortunately, his relationship with the railroad was short-lived; Lee died shortly thereafter. The Valley Railroad later became a part of the Baltimore and Ohio Railroad system.

Sinclair Lewis (Scott #1856) established a reputation in the early years of the 20th century as an author of short stories, mostly about business and many about salesmen. One of these, *Number Seven to Sagapoose,* has salesman Rabbitt arriving at Sagapoose on train number seven and waiting for a connection with the 10:16 branch train. But critical literary recognition of Lewis's work came with publication of a novel, *Main Street*, written in 1920.

In *Main Street*, Lewis presented an interesting and accurate observation about railroads in the midwest when he wrote, "here the railroads had been before time was." His point was that many prairie towns had been established as convenient stopping places for that "new god; a monster of steel limbs, oak ribs, flesh of gravel, and a stupendous hunger for freight." In this he was correct. The midwest (and the far west) with relatively meager population allowed the railroad to determine where a town should spring up. Depots and water tanks were erected at intervals convenient for the railroad.

Speaking then of established towns, Lewis wrote, "If a town was in disfavor, the railroad could ignore it, cut it off from commerce, slay it." Sometimes, the proffer or withholding of local subsidies influenced location to an area that would otherwise not have been considered. There are numerous examples where, when a community refused to subsidize construction, it was told that the railroad, "could not afford to swerve their line to the right or to the left to accommodate any little town" and, instead, a new town was created a few miles away.

Finally, Lewis noted, "Even in this new era...the citizens went down to the station to see the trains go through. It was their romance, their only mystery..." But more than that, it was the hub of activity for the town. It was here that strangers arrived and news from the wider world was first received; it was from here that loved ones departed; it was through here that goods and foodstuffs were shipped and accepted. The townsfolk gathered at the depot to hear speeches by political candidates or to mourn beloved personages as a train bore their body to a final resting place. A *Fortune* magazine writer noted that "These places were to be the very pivots of life in all its most tumultuous departures and arrivals."

Most of **Jack London's** stories are about the sea or the north country but a few describe locales with railroad associations. One described his fear upon being caught in the perilous currents in the Straits of Carquinez. This was the body of water crossed by the Central Pacific ferries when the transcontinental railroad tracks ended at Benecia, California. Another, from *The Valley of the Moon*, was of the time of a strike in the railroad shops. It is a story of people told from London's socialist point of view— of people questioning justice, of politics, and class struggle. A battle between the strikers and the strikebreakers is narrated in chilling and sobering prose. London is depicted on Scott #2182.

James Russell Lowell (Scott #866) took advantage of the democratic nature of an American railroad coach by using it for the setting of *An Incident in a Railroad Car*. The poem, in which a narrator reads Robert Burns to a group of "rude and rough" men, has nothing to do with railroading per se. But it does highlight the fact that American railroad cars were essentially classless and anyone who could afford a ticket was granted occupancy, regardless of rank or station.

Thurgood Marshall's (Scott #3746) father, William, worked as a waiter on the Baltimore and Ohio Railroad and instilled in his sons a love of railroading. During regular excursions to the B&O depot, William would tell them tales of his days on the road and he would explain how the trains worked. Following in his father's footsteps, while a college student Thurgood spent summers as a B&O dining car waiter. He carried his interest in trains into his adult life and, when he was a successful lawyer, some friends gave him an electric train set as a Christmas gift. Wearing a striped engineer's cap, he invited neighborhood children into his home to watch the toy trains speed around the track. Marshall's railroad connections are trivial compared to his achievements in the legal field, including his argument to the United States Supreme Court in the landmark case, Brown vs. Board of Education. His appointment as a Supreme Court justice capped an illustrious and controversial career.

It was **Edna St. Vincent Millay** (Scott #1926) in her poem, *Travel*, who saw the engine's "cinders red on the sky", heard the shrieking whistle and despite the pangs of parting with friends, felt "Yet there isn't a train I wouldn't take, no matter where it's going."

The song *Chattanooga Choo Choo* was written in 1941 by Mack Gordon (lyrics) and Harry Warren (music) but was popularized by **Glenn Miller** (Scott #3098) and his orchestra. It memorialized a fictional train that left "the Pennsylvania Station 'bout a quarter to four." The song was featured in the movie *Sun Valley Serenade* and sung by Tex Beneke and the Modernaires. Miller, one of the most famous of the "big band" leaders, was lost in an airplane crash during World War II.

Edward R. Murrow (Scott #2812) worked for the Bloedel-Donovan logging company in his youth. However, his tenuous connection to railroading was, like James Whistler (mentioned later), through his father. Bloedel had built a railroad from their lumber camp in the deep woods of Washington State to a bay where logs were assembled into rafts and floated to a sawmill. The elder Murrow was the engineer of a logging locomotive on that railroad. Although unrecorded, it is likely that he operated a geared locomotive because Bloedel, like most lumber companies, used Shay, Heisler, or Climax locomotives for such tasks. These

186

short wheelbase machines could negotiate the sharp curves and tempo-rary, irregular tracks laid in the forest. Their gear drives made these little giants extremely powerful for their size and thousands were employed in logging and other industrial service.

Ogden Nash (Scott # 3659) was noted for his very short poems but his poem *Riding on a Railroad Train* is not so terse and offers that his "pri-vate joy, both man and boy, is being a railroad rider." In a few stanzas, Nash paints a picture of the pleasures of railroad travel that bypasses the choking dust of the highway, where he can call for a "long cool drink" while relaxing on "a soft settee in an "air-conditioned smoker." He also laments the passing of the steam locomotive yet is convinced that despite the motive power, "a train is a train and will so remain, while the rails glide glistening under."

Dorothy Parker (Scott #2698) used a Pullman compartment as the set-ting for her short story, *Here We Are*. In it, a newly married, nervous cou-ple are on their honeymoon, "negotiating new territory," both geographically and emotionally, while speeding to New York City. As the train "leaped at curves and bounced along straightaways," the bride looks out at "big weathered signboards" flashing by. Her sensitivity and "fearful hesitancy" precipitates an argument, ostensibly about her hat but really about his tactlessness and "jocular anticipation." It expresses an age-old difference between the genders. In this case, their differences are mended before the trip ends.

As a congressman and then as governor of Tennessee, **James Polk** (Scott #2587) supported "a judicious system of (internal) improvements," including the construction of macadamized turnpikes and railroads. However, later, as President (1845-49), he reduced federal expenditures for internal improvements. Polk came to believe that the " 'American System' consisted of several closely allied branches: a federal bank, protec-tive tariff, distribution of the land fund, and internal improvements." All but the last had been discarded and it was his fear that if he encouraged federal support of railroad building (the principal recipient of funds), the others might revive. He saw himself as the challenger of special privileges conferred under the Hamiltonian system.

Ayn Rand's (Scott #3308) 1957 novel, *Atlas Shrugged*, is about rail-roads—and a whole lot more. A classic, considered a "great work of art," the book has a complex story line interwoven with profound philosophical ideas. Rand wrote the action against a railroad background because she believed that the railroad "touched all other industries and was the circulatory system that kept America alive."

It is impossible to distill the plot of this long, 1200 page book into a few sentences but it concerns a man who threatens to "stop the motor of the world." Dagny Taggart, the leading female character, is Vice President of Operations of Taggart Transcontinental, a railroad founded by her father. She struggles to build and preserve the road and to solve a number of conundrums that are presented, one involving the identity of a mythic character, John Galt, with whom she falls in love. A second puzzle concerns an extraordinary motor she finds in an abandoned factory. The novel has been characterized as a mystery story by some, as science fiction by others. Other interpretations perceive it as a feminist fable with a strong-minded, independent protagonist-heroine who must weigh love against her career responsibilities and, finally, as Arthurian romance.

Ayn Rand went to great lengths to make her books technically accurate and her preparations for writing scenes in *Atlas Shrugged* included riding in the diesel engine of the *Twentieth Century Limited* and, for a short time as it passed through Indiana, operating it herself. Speaking later of that 80 mile per hour ride, she said, "I am completely ruined now as a train passenger...That's much too tame. I would love to travel across the whole continent in the engine." The scene in the novel which she based on her experience "is one of the most movingly beautiful in any of Ayn's writing."

James Whitcomb Riley (Scott #868) also wrote of a locomotive in *The Iron Horse* where he defied the reader "...to point Me out a steed the half so fine...As this old iron horse of mine." He describes its many splendid characteristics...its "gait" and "burnished mane," the "thunder of thy hooves" and the "star that on thy forehead gleams..." as it races along to reunite lovers and families.

Will Rogers (Scott # 1801) had an incidental connection to railroading through his wife, Betty Rogers. Betty had worked as a clerk for the Iron Mountain Railroad in Arkansas where her responsibilities included checking cars in the yard adjacent to the station. An irreverent western humorist, it was Rogers' practice to poke fun at many of the institutions and icons of the day and he found a target in the New York, New Haven and Hartford Railroad. That road experienced a number of accidents during the early years of World War I and, after a particularly bad one in which 50 people were killed, Rogers' commentary was: "I see where the NY, NH & H have started in on their spring drive." Recriminations from annoyed officials of the road followed but, in the end, Rogers had the last word when he observed, "You see friends bidding each other goodbye at their depots just as though they are going to war." Will had a lifelong fascination with aviation. He took his first flight in a pre-World War I Curtiss pusher seaplane and continued to take to the air during those days when flying was exceptionally dangerous. He was involved in several airplane crashes and his final flight (1935), piloted by Wiley Post, ended in Alaska with the loss of the two men.

Numerous other personages who have been honored on United States postage stamps have employed railroad locales or backgrounds in an incidental way. **William Saroyan** (Scott #2538) opens *The Human Comedy* by telling of Ulysses Macauley seeing "the passing of the whole train, from locomotive to caboose." Although he waves to the engineer and others, he receives only one answering wave from a rider in a gondola car. At a later time, Saroyan describes a train filled with soldiers in uniform on their way to war.

John Steinbeck (Scott # 1773) in his tale, *How Edith McGillicuddy Met R. L. S.*, relates a story about a little girl taking a train with a "little engine rolling black smoke out of its head and puffing steam out of its belly" to a funeral. Flat cars carried benches for the mourners and "the train bell tolled mournfully." The highlight of the trip for Edith was meeting Robert Louis Stevenson and his lady friend who "smokes cigarettes."

Henry Thoreau (Scott #1327), writing at (and about) his sylvan retreat on Walden Pond, made many references to the Fitchburg Railroad which skirted the pond. He heard the locomotive's whistle "sounding like the scream of a hawk" and then heard "the iron horse make the hills echo with his snort like thunder, shaking the earth with his feet, and breathing fire and smoke from his nostrils." The portrait on the stamp is by Leonard Baskin and is based on an 1856 daguerreotype.

Jim Thorpe (Scott #2089) was an American Indian (with Irish and French blood as well) who became one of the most renowned athletes in the country. Born in the Indian Territory (now Oklahoma) in 1888, Thorpe was one of a few boys selected to attend the Carlisle Indian School at Carlisle, Pennsylvania. There, he played football under the tutelage of "Pop" Warner, the famous coach. In the summer Olympic games held at Stockholm in 1912, Thorpe received gold medals in the pentathlon and the decathlon events. He later played major league baseball and professional football and in 1950 was named by the Associated Press as the "greatest all-round athlete of the twentieth century." Thorpe's connection to railroading lies in the fact that when the town of Mauch Chunk, Pennsylvania, famous for the nearby "Switchback Railway" (see vignette titled, *Ubiquitous Little Jimmies*"), consolidated with the Upper and East Mauch Chunk regions, it was renamed Jim Thorpe, Pennsylvania, in the athlete's honor. The area has recharacterized itself with a dominant railroad theme centering about the switchback road, the mansion of Asa Packer, the founder of the Lehigh Valley Railroad, and the restored Jersey Central Railroad station, from which a tourist steam train is operated.

Although best known as a humorist, in words and drawings, **James Thurber's** (Scott #2862) story, *That Man on a Train*, is anything but funny. Sigmund Freud had related dreams of death to journeys, some involving train trips. Thurber, harking back to Freud's writings, employs a commuter train as a setting for a story concerning death. In the story, the conductor, speaking to the narrator, comments about another passenger, "Poor fella just lost his little girl." The description of "that man" is actually of a neurotic Thurber, who, although she had not died, feared the custodial loss of his little girl as a result of a pending divorce. Thurber used a train in another work titled, *The Train on Track Six*. A publication announcement was made in 1955 but the novel was never completed. Interestingly, he vacillated between dropping it and finishing it and at one point declared that he would publish it as *The Train on Track Five*. Obviously, the change of track made no difference because the train never left the station; Thurber dropped the project.

Earl Warren (Scott #2184) was influenced by his own and his father's experiences as Southern Pacific Railroad (Espee) employees. Methias Warren worked for the Espee but was blacklisted after joining fellow workers in the 1894 Pullman strike. He did find other railroad jobs however. Earl, his son, worked as a call boy for the road and as he wrote of his railroad observations in his memoirs. He abhorred the power exercised by the railroad: layoffs that were ordered to increase dividends; cheap labor imported and then "fleeced...at the company store;" men crippled "because there were no safety appliances;" and, "crime and vice...countenanced by corrupt government." Warren believed that his railroad experiences taught him "valuable lessons that would tend to shape my career throughout life." He brought those lessons to his political career and as a guide during his Supreme Court tenure.

John Wayne, the star of the motion picture Stagecoach, is pictured on Scott #2448 (another John Wayne stamp is planned for issue in late 2004). Wayne first appeared in the movie *Brown of Harvard* as an unbilled double for Francis X. Bushman, Jr. in 1925. From that time on, he was one of the busiest actors in Hollywood with a career spanning five decades. His early acting days involved grinding out short, unmemorable, low budget westerns but his star quality was recognized after he appeared in *Stagecoach* in 1939. Although the opening of the west was inextricably related to railroads and although Wayne played in innumerable westerns, only three of his films had railroad themes. The first, *Hurricane Express*, was a serial in 12 chapters, made in 1932. This thriller, with the usual cliff-hanging escapades in chapters titled "The Masked Menace," "Buried Alive," and "Wings of Death", had Wayne solving a series of mysterious train wrecks. In *Tycoon*, released in 1947, Wayne attempted to bore a railroad tunnel through a South American mountain. Failing in this, he then constructed a bridge on an alternate route, thereby redeeming himself and "winning the girl." Finally, in the film *The Train Robbers* (1973), the railroad is incidental to the story which involves a deceitful widow and gold stolen from a train.

Daniel Webster (Scott #725), as a United States senator and later, expressed his support for railroads a number of times. Very early on (1829), at the dawn of the railway age in this country, Webster presented a petition to Congress from the South Carolina Canal and Railroad Company that requested federal support for their proposed undertaking. Robert Hayne, the senator from South Carolina, demurred. One argument Hayne raised was that the people of his state had no legitimate interest in canals or roads in other states. Webster disagreed, stating that the most important consideration should be whether some national interest was served by an interstate railroad. In 1847, Webster supported the completion of a southwestern railroad from Savannah to Pensacola. Later that year, he was asked to preside over the opening of the Northern Railroad in New Hampshire.

The setting of **Edith Wharton's** short story, *A Journey*, is a sleeping car. In this car, a woman is bringing her dying husband home and, as she tosses in her berth, she reflects on her life with him. When morning comes and she enters her husband's berth she finds that he is dead. Realizing that she might be removed from the train with her husband's body, she stages an elaborate deception of the passengers and porter, convincing them that he still lives and wishes to remain sleeping. The author, who is shown on Scott #1832, provided an enigmatic ending to the story as the train approached Grand Central Station in New York.

Walt Whitman (Scott #867), in addition to several incidental refences to trains in his *Leaves of Grass,* wrote an ode *To a Locomotive in Winter.* In it, he lyrically described a locomotive with its "train of cars behind, obedient, merrily following...the fierce-throated beauty."

James Greenleaf Whittier (Scott #865) wrote a poem about a railroad conductor who lost his life in an accident on a Connecticut railroad in May 1873. The poem, simply titled, *Conductor Bradley,* tells us that despite his grievous injuries, this railroad man's last words were, "Put out the signals for the other train!" "That last act of failing tongue and brain!" prevented the further tragedy of the following train crashing into the already wrecked one.

Pullman Car Hiawatha, written in 1931 by **Thornton Wilder**(Scott #3134) tells of passengers on a train speeding across Ohio in a sleeping car while, at the same time, moving through the cosmos. Although the play lacked a plot, it attempted to portray the order of the cosmos in which man is an important part...its intent is to embrace the whole of human experience. Like several of Wilder's offerings, he employs the device of a "Stage Manager" who not only comments and introduces various characters but also takes part in the action. The travelers include an unmarried woman, a young couple, a doctor but, unusually, inanimate objects and quantities and measures such as planets, cities, and units of time, are played by actors. The town of Grover's Corners comes onstage, followed by a field, then a tramp. One of the passengers expires and the play continues...a blend of realism and fantasy that ignores the "dimensions of time and distance" in order to present a universal human experience.

The works of **Thomas Wolfe** (Scott #3444) are sprinkled liberally with allusions to trains. Holman, writing of Wolfe, mentions that he "imprisons images in the imagination through being glimpsed from a train." For example, the author writes, "To anyone outside, a speeding train is a thunderbolt of driving rods, a hot hiss of steam...a wall of movement and of noise, a shriek, a wail." "But if one is *inside* the train, everything is different. The train itself is a miracle of man's handiwork...one's own sense of manhood and mastery is heightened by being on a train." Yet many of the train passages are not allegorical or mere representations of the passing scene but, instead, are excellent descriptions of railroad subjects. From "the brakeman (who) came draftily into the dirty plush coach and emptied a scuttle of coal into the big stove at the end" to "the faint and ghostly tolling of (the train's) bell, the short explosive blasts of its hard labor...and the long heavy rumble of its wheels," Wolfe's railroad word pictures are authoritative. Absorbing "the flare of the rails, the switch-lights of the yard, small, bright, and hard, green, red, and yellow, poignant in the dark, and on other tracks...the strings of darkened trains all empty," the reader becomes an observer to a realistic scene. As they lay in their berths "with hot sleepless eyes" and hearing the "sad lulling magic of the car wheels," Wolfe's readers can forget that they are perusing a tale about a train. Instead, they are there, in a hot berth, kept from sleep by the "clackety-clack" of the wheels passing over the rail ends. Few authors have painted images of train life as realistically as Wolfe.

Although the **Brooklyn Bridge** (Scott #2041) was not built as a railroad bridge, there were those, as evidenced by contemporary articles in the *Brooklyn Eagle*, who believed that a regular passenger train should traverse it. Starting at a terminal in Brooklyn, these advocates saw a connection made with the New York Central and Hudson River Railroad so that a traveler could travel uninterruptedly throughout the Central's system. Washington Roebling, the bridge's engineer, disabused the proponents of that scheme by pointing out that the bridge was not designed to carry heavy road locomotives and Pullman cars and its grade was too steep for ordinary locomotives. He did however, endorse his father's plans for a mile long cable railway to cross the bridge. John Roebling, the designer of the structure, foresaw trains of cable cars moving as fast as 40 miles per hour and carrying as many as 1,000 people. In practice, the cars, hauled by wire rope cable that was driven by two 300 horsepower steam engines, took five minutes to cross the bridge. Despite continued investigation into the application of conventional light locomotives similar to those used on the elevated rapid transit lines, the cable railway endured for more than two decades from the bridge's opening in 1883. In 1898, trolley car tracks were added at the roadway level and in June of that year, the Brooklyn Elevated Railway Company began to run electric trains from Park Row in Manhattan to Coney Island. The cars were equipped with cable grips, which were used for transiting the bridge. Eventually (1908), the cable apparatus was supplanted and the trip was made exclusively by electrically-powered cars.

A stamp depicting the **San Francisco-Oakland Bay Bridge** (Scott #3565), is one of a pane of 50 stamps of the "Greetings from America" group, issued in 2002. Each stamp carries a different design, which represent familiar images from the state that they celebrate. The California stamp shows the Bay Bridge, which connected San Francisco and Oakland and was opened in 1936. This two level bridge carried automobile traffic on its upper deck and was shared by truck and rail traffic on the lower. An interurban railway and local street cars were carried across the bay. Tracks were shared by the Southern Pacific, Sacramento Northern, and Key System trains. In the late 1950s, the bridge was reconfigured; the railway system was removed and replaced by additional vehicular traffic lanes.

The Detroit People Mover (Scott #3582), a fully-automated light rail system that operates on an elevated single track loop in Detroit's central business district, is displayed on the Michigan stamp that is another of the "Greetings from America" group. Twelve fully automated, computer controlled, driver-less vehicles provide service over an approximately three mile long system. The vehicles are each powered by a linear induction motor that can provide a maximum velocity of 56 miles per hour. Frequent service is provided from the 13 stations distributed along the route.

The **Veteran's Memorial Bridge** in Cleveland (known as the Detroit Superior Bridge when it was opened in 1918) is represented on Scott #3595, another of the "Greetings from America" group. The bridge, shown on the Ohio stamp, had two decks and carried streetcars on the lower deck during the years 1918 to 1954. Another railroad connection is the tall building shown on the right side of the stamp. This is the Cleveland Terminal Tower, headquarters of the Chesapeake and Ohio Railroad, and the hub of rail traffic in the city.

A stamp issued in 1955 (Scott #CZ147) commemorated the hundredth anniversary of the building of the Panama Railroad, the first transcontinental railroad. Although it definitely shows a railroad subject, this stamp has not been described at length because it was intended for Canal Zone postage use rather than use in the United States. It shows a 4-4-0 steam locomotive, the *Nueva Granada*, which was built in the U. S. in 1852.

Finally, there is another famous American who was not involved with railroads but is worthy of mention because of a familial tie to trains. The father of **James A. McNeill Whistler**, the famous painter, whose visage is shown on Scott #885, was a West Point graduate and a well-known railroad pioneer. George W. Whistler, worked with Colonel Long on the Baltimore and Ohio Railroad but was best known for his employment by the Tsar Nicholas I to build the first railroad in Russia. While in Russia, he contracted cholera and died in St. Petersburg.

In closing, I would like to apologize if I have overlooked any other United States postage stamps with railroading associations. Although I believe that I have mentioned all those with obvious and important railroad themes, I am equally certain that, considering the pervasive influence that railroads have had on all Americans and their activities, I have probably omitted a few.

It is evident that this history, based on United States postage stamps, has many gaps. Several important developments and personages important to railroad history are missing. A few candidates for inclusion on postage stamps are James Andrews, General Herman Haupt, George Pullman, and George Westinghouse.

Although Andrews, the executed spy who led the raiders that stole the General, and Pullman are discussed above, they have not been honored with stamps. Haupt was a talented engineer who headed the United States Military Railroads during the Civil War. His organizational genius and ability to keep the railroads operating despite enemy incursions and materiel shortages contributed greatly to final Union victory. George Westinghouse deserves recognition on a postage stamp for his many contributions to the improvement of American life, railroad and otherwise. His air brake was probably the single most important invention that allowed railroad trains to break the low speed barriers that restrained them. Trains could attain high speeds early on; controlled speed runs exceeding 60 miles an hour were made in the mid-19th century. But until it was possible to slow and stop a speeding train in a reasonable distance, high speeds could not be scheduled as a matter of course. Westinghouse also brought his talents to bear on many other railroad problems, notably in the area of signal development, another important element necessary to high speed railroading. There are surely many others who might be included as the subject of postage stamps

An interesting stamp series might include views of various railroad stations—maybe from a typical 19th century country station to massive metropolitan terminals (for example, Grand Central or Pennsylvania station in New York City). Another series might show some famous railway bridges and should certainly include the beautiful and spectacular Hell Gate Bridge. Signal development is another area of great interest and possibilities. From simple smashboards to banner box signals to semaphores, an exciting story waits to be told. Locomotive anomalies such as the Shay geared engine or some of Ross Winans's unusual machines would make great stamps.

Finally, except for a few depictions of diesel locomotives, United States postage stamps chronicle no elements of railroad history more recent than the 1960s. Granted, as a mature industry where progress is measured in evolutionary, not revolutionary, steps, there are few, if any, exciting or inspiring developments since that time. But, there have been developments that might be represented on future stamps. The creation of ConRail and Amtrak should be documented. Perhaps it is too early to determine whether some of the newest innovations, the *Acela* train, for example, should be memorialized but some other advances—perhaps light rail developments—might be.

The author, and surely, railroad enthusiasts and and philatelists look forward to and eagerly await new postage stamps about railroads.

SOURCES

INTRODUCTION
Brookman, V. 1, 8; V. 2, 154; V. 3, 163, 189, 190; Martin, 122; Marzulla, 212-13; *Train Sheet*, Fall 1993, Thomas McConkey, "Last Steam on the Panama Railroad"

RAILROAD INFANCY (1825-1850)

America's First Railroad (Scott #1056)
Appleton, 1; Bartlett, 108-110; Dalzell, 5; Dunaway, 596; *Facts and Arguments in Favour of Adopting Railways in Preference to Canals in the State of Pennsylvania*, 24; Harlow, 18; *Merchants' Magazine...*, October 1844, 372; *Pioneer Railroads of the Old and New Worlds, The*, 12; *Railroad History*, #168, 5-16; Starr, 27, 33, 34; *Trains*, April 1975, 28-32; Webb, 25, 148

Ubiquitous Little "Jimmies"
Adams, Ramon, 87; Alexander, *Civil War Railroads and Models*, 202; *American Journal of Railway Appliances*, April 1886, 156; *American Railroad Journal*, May 21, 1853, 329; Bendel, Plates 3 and 17; Colby, 19; *Engineering*, August 18, 1871, 104; Hare, 282; Hilton, *American Narrow Gauge Railroads*, 27; *J. Franklin Institute*, February 1851, 143, 144; Lucas, 45; MacGill, 390; *Passenger, Freight and Work Equipment of the Delaware and Hudson*, 9; *Railroad and Engineering Journal, The*, April 1892, 165; *Railroad History*, #97, 68-73; *Scientific American*, May 3, 1879, 276; Smithsonian Institution, (NMAH) Exhibit; Summers, 96; *Technology and Culture*, January 1970, 75; Train Sheet, Fall 1995, Harold Fredericks, "Switchback Railroad History," 5; Voss, 53; White, *The American Railroad Freight Car*, 156, 157, 554, 555, 557; Wood, Nicholas, 524

Stourbridge Lion locomotive, 1829
Phillips, Lance, 44, 45; Railroad History, #91,14, #107, 89, #116, 58; Scientific American, February 13, 1892, 104; Shaughnessy, 31-2, 34-5; Transactions of the Newcomen Society, 1923-24, L. F. Loree, "The Four Locomotives Imported into America in 1829 by the Delaware and Hudson Company," 69, 72; Wilson, Mitchell, 149

Novelty Locomotive, 1829
Brophy, 45-7; Ellis, 44-5; *Encyclopedia Brittanica*, 15th Ed., 1989, V.4, "Ericsson," 540; Jacob, 116-118; Snell, 26, 27; Proceedings and Addresses, 165; Wilson, Mitchell, 204

Early Railroad Surveys
Cunningham, John, 19, 43, 45; Dilts, 49; Harwood, 8, 35; *J. Franklin Institute*, September 1830, S. H. Long, "On the principles which should govern the location and construction of Rail-roads," 182; Lane, 288; Long, 5; Modelski, xvii, xviii, 6, 7; Pangborn, 40, 43, 54, 86; *Railway History Monograph*, Crete, NE, 6, 29; Stover, *History of the B&O*, 20; Watkins, 21, 22, 41-48; White, *The John Bull*, 88-93; Withuhn, 11; Wood, Nicholas, 530

B&O Railroad, the First Common Carrier
Archer, Robert 11; Bell, 7, 16-18; Brown, William, 119, 124, 205; Comstock, 27, 31; Dilts, 95, 98, 99; Dunbar, 953; *Ellicott City* (MD) *Bicentennial Journal* , 1; Harwood, 8, 35; Kay, 34; Klein, Aaron, 27, 56; Marzulla, 104; Pangborn, 42, 45, 55, 71; *Railroad Gazette*, January 4, 1878; February 25, 1881, 107; *Railroad History*, #10, 5; #52, 12; #73, 48, 49; #127, 23; Reinfeld, p.302; Reinhardt, 34-37; *Scientific American*, January 6, 1872, 24; June 15, 1889, 376; Sinclair, 63-64, 67-68; Solomon, 51, 62; Stover, *Routledge...*, 12, 13, 16; Stover, *History of the B&O...*,16, 35, 36; *Train Sheet*,; Winter 1985, 2, 3; Waitley, 15, 19; Webb, 31, 32, 53-56; White, *American Locomotive Builders*, 41; Wright, Norman, U-7

Best Friend of Charleston Locomotive
Adams, Charles F., Jr., 40; *American Railroad Journal:*, April 17, 1852, 248; *Augusta Chronicle, The*, November 19, 1944, "Timbers of Historic Railway Line Bared at Warrenville"; Brown, William, 24-26, 137-40; Carter, Charles F., 1908 ed., 24; *Civil Engineer and Architect's Journal, The*, October 1837, 1-3; Comstock, 33-35; *Encyclopedia Brittanica*,1969, V18, 1106; *Engineering*, September 21, 1877, 222, 223; *First Semi-Annual Report...*, 5, 13-17; Henry, *Trains*, 9; Klein, Aaron, 13, 14, 31; Letter from E. Milby Burton...dated July 28, 1960; Letter from Moses Kimball...dated December 21, 1830; MacGill, 422; Nock, #54; Ogburn, 16; Overby, 6; Pangborn, 42, 76; Phillips, Lance, 44, 46, 53, 187; Phillips, Ulrich, 143, 144; *Railroad History*, #7, 9; #65, 77; #91, 10, 15; #129, 43; #150, 115, 116; Reed, *New York Elevated...*, 25;

RAILROAD ADOLESCENCE (1850-1875)

Rae, 3, 57, 67; *Railroaders, The*, 17, 20, 41, 55, 68, 78, 79, 81; Reck, 146; *Scientific American*, May 29, 1847, 286; Stover, *Routledge...*, 33; Sunderland, 5-9; Thompson, 11; Wilson, Neill C., 13

Abraham Lincoln: The Most Famous American Railroad Employee
Abdill, *Rails West*, 48; *American Railroad Journal*, September 30, 1854, 615; Brown, Dee, 7- 9, 12; *Civil Engineer and Architect's Journal*, The, August 1856, 264; Cook, *The Beauty of Railroad; Bridges*, 123; Gies, 150, 151; Gross, 38; Henry, *Trains*, 32; *Journal of the Association of Engineering Societies*, May 1894, 257; Marzulla, 120; McClure, 382, 383; *Postage Stamps of the United States*, 168; Miers, 86-89; Rae, 62; *Railroad History*, #30, 23, 24; #56, 60-62; Riegel, 100; Robertson, Donald, 39; Russell, 37-39; Stover, *Iron Road ...*, 114, 147; Sunderland, 16-19; *Technology and Culture*, October 1982, 542, 543

Andrew Carnegie: Immigrant, Industrialist, Philanthropist, and Railroad Man
American Railroad Journal, October 30, 1847, 690; Bates, 20-25; Botkin, 10-12; Bridge, 42, 75; Carnegie, 37-38, 55, 56, 63, 64, 69-72, 83; *Cassier's Magazine*, December 1898, 95; Heilbroner, 4, 6, 9, 107, 111; Kent, 24, 28, 30, 33, 34, 36, 40-41, 45-47, 50-51, 54-59, 60-61, 63, 103-5; Livesay, 80, 95, 96; Meltzer, 25, 27, 34-37, 43, 44, 49, 50, 55, 58, 61, 66, 67; Stover, *Iron Road to the West* , 206; Wall, 72, 87, 89-91, 114-117, 138-144, 157-166, 177, 192, 204-207, 239, 264, 828, 829, 832; White, *The American Railroad Passenger Car* , 213, 214

Within the "Range of Our Sure and Easy Guardianship"
Ames, 7, 8; Andrews, 394; Bloomgarden, 69; *Brown*, Dee, 34; *Collier's Encyclopedia*, 1964 ed., V.10, "Gadsden," 519 and V.17, "New Mexico," 437; Daniels, 44, 45; Gadsden [on line]; Galloway, 38, 48, 49; *Golden Spike*, The, 63; Marzulla, 108; *Merchant's Magazine...*, February 1850, 149; *December 1856*, 672; *Railroaders, The*, 28, 30; Stover, *Iron Road ...*, 110; Thomas, Richard, 289; *Transactions of the Newcomen Society*, 1937-1938, 209

Spanning the Niagara Gorge
American Railroad Journal, May 29, 1852, 344, 345; November 5, 1853, 717; March 24, 1855, 188; June 30, 1855, 402; Billings, 49-51; Bloomgarden, 66-67; Brown, David J., 79, 106; *Civil Engineer and Architect's Journal*, The, May 1855, 160, 174; June 1855, 211; Clemens,

17; Cook, *The Beauty of Railroad Bridges*, 41-47, 109-111; Edwards, 167-171; Finch, 280; Gies, 182; *J. Franklin Institute*, April 1855, 233; January 1861, 17, 23; McCullough, *The Great Bridge*, 71; *Papers and Practical Illustrations*, 3-21, 22, 26-30; Marzulla, 98; Roebling, 6-31, 32; *Scientific American*, April 21, 1877, 249; May 12, 1877, 297; July 14, 1883, 19; February 22, 1896, 119; June 17, 1899, 396, 397; *Scientific American Supplement*, March 12, 1892, 13,499; Seibel, 5, 14, 16, 31, 44, 49-56, 241; Steinman, *The Builders of the Bridge*, 157, 164, 165, 172, 188, 189; *Train Shed Cyclopedia*, #54, 27; *Train Sheet*, Winter 1985, 2; Wright, Norman, U-6, U-7

Johns Hopkins...Savior of the Baltimore and Ohio Railroad
Collier's Encyclopedia, 1964 ed.,V.15, "Maryland," 489; Harwood, 53, 58; Hungerford, 321-29, 350, 351, 369, 370; *Johns Hopkins Magazine, The*, January 1974, Jacob, Kathryn A., "Mr. Johns Hopkins," 13-17; *Maryland Magazine*, Spring 1983, Gerry O. Myers, "The Legacy of Johns Hopkins," 26-29; Thom, 1-13, 30-36, 39, 40, 72, 125; Wright, Norman, U-8

Palaces on Wheels
A. Phillip Randolph [on line]; Allen, 123; Anderson, 5, 6, 153-169, 224-225, 286, 347-349; Bradlee, *The Eastern Railroad...*, 71; *Brazeal*, 16-18, 147-150; *Cassier's Magazine*, December 1898, 95; Harlow, 390; Henry, *This Fascinating Railroad Business*, 253; Holbrook, 318; Hubbard, 265; Husband, 48, 101, 157; Klein, Aaron, 175; Leyendecker, 74, 75, 98; Mott, 398; *National Car and Locomotive Builder*, October 1889, 146; Ogburn, 86; Pfeffer, 22-29; *Railroad History*, #59, 32, 33, 35, 36; #82, 45; *Scientific American*, June 15, 1872 / 392; November 12, 1892; *Scribner's*, September 1888, unnumbered; Stover, *Iron Road...*, 206; White, *The American Railroad Passenger Car*, 203, 205, 213, 247, 661; Wright, U-13

Carrying Cows
American Railroad Journal, December 18, 1847, 690; Beebe, 133; Daniels, 51; *Engineering*, February 23, 1894, 263; Harlow, 359; Hilton, *American Narrow Gauge Railroads*, 70;; Riegel, 269; *Scientific American*, November 11, 1868, 314; June 10, 1871, 374; December 11, 1880, 374; February 4, 1882, 65; April 18, 1885, 248; Stover, *History of the Baltimore and Ohio Railroad*, 58; Taber, 277; Voss, 40; White, *The*

American Railroad Freight Car, 259, 265 and *The Great Yellow Fleet*, 29

Stonewall" *Jackson Deceives the B&O Railroad – True or False?*
Bowers, 119, 120; Farwell, 160, 162, 166, 167; Henderson, 91, 92, 95; Hungerford, 6-14; *Railroad History*, #104, 7-25; Letter from Anne Calhoun; Robertson, James, 229, 230, 245, 246

The Great Locomotive Chase
Abdill, George B. Civil War Railroads, 70; *American Heritage*, December 1977, 37, 44, 45; Brochure from the Big Shanty Museum; Carter, Ernest F., 59; *Dispatcher*, The, January-February 2001, 5; Douglas, 113; Dow, 20; *Engineering*, March 23, 1894, 385; *Landmarker, The*, Winter 1979-80, 3, 7, 8, 12; Nock, 172; Oliver, Smith H., 84; Pittenger, 4, 69, 70, 85-118; *Railroad History*, #3, 38; #106, 7; #132, 38; Roper [on line]; *Southern Confederacy*, April 15, 1862; Talbot, 626; U. S. Army [on line]; White, *A History of the American Locomotive*, 467 and *Early American Locomotives*, #25

Emigrants to the West
Adams, Ramon, 178; Beebe, *Hear the Train Blow*, 164; Bettmann, 174; Burgess, 749; Daniels, 93; Galloway, 21; Hubbard, 197; Kirkland, 300; Marzulla, 108; *Scientific American*, May 31, 1879, 341; October 23, 1869, 258; Stevens, 128; *Train Sheet*, Winter 1985, 3; White, *The American Railroad Freight Car* , 184

The Little Red Caboose
Hubbard, 47-50; *Illinois Central Magazine*, February 1925, 27; Knapke, 26-28; 36, 37; Marshall, John, 169; O'Connell, 6; *Railroad Car Journal*, The, September 1894, 190, 191; February 1895, 33; Stein, Jess, "caboose"; Oxford English Dictionary, "caboose"

Mail by Rail
Barrett, 195; Brown, Abram, 48; Drury, 272, 273; Foster-Harris, 180; Fuller, 160-168; Holbrook, 301-304, 311, 12; Hubbard, 213; Marzulla, 87; Modelski, 64, 65; O'Connell, 7; O'Dell, 184; Pangborn, 104; *Railroad Car Journal*, The, June 1894, 107; *Railroad History*, #21, 7; Reinhardt, 239-247; Russell, 40; *Scientific American*, October 4, 1879, 209; *Scientific American Supplement*, March 13, 1897, 17,679; *Scribner's*, June 1873, unnumbered; *Stamps and Stories*, 245; Voss, 82; Weber, 230; Wright, Norman, U-7, U-9, U-10, U-11, U-13

Railroad Navies

Billington, 113; *Cassier's Magazine*, August 1894, 277, 292; April 1898, 519-524; *Engineering*, January 8, 1892, 38, 39; January 15, 1892, 69-72; Henry, *This Fascinating Railroad Business*, 106; Hilton, *The Great Lakes Car Ferries*, 1, 2, 9, 12, 55; *Leslie's Weekly*, May 11, 1878; Letter from Jean D. Schlademan, USPS, to the author, dated August 23, 2001; *Linn's Stamp Yearbook* 1995, 393-397; *Railroad History*, #174, 7, 8; *Scientific American*, December 8, 1888, 351, 352; October 7, 1893, 234; May 5, 1894, 279; *Scientific American Supplement*, November 1, 1890, 12,359-12,361; November 23, 1895, 16,587, 16,588; January 30, 1892, 13,400; Scull, 12

Moving Liquid Gold

Carr, 7, 12, 22, 51, 129-30, 347; *Collier's Encyclopedia*, 1964 ed., V.18, "Petroleum," 629-30; Darrah, 114; Heller, unnumbered; Hubbard,123; Marzulla, 122; *National Railway Historical Society Bulletin*, V.38, #1, F. J. Heller, "A History of Tank Cars," 17, 18; Robertson, Donald, 39; Wall, 172-75

Dinner in the Diner (Scott #3101, Issued 1996)

Brochure of the Baltimore and Ohio Railroad Transportation Museum, 33; Brown, Dee, *Hear That Lonesome Whistle Blow* , 223; *Cassier's Magazine*, December 1898, 106; Douglas, 181, 186 Foster-Harris, 180; Hollister, 10; Husband, 49-52; *J. Franklin Institute*, September 1829, 199; Klein, Maury, 507-509; Leyendecker, 87; Morris, 12; Ogburn, 89, 92; Rae, 30; *Railroad History*, #32, 61 and #164, 16; Talbot, 663; White, *The American Railroad Passenger Car*, 313; Withuhn, 20

National Grange, 1867-1967

Andrews, 410, 411; Railroaders, The, TIME-LIFE, 223 ; Stover, *Routledge Historical....*, 46, 47

Walter McQueen - From Old Puff to Jupiter

Ambrose, 361, 366, 367; Bianculli, V.1, 105; Dunn [on line]; *Brotherhood of Locomotive Firemen and Engineman's Magazine*, November 1948; Growing With Schenectady [on line]; Harte [on line]; Hollingsworth, 37; Lounsbury, 465; Phillips, Lance, 118; Russell, 63; Sinclair, 296; White, *History of the American Locomotive*, A, 320, 321

Spanning the Continent: The First Transcontinental Railroad
Abdill, *Pacific Slope Railroads*, 45, 46 and *Rails West*, 52; Ambrose,
360-67; Ames, 4, 7, 8, 9, 25, 26, 60, 224-226; Bianculli, 105;
Bloomgarden, 101; Brown, Dee, 64, 78, 85, 86, 105; Davidson, Charles,
112; *Dispatcher*, The, March-April 2001, 10; Dunbar, 1320, 1321;
Galloway, 27; *Golden Spike*, The, 63; Hogg, 17, 35, 46, 51, 54, 55, 114,
115, 138; Howard, 201; Klein, Aaron, 218; Klein, Maury, 7, 149, 499,
500; Lewis, Oscar, 93, 94; Marzulla, 89; *Merchant's Magazine...*,
October 1862, 320; Moody, 18; O'Dell, 31; Photograph from Union
Pacific Railroad Museum; Quiett, 84; *Railroaders*, The, 20, 28;
Reinhardt, 46; *Report of Board...*, 10; *Scientific American*, May 29,
1847, 286;*Transactions of the Newcomen Society*, 1937-1938, Ralph
Budd, "Railway Routes Across the Rocky Mountains," 209; Weber, 43;
Wellington, 775-777; Williams, John, book title

Taming the Missouri River
Dictionary of American Biography [on line]; *Encyclopedia Americana*,
1997 ed., V.6, "Chanute, Octave"; Maw, 120, 121; *J. Franklin Institute*,
September 1869, 179-184; Lienhard [on line]; "Octave Chanute" [on
line]

Rack and Roll
Allen, 16; American Society of Mechanical Engineers, Annotated List
of Designated Landmarks..., 11; Bray, 14; Ellis, 27; *Engineering*, August
18, 1876, 140; September 4, 1891, 264; *History of the Baldwin
Locomotive Works*, 1831-1923, 43, 44, 82; Hollingsworth, 45; *Railroad
History*, #4, 19, 20, 22; #8, 16, 17; #123, 30, 31; Ransome-Wallis, 473;
Scientific American, May 16, 1885, 303; *Scientific American
Supplement*, May 1, 1886, 8,604, 8,605; Weightman, 2, 14; Wright,
William, 48

U.S. Grant: Crédit Mobilier and Other Railroad Affairs
Ames, 46, 60; Andrews, 260, 61; Carter, Charles F., 1926 ed.,93;
Galloway, 206; Grant, Ulysses, 301-303, 324-25; Holbrook, 171; Jensen,
91-93; Kent, 72, 76, 77; McFeeley, 322-28, 487-89; Mercer, 39; Perret,
389-93, 435, 36; Weber, 43

George Westinghouse and Jimmy Rodgers, Famous "Brake" Men
Dunbar, 1028; *Encyclopedia Brittanica*, "Railway," 1123; *Engineering*,
May 1, 1874; Henry, *This Fascinating Railroad Business*, 238; Henry,
Trains, 58; Holbrook, 292; Interstate Commerce Commission, Third

Annual Report, 33, 338-340; Jensen, 189, 256; Kinert,130; Kirkman, 336-340; *National Car and Locomotive Builder*, October 1889, 146; *National Railway Historical Society Bulletin*, Volume 40, #5, 17; Phillips, Lance, 322, 353; *Railroad History*, #105, 13; *Reference Book of The Westinghouse Air Brake Company*, 11; Rodgers, xxii, xxv, 7, 10-12, 32, 62, photo ff. 86, 94, 129, 152; *Scientific American*, March 8, 1873, 144, 145; January 1, 1887, 3; Stevers, 73, 74; Thomas, Richard, 315; *Train Sheet*, Winter 1985, 3; *Trains*, October 1975, 47, 48.; White, *The American Railroad Passenger Car*, 552

John Henry, A Steel-Driving Man

Adler, 122, 132; *American Railroad Journal*, 1 December 1849, 758, 759; Botkin, 402-405; *Civil Engineer and Architect's Journal, December 1855*, 418; *Contributions from the Museum of History and Technolgy*, Bulletin 240, 210; Couper, 127-173; Drinker, 483, 484; Howard, 232; Jacobs, David, 42; *Kaempffert*, 363; *Railroad History*, #129, 51, 52; *Sandström*, 98-100, 290-92; *Scientific American*, 1 July 1868, 9; Stine, 145

Eads Mississippi River Bridge

Billings, 50, 51; Brookman, V.1, 190; Brown, David, 20; *Dispatcher, The,* April 2001, 13; Ellet, 21-26; *Engineering*, October 4, 1872, 245-247; Finch, 289, 291; Gies, 158, 166, 173; Jacobs, 61, 65; *Journal of the Association of Engineering Societies*, March 1898, 194, 195; *Journal of the Franklin Institute*, September 1868, 147-152; October 1868, 248, 249; *Mystic's 2001 U. S. Stamp Catalog*, 1, 2, 12, 101; Petroski / 159; Sandhurst, 412; *Science Record*, 1875, 262; *Scientific American*, December 17, 1870, 391; December 24, 1870, 401; November 15, 1873, 311; July 18, 1874, 42; March 2, 1889, 136; *Scientific American Supplement*, August 2, 1890, 12,152; Steinman, *Bridges and Their Builders*, 185, 174-206; *Technology and Culture*, October 1982, 539

Eddy and His Clocks

Bradlee, *The Boston and Lowell Railroad...*, 23; Colburn, 81; *J. Franklin Institute*, December 1876, 28; Kinert, 134; Kirkland, V.1, 308; *Railroad Gazette*, The, September 24, 1880, 501; *Railroad History*, #69, 79, #7, 4; #114, 29, #2, 17; #69, 80; Sinclair, 206-8, 214-16, 241, 242; Talbot, 621-623; Wardwell, unnumbered; White, *History of the American Locomotive*, A, 95-97, 451, 452; *World of Hibernia, The*, Spring 1999, 33, 35

RAILROAD MATURITY (1875-1900)

Workin' on the Railroad

Bostonian, The, 306; *Cassier's Magazine*, May 1895, 78; *Engineering*, January 18, 1878, 43, 44; October 27, 1893, 509; January 19, 1894, 87; Forney, *The Car-Builder's Dictionary*, 1879 ed., 49, Figs. 43, 45; Hubbard, 58, 59; *J. Franklin Institute*, June 1899, 491; Parsons, 8; *Railroad and Engineering Journal*, The, August 1891, 377; *Railroad Gazette*, The, January 13, 1872, 11; February 28, 1879, 107; *Railroad History* #127, 66, 67, 74; #49, 26; *Scientific American*, August 5, 1876, 79; April 20, 1878, 239, 240; December 30, 1882, 420; July 11, 1896, 21; October 31, 1896, 335; *Scientific American Supplement*, May 25, 1889, 11,163; June 12, 1897, 17,881; Wait, Figures 5589-5600

Thomas Edison: The Electric Locomotive and the "Movies"

Bloomgarden, 111; Josephson, 21, 22, 238-42, 392-401; *Railroaders, The*, 226-33; Reinfeld, 345; United States Postal Service, stamp Scott #3182c; Wright, Norman, U-7, U-11

Ely's Locomotive #10

Alexander, *Iron Horses*, 184; Ellis, 128; *Engineering*, December 2, 1881, 552-3; December 16, 1881, 596-7; *J. Franklin Institute*, July 1880, 6, 7; Letter from Thomas T. Taber dated March 13, 2001; Lovell, 45; Pangborn, 157; *Railroad History*, , #52, 23, 27; #59, 9-11; #64, 58; #90, 137, 138; #96, 46-50; *Railroad Men*, September 1904, 445, 478; *Scientific American*, September 24, 1892; 197; October 28, 1893; 283; Westing, *Pennsy Steam and Semaphores*, 9

Blockade!

American Journal of Railway Appliances, December 15, 1883, 290; Best, 13, 46, 55, 56, 70, 71; Clemens, 9-16; Dunbar, 1068; *Engineering*, October 17, 1884, 356, 359; April 5, 1889, 326; Grant, H. Roger, *We Took the Train*, 41; Hubbard, 294; *Journal of the Franklin Institute*, May 1841, 341, 342; Reinhardt, 175, 178-80, 182, 184; *Rotary Snow Plow*, introductory notes; *Scientific American*, August 26, 1865, 142; May 5, 1885, 323; May 23, 1885, 323; May 5, 1888, 271, 277; *Scientific American Supplement*, December 15, 1888, 10,792; Smith, Stephen, 233; White, *The American Railroad Freight Car*, 97

#999: The Speed Queen and the Empire State Express
Alexander, *Iron Horses*, 208; Botkin, 77; *Cassier's Magazine*, May 1893,
5, 7; June 1893, 137-43; Colburn, 80; *Dispatcher, The*, Mar/Apr 2000,
15; Mar/Apr 2001, 14; *Engineering*, July 28, 1893, 110; September 15,
1893, 330; September 22, 1893, 359; September 29, 1893, 388-90;
October 6, 1893, 418, 419, 432, 433; Dow, 52; Ellis, 128; Grant, H.
Roger, *We Took the Train*, xix; Hollingsworth, 44, 45 ; *Jersey Central
Lines*, January 1981, Walter Matuch, "Steam Power... C.N.J. Style: The
Camelbacks," 34; Marzulla, 46; *National Geographic Magazine*, August
1902, Henry H. McClure, "Shortening Time Across the Continent,"
319; *National Railway Historical Society Bulletin* V.58, #1, 1993,
James E. Kranefeld, "The Number that Became a Name," 6-10; Oliver,
Smith, 88; Pangborn, 124; Phillips, Lance, 354, 355; *Railroad History*,
#142, 32; *Scientific American*, May 13, 1893, 294; May 20, 1893, 306;
June 3, 1893, 341; June 6, 1893, 34; September 3, 1898, 152, 153;
Scientific American Supplement, October 10, 1891, 13,144; November
25, 1899, 19,996; Sinclair, 182; *Train Sheet*, Winter 1985, 1-3; *Trains*,
March 1967, 38-46; *Transport Heritage*, April 1996, 3; Wright, Norman E., U-
6, U-10

THE GOLDEN YEARS OF RAILROADING (1900-1930)

Railroad Station Transfer
Book of the Royal Blue, April 1900, "B&O Electric Automobile Service
at Washington, D.C.," unnumbered; October 1900, "B&O Electric
Automobile Service at Washington, D.C.," unnumbered; May 1901,
"Electro-mobile Service of the Baltimore & Ohio Railroad," unnum-
bered; Letter from Anne Calhoun, Librarian/Archivist, B&O Railroad
Museum, to the author, dated June 22, 2001; *Linn's Stamp News*,
October 19, 1998, 12; *National Railway Historical Society Bulletin*,
Volume 61, Number 5/6, 14-23; Wright, Norman, U-6

"The Story of a Brave Engineer"
Ballad of Casey Jones [on line]; Botkin, 40-51, 456; Casey's Engine [on
line]; *Dispatcher, The*, September/October 2000, 40 and January-
February 2003, 3; Marzulla, 102; Reinfeld, 289; Schafer, *Classic
American Streamliners...*, 73-76, 124, 125, 140, 141; Details of the
Wreck [on line]; Sullivan [on line]; Thomas, Richard, 185; *Train Sheet*,
Winter 1985, 2; The (Trenton, NJ) Times, September 4, 1988, BB-1 and
BB-6; True Story... [on line]; Webb, 123, 124; Wright, Norman, U-7

Mules Along the "Big Ditch"
Bianculli, 202; Cameron, 248-252; Harper's Monthly Magazine, January 1859; Martinez, 130; Marzulla, 79; McCullough, *The Path Between the Seas*, 35, 277-87, 299, 600-602; Wright, Norman, U-6, U-11

From Tinplate to Golden Perfection
Comstock, 50, 51; *Dispatcher, The,* September-October 2000, 37 and May-June 2002, 1; Dow, 5, 23; *Journal of the Association of Engineering Societies*, September and October 1884, Wellington Adams, "Evolution of the Electric Railway," 261; Kay, 72; May, 7; *Railroad Magazine*, April 1943, 11; *Scientific American Supplement*, June 25, 1881, 4,554; Sutton, 1-14; *Transactions of the Newcomen Society*, 1949-1951, F. J. G. Haut, "The Early History of the Electric Locomotive,"153; Westing, *The Locomotives That Baldwin Built* , 9; Wright, Norman, U-7, U-9, U-11

RETREAT AND RENAISSANCE (1930-1950)

1930s: Streamlining Brings a New Look
American Heritage of Invention & Technology, Fall 1986, Margaret Coel, "A Silver Streak," 10, 17; Kisor, Henry, 15, 16; *Railroad History* #173, 70-84; Solomon, 43-47; Stover, *American Railroads*, 215; *Trains*, September 1997, 46-7, 71

Hiawatha Train
Alexander, Edwin P. *American Locomotives*, 192; Longfellow, 149; *Railroad History* #136, 18; Solomon, 47; Wright, Norman, U-12

Congressional Limited Train
Haine, 11, 112; *National Geographic Magazine*, November 1936, 554; Phillips, Lance, 72; Reed, Train Wrecks, 128; Schafer, *Pennsylvania Railroad*, 70, 71, 74, 109, 110; Wright, Norman, U-12

Super Chief Train
Railroad History #173, 86; Solomon, 40, 52; Wright, Norman, U-12

Daylight Train
Alexander, Edwin P. *American Locomotives*, 204; Church, R. J., 6, 51, 55, 59, 67, 73, 81, 93, 94; *Dispatcher, The*, September-October 2000, 33; *Model Railroader*, April 1972, 42-51; Schafer, *Classic American Streamliners...*, 156-159; *Trains,* June 1993, 46-51; Wright, Norman, U-12; Wright, Richard K., 17-47; Yenne, 142

Twentieth Century Limited Train

Cook, *The Twentieth Century Limited*, 1-4, 15, 16, 45, 63-65; *National Geographic Magazine*, August 1902, 319-21; Phillips, Lance, 104-106; *Railroad History*, # 119, 61, 62; #184, 47-50; *Railway Age*, October 13, 1905, as mentioned in *Railroad History* #138, 108; Solomon, 67, 70; Wright, Norman, U-12

The Diesel Takes Over

Allen, 192; *American Heritage of Invention & Technology*, Winter 1991, Maury Klein, "The Diesel Revolution," 16-22; *Century of Progress...*, 1924, 5; Henry, *This Fascinating Railroad Business*, Introduction; Marre, Louis A. *Diesel Locomotives...*, 10, 205, 288, 330, 355, 382 and *The Contemporary Diesel...*5, 116; Marzulla, 95; *Railroad History*, #184, Spring 2001, 9-19; *Railway and Locomotive Historical Society Newsletter*, Fall 1996, Kyle Wyatt, "The First Diesel Electric Locomotive," unnumbered; Reinfeld, 283, 345; *Trains*, September 1997, 36-7, 66-7, 70-9, 82-4; *Train Sheet*, Winter 1985, 2

IS THERE LIGHT AT THE END OF THE TUNNEL? (1950-Present)

Yenne, 114, 115, 144, 150, 151

Balanced On One Rail

About Las Vegas Monorail [on line]; ASME; Associated Press news release, May 18, 2001; Brief Monorail History [on line]; Cudahy, *How We Got to Coney Island*, 99; *Encyclopedia Americana*, 1997 ed., V.18, 446; V.19, 376, 377; *Encyclopedia Brittanica*, 15th ed., V. 6, 144; V. 8, 265; V. 19, 376; *European Scientific Notes; Journal of the Franklin Institute*, March 1874, 197-202; Marzulla, 132, 133; Monorails of... [on line]; Scientific American, July 10, 1886, 15, 21; September 7, 1889, 150; March 28, 1891, 191, 192; February 17, 1894, 97, 100; March 24, 1894, 182; *World Book 2000*, V. 13, 732; V. 21, 47; Wright, Norman, U-7

LABOR AND LEGISLATION

Railroads, Labor, and the Law: Strikes, Regulation, and Administration

American Heritage, February/March 1978, 56-8; Andrews, 525-28, 530, 534, 793, 868,69; Auchincloss, 51-53, 82; Brogan, 136-141; *Collier's Encyclopedia*, 1964 ed., V. 6, 624, "Cleveland," V. 11, 731, "Hayes," V.

MASS TRANSIT BY RAIL

Going Out on the Town - from Horses to Horsepower

Horsecars, First to Last, 1832-1926

16, 21, 24, 27; Miller, John, 1, 2, 16-23, 25, 32; Pangborn, 60, 61; Railroad History, October 1962, 9; Reed, 17, 19; *Train Sheet*, Winter 1985, 4; Wright, Norman, U-8

Climbing Halfway to the Stars Via Cable Cars

Cassier's Magazine, August 1899, 403-405; Middleton, *The Time of the Trolley*, 35-51; Miller, John, 35-53; *Scientific American*, April 17, 1875, 239; July 14, 1888, 22; *Scientific American Supplement*, Sept. 17, 1881, 4,743-4,748; August 22, 1885, 8,027; Wright, Norman, U-8, U-9

Underground Railways

American Heritage of Invention & Technology, Winter 1997, Oliver E. Allen, "New York's Secret Subway," 44-48; *Collier's Encyclopedia*, 1964 ed., "Subways, electric"; *Contributions from the Museum of History and Technology*, Bulletin 240, Paper 41, 232; Cudahy, *Under the Sidewalks of New York*, vii, 8, 9, 18, 72-75, 112, 119; Derrick, 15; Dwyer, 1-14, 16-17, 44, 66, 147, 170-1; Fischler, 7; Hood, 2, 11, 44-48, 82-84, 101; *Interborough Rapid Transit* / 13, 23-25; McCormick, 8; Middleton, *The Time of the Trolley*, 357, 359, 372, 374, 377; Miller, 82-93; *Science Record*, 1874, 337; *Scientific American*, February 13, 1897, 99; August 21, 1897, 114; April 8, 1899, 212; April 15, 1899, 234; Snyder, xiii, xiv, 35-36; United States Postal Service, stamp Scott #3187j

Antecedents of the Toonerville Trolley

Fischler, Stan, 180, 181; Middleton, *The Time of the Trolley*, 245; Photograph from the Toledo-Lucas County Public Library; *Railroad Gazette*, as reported in *Scientific American*, January 1, 1887, "The Anchor Brake," 3; Railroad History, October 1962, 9; Rowsome, 14; Young, 162

A Streetcar Named Desire

Cudahy, *How We Got to Coney Island*, 24; *International Herald Tribune*, May 5-6, 2001, 20; Middleton, *The Time of the Trolley*, 25, 34; Miller, John, 20, 132, 133, 141; *New Yorker, The*, March 6, 1989, Tony Hiss, "Annals of Transportation (Trolleys)," 70, 71; Rowsome, 15; *Train Sheet*, Winter 1985, 4; *Trenton (NJ) Times*, August 5, 2001, B6; United States Postal Service, stamp Scott #3186n; Williams, Tennessee, 6; Young, 175, 177, 198, 199, 208

POST SCRIPT: A FEW OTHER STAMPS

Alcott: Saxton, 157

Barton: Barton, xv, 121, 176, 183, 282; Bolotin, 10, 11

Benét: Benét, Stephen, 59-74; Benét, Rosemary, 95,96

Berlin: American Heritage Foundation... [on line]; Furia; 56, 73-76; Freedland, 42, 48, 49; Freedon Train [on line]; Hamm, 208, 232, 235; Peach [on line]; Sam DeVincent Collection... [on line]; Stackman [on line]; *National Geographic Magazine,* October 1949, 532; United States Postal Service... [on line];*When That Midnight...* [on line]

Bly: Davidson, Sue, 8, 46; Ehrlich, 13, 30-38, 57-67, 79-93, 96, 97; Kroeger, 43, 44, 139, 168, 169, 230-232; *Train Sheet,* Winter 1977-78, 1-3

Cather: Cather, *Collected Short Fiction,* xxxix, 339-52, 381-93; Cather, *Collected Stories,* 421-463

Cohan: McCabe, 115

Dickinson: Dickinson, 286; Marzulla, 166

DuBois: DuBois [on line]; Hynes [on line]; Underground Railroad [on line]; Wager [on line]

Eisenhower: *Classic Trains,* Spring 2002, 81; Perret, 9-11

Eliot: *Cats* souvenir brochure...[on line]; *Collier's Encyclopedia,* 1964 ed., V 9, 91-93, "Eliot;" Eliot, 167-169

Emerson: Emerson, 219, 224

Faulkner: Faulkner, *Collected Stories,* 431, 673 and *The Faulkner Reader,* 353-432

Ferber: Edna Ferber [on line]; Saratoga Trunk. [on line]

Fitzgerald: Bruccoli, 342-3: A review of *The Vegetable in the New York Post* by John F. Carter, Jr. and 399: A review of *Taps at Reveille* in *The Nation* byWilliam Troy; Fitzgerald, 211-15, 273-293; Gallo, 126-7; LeVot, 133-4

Frost: Frost, 376-8

Garfield: Caption on a photograph from the author's collection; *Colliers Encyclopedia,* 1964 ed., V.10, "Garfield, James Abram," 576; Marzulla, 36

Gompers: Livesay, 142, 43.

Grant: Buehrer, 50, 51, 70-73, 140-43; Cary Grant Press Release [on line]; Colliers's Encyclopedia, "Fisk, James"; Deschner, 110-12; Gordon, various; McCann, Filmography #28; Moore [on line; Railroad Network, The [on line];Toast of New York, The [on line]

Greeley: Archer, Jules, 127, 159; *Collier's Encyclopedia,* 1964 ed., "Greeley, Horace," V.11, 429; Isely, 44-5

Griffith: An Arcadian Maid [on line]; Bennett [on line]; Lonedale

Operator, The [on line]

Harrison: Sokolofsky, 74

Hart: Bach, 25-30, 50-62, 66-69; Hart, 43, 44, 58-65, 78-88, 238-40, 279-81, 384-6, 393-7, 401, 402, 427

Harte: Harte [on line]; Learned, 195

Hawthorne: *Collier's Encyclopedia*, 1964 ed., V. 11, 722, "Hawthorne;" Hawthorne, 1070-82; Myerson, 80-101

Hemingway: Hemingway, 119 et seq.; 163 et seq.; 211 et seq.; 258 et seq.; 322 et seq; 557 et seq.; 571 et seq.

Irving: Wood, James, 163, 164

Jackson: Curtis, James, 33; Daniels, 66; Postcard sold by the Baltimore and Ohio Railroad at the New York World's Fair, 1939; Remini, 102; Stover, *The Life and Decline of the American Railroad*, 8

Johnson, Andrew: Trefousse, 38-40, 73, 77-79, 93, 117, 137, 301

Joplin: Berlin, vii, 27, 28; Curtis, Susan, 41; Encyclopedia Brittanica, The [on line]; Haskins, 41; Stein, Jess

Julian: *Ebony* Magazine, March 1975

Kennedy: Stein, Jean, dust cover, 32

Kern: Bordman, 172-4; 403-4

LaGuardia: Hood, 228, 233-39

Lee: Thomas, Emory, 410-411

Lewis: Alvarez, 162; Botkin, 178; Bradlee, *Boston and Maine Railroad*, 29; DiRenzo, 352; Grant, *Country Railroad Station in America*, 10; Henry, Trains, 41, 42; Holbrook, 263; Lewis, Sinclair, 229; McAfee, 123; Russell, 23; Taber, 278; Vose, *Manual for Railroad Engineers*, 422, 423;
London: Shepard, 232-243

Lowell: Scudder, 45

Marshall: Haskins, 6, 9, 10, 23, 71, 72; MCCSC Learning Network [on line]; Metcalf, 113-141; Montgomery County...[on line]; Oran Z [on line]; Supreme Court Historical Society, The [on line]; Thurgood Marshall Press Release [on line]

Millay: Millay, 78

Miller: Chattanooga Choo Choo [on line]

Murrow: Kendrick, 89, 97-99

Nash: Nash, 210

Parker: "Dorothy Parker" [on line]; Kimbel, 223-233; Lopata [on line]; Parker, 199-210

Polk: *Collier's Encyclopedia*, 1964 ed., V. 19, 216-7, "Polk, James Knox;" McCormac, 684,5; Sellers, 396-8

Rand: Atlas Shrugged [on line]; "Ayn Rand." [on line]; Branden, 219, 300; Gladstein, 34-63; Sobczak, 111

Riley: Riley, 47

Rogers: Ketchum, 68, 130, 152, 226, 374-5

Saroyan: Saroyan, 4, 198

Steinbeck: Covici, 557-72

Thoreau: Marzulla, 149; Thoreau, x, 25, 68, 69, 151-154, 157-161, 163

Thorpe: Brochure, "Visit Old Mauch Chunk," *Colliers Encyclopedia*, V. 22, "Thorpe, James Francis," 293

Thurber: Holmes, Charles S., 293; Kinney, 553-4

Truman: McCullough, 493-507

Warren: Katcher, 12-16, 23; White, G. Edward., 10-12

Wayne: Eyles, 98, 244, 259; Ricci, 44; Shepherd, 335, 348, 355

Webster: Bartlett, 118, 232; Dalzell, 26, 27

Wharton: Brookner, V.2, 20-30

Whitman: Whitman, 54, 97, 187, 583

Whittier: Whittier, 117

Wilder: Goldstone, 87; Meitche [on line];Stresau, 46-48, 100; "Thornton Wilder." [on line]

Wolfe: Holman, 60, 129, 171, 258, 448, 480, 576

Brooklyn Bridge: Cudahy, How We Got to Coney Island, 157-69; Grafton, 31, 35; Hood, 25; Kouwenhoven, 423; McCullough, 32, 436, 481, 515, 518-19; Railroad History, October 1957, 7-20; *Scientific American*, 12 June 1883, 335, 336; 13 October 1883, 230; 26 March 1898, 195; 9 July 1898, 20; Younger, 8,9

San Francisco-Oakland Bay Bridge: "Bridging the Bay." [on line]; Dillon, 68, 71; *Dispatcher, The*, March/April 2002, V.49,#02-2, 13; San Francisco-Oakland Bay Bridge, The [on line]

Detroit People Mover: Dispatcher, The, May-June 2002, V.49, #02-3, 1; People Mover [on line]; Woodward Heritage [on line]

Veteran's Memorial Bridge: *Dispatcher, The*, July/August 2002 and September/October 2002

Whistler: Bianculli, 60; *Colliers Encyclopedia*, 1964 ed., V.23, "Whistler, James Abbott McNeill," 464; Gould, Levi, 38; Marzulla, 85

BIBLIOGRAPHY

A. Phillip Randolph: For Jobs and Freedom. Public Broadcasting System (PBS). [on line] <http://www.pbs.org/weta/apr/aprbio.html> (30 June 2003)

A. Phillip Randolph, labor and civil rights leader. The African American Registry.® Published by Media Business Solutions.® [on line] <http://www.aaregistry.com> (28 June 2003)

AAA TourBook, Illinois, Indiana & Ohio. Heathrow, FL: AAA Publishing, 2001

Abdill, George B. *Civil War Railroads*. Bloomington, IN: Indiana University Press, 1999 (Reprint of the Superior Publishing Company edition of 1961)
———. *Pacific Slope Railroads*. New York: Bonanza Books, 1959
———. *Rails West*, New York: Bonanza Books, 1960

About Las Vegas Monorail. [on line] <http://www.lvmonorail.com/about.html> (30 June 2003)

Adams, Charles F., Jr. *Railroads: Their Origin and Problems*. New York: G. P. Putnam's Sons, 1893

Adams, Ramon F. *The Language of the Railroader*. Norman, Okla.: University of Oklahoma Press, 1977

Adler, Dorothy. *British Investment in American Railways, 1834-1898*. Charlottesville: The University Press of Virginia, 1970

Alexander, Edwin P. *American Locomotives, 1900-1950*. New York: Bonanza Books, 1950
———. *Civil War Railroads & Models*, New York: The Fairfax Press, 1989
———. *Iron Horses*, New York: W. W. Norton and Company, 1941

Allen, G. Freeman. *Railways, Past, Present & Future*. New York: William Morrow and Company, Inc., 1982

Alvarez, Eugene. *Travel on Southern Antebellum Railroads, 1828-1860*. University, AL: The University of Alabama Press, 1974.

Ambrose, Stephen E. *Nothing Like It in the World*. New York: Simon and Schuster, 2000

American Heritage. New York

American Heritage Foundation Freedom Train. National Archives and Records Administration. [on line] <http://www.archives.gov/publications/prologue/spring_1997_railroad_records_2.html> (29 June 2003)

American Heritage of Invention & Technology. New York

American Journal of Railway Appliances. New York

American Railroad Journal. New York

American Society of Mechanical Engineers. New York

Amerman, John W. *The Illinois Central Railroad Company Offers for Sale Over 2,000,000 Acres Selected Farming and Wood Land,* mentioned in Modelski, *Railroad Maps of North America*

Ames, Charles Edgar. *Pioneering the Union Pacific.* New York: Appleton-Century-Crofts, 1969

An Arcadian Maid. Internet Movie Database, Inc. (IMDb Review). [on line] <http://www.imdb.com/Title?0001118> 7 June 2003)

Anderson, Jervis, *A. Philip Randolph; A Biographical Portrait.* New York: Harcourt Brace Jovanovich, 1973

Andrews, Wayne, Editor, *Concise Dictionary of American History.* Charles Scribner's Sons, New York, 1962

Appleton, Edward. *History of the Railways of Massachusetts.* N.p.: The Railroad Enthusiats, Inc., 1952 (A reprint of the original article published in *Walling's Atlas of Massachusetts* in 1871)

Appletons Mechanics' Magazine and Engineers' Journal. New York

Archer, Jules. *Fighting Journalist.* New York: Julian Messner, 1966

Archer, Robert F. *The History of the Lehigh Valley Railroad.* Berkeley, Calif.: Howell-North Books, 1978

ASME National Mechanical Engineering Landmark citation #N84

Associated Press. New York

Atlas Shrugged. Powell's Books. [on line] <http//www.powells.com/cgi-bin/biblio?inkey=62-0452011876-0> (21 March 2002)

Auchincloss, Louis. *Theodore Roosevelt.* New York: Times Books, 2001

Augusta (GA) *Chronicle, The*

"Ayn Rand." *Dictionary of Literary Biography*, V. 227, *American Novelists Since WWII, Sixth Series.* Literarature Resource Center. [on line] Gale Group Databases. Mary Jacobs Library, NJ. <http://www.infotrac.galegroup.com> (20 March 2002)

Bach, Stephen. *Dazzler, The Life and Times of Moss Hart.* New York: Alfred A. Knopf, 2001

Ballad of Casey Jones, The. Casey Jones Railroad Museum State Park. [on line]. <http://www.trainweb.org/caseyjones/song.html> (14 February 2003)

Barrett, Richard C. *Boston's Depots and Terminals.* Rochester, New York: Railroad Research Publications, 1996

Bartlett, Irving H. *Daniel Webster.* New York: W. W. Norton and Company, 1978

Barton, William E. *The Life of Clara Barton, Volume 1.* A reprint of the 1922 edition. New York, AMS Press,1969.

Bates, David Homer, *Lincoln in the Telegraph Office.* Lincoln, NE: University of Nebraska Press, 1995 (Reprinted from the original 1907 edition by The Century Company, New York)

Beebe, Lucius and Charles Clegg. *Hear the Train Blow.* New York: E.P.Dutton and Company, 1952

Bell, J. Snowden. *The Early Motive Power of the Baltimore and Ohio Railroad.* New York: August Sinclair Company, Publishers, 1912

Bendel, A. *Aufsatze Betreffende Das Eisenbahnwesen in Nord-Amerika.* Berlin: von Ernst and Korn, 1862

Benét, Stephen Vincent. *Selected Works of Stephen Vincent Benét.* New York: Rinehart & Company, 1942

Benét, Rosemary and Stephen Vincent Benét. *A Book of Americans*. New York: Farrar and Rinehart, Inc., 1933

Bennett, Carl. Progressive Silent Film List - *An Arcadian Maid*. [on line] <http://www.silentera.com/PSFL/data/A/ArcadianMaid1910.html> (7 June 2003)

Berlin, Edward A. King of Ragtime, *Scott Joplin and His Era*. New York: Oxford University Press, 1994

Best, Gerald M. *Snowplow*. Berkeley, Calif.: Howell-North Books, 1966

Bettmann, Otto L. *The Good Old Days-They Were Terrible!* New York: Random House, 1974

Bianculli, Anthony J. *Trains and Technology, V. 1*. Newark, DE: The University of Delaware Press, 2001

Billings, Henry. *Bridges*. New York: The Viking Press, 1966

Billington, David P. *The Innovators*. New York: John Wiley and Sons, Inc., 1996

Bloomgarden, Henry S. *American History through Commemorative Stamps*. New York: Arco Publishing Company, 1969

Bolotin, Norman. *Civil War, A to Z*. New York: Dutton Children's Books, 2002

Book of the Royal Blue. Published by the Passenger Department of the Baltimore & Ohio Railroad, Baltimore, N.d.

Bordman, Gerald. *Jerome Kern, His Life and Music*. New York: Oxford University Press, 1980

Bostonian, The. Boston

Botkin, B. A. and Alvin F. Harlow, Editors. *A Treasury of Railroad Folklore*. New York: Bonanza Books, 1953

Bowers, John. *Stonewall Jackson, Portrait of a Soldier*. New York: William Morrow and Company, Inc., 1989

Bradlee, Francis B. C. *The Boston and Lowell Railroad, The Nashua and Lowell Railroad, and the Salem and Lowell Railroad*. Salem, MA: The Essex Institute, 1918

————. *The Boston and Maine Railroad.* Salem, MA: The Essex Institute, 1921
————. *The Eastern Railroad,* Salem, MA: The Essex Institute, 1917

Branden, Barbara. *The Passion of Ayn Rand.* Garden City, NY: Doubleday & Company, 1986

Bray, Donald. *Cog Railway.* Mount Washington, NH: Mount Washington Railway Company, 1991

Brazeal, Brailsford R. *The Brotherhood of Sleeping Car Porters.* New York: Harper Brothers, 1946

Bridge, James Howard. *The Inside History of the Carnegie Steel Company.* New York: Arno Press, 1972

"Bridging the Bay." University of California Berkeley Library [on line] <http://www.lib.berkeley.edu/Exhibits/Bridge/sfobay.html> (10 May 2002)

Brief Monorail History, A. Seattle Monorail Services. [on line] <http://www.seattlemonorail.com/history.htm> (30 June 2003)

Brochure from the Big Shanty Museum. Kennesaw, Georgia.

Brochure of the Baltimore and Ohio Transportation Museum. Baltimore: Baltimore and Ohio Railroad

Brochure, "Visit Old Mauch Chunk," published by the Jim Thorpe Chamber of Commerce

Brogan, Denis W. *The Era of Franklin D. Roosevelt.* New Haven: Yale University Press, 1950

Brookner, Anita, Ed. *The Stories of Edith Wharton.* Vol. 2, New York: Carroll & Graf Publishers, Inc., 1989

Brookman, Lester G. *The United States Postage Stamps of the 19th Century.* New York: H. L. Lindquist Publications, Inc., 1966

Brophy, Ann. *John Ericsson and the Inventions of War.* Englewood Cliffs, NJ: Silver Burdett Press, 1991

Brotherhood of Locomotive Firemen and Engineman's Magazine

Brown, Abram E. *History of the Town of Bedford.* Bedford, Mass.: Privately published, 1891

Brown, David J. *Bridges*. New York: Macmillan Publishing Company, 1993

Brown, Dee. *Hear That Lonesome Whistle Blow*. New York: Holt, Rinehart and Winston, 1977

Brown, William H. *History of the First Locomotives in America*. New York: D. Appleton and Company, Revised Edition, 1874

Bruccoli, Matthew J. *F. Scott Fitzgerald, In His Own Time: A Miscellany*. Kent, OH: The Kent State University Press, 1971

Buehrer, Beverly Bare. *Cary Grant: A Bio-Bibliography*. New York: Westport Press, 1990

Burgess, George H. and Miles C. Kennedy. *Centennial History of the Pennsylvania Railroad*. Philadelphia: The Pennsylvania Railroad Company, 1949

Cameron, Ian. *The Impossible Dream: The Building of the Panama Canal*. New York: William Morrow & Company, Inc., 1972

Carnegie, Andrew, *Autobiography*. Boston: Houghton Mifflin Company, 1920

Carr, Albert Z. *John D. Rockefeller's Secret Weapon*. New York: McGraw-Hill Book Company, 1962

Carter, Charles F.*When Railroads Were New*. New York: H. Holt, 1908 ed.
——. *When Railroads Were New*. New York: Simmons-Boardman Publishing Company, 1926 ed.

Carter, Ernest F., *Unusual Locomotives*. The Macmillan Company, New York, 1960

Cary Grant Press Release. United States Postal Service. [on line]
<http//www.usps.com/news/2002/philatelic/sr02_067.htm> (16 July 2003)

Casey's Engine. Casey Jones Railroad Museum State Park. [on line].
<http://www.trainweb.org/caseyjones/382.html> (14 February 2003)
<http://www.trainweb.org/caseyjones/638.html> (14 February 2003)

Cassier's Magazine, New York

Cather, Willa. *Collected Short Fiction, 1892-1912*. Lincoln, NE: University of Nebraska Press, 1965
——. *Collected Stories*, New York: Vintage Books, 1992

Cats souvenir brochure for the Fourth National Touring Company. The Poems. [on line] <http://www.geocities.com/broadway/alley/1711/cats/poems/html> (16 July 2003)

Century of Progress, A, The General Electric Story. Schenectady, NY, Hall of History Foundation, Schenectady, 1981

Century of Reading Company Motive Power, A. Published by the Reading Company, Philadelphia, 1941.

Ceremonies upon the Completion of the Monument Erected by the Pennsylvania Railroad Co. at Bordentown, New Jersey, November 12, 1891. Washington: Gedney & Roberts

Chanute, Octave. Biography. [on line] <http://invention.psychology.msstate.edu/i/Chanute/Chanute.html> (30 June 2003)

Chanute, Octave. Biography in the Inventors Gallery. [on line] <http://invention.psychology.msstate.edu/i/Chanute/Chanute.html> (30 June 2003)

Chanute, Octave. *Progress in Flying Machines*. Long Beach, CA: Lorenz & Herweg, 1976. A Facsimile of the 1894 Edition.

Chanute, Octave Alexander. American Aerospace Pioneers. Hill Aerospace Museum. [on line] http://www.hill.af.mil/museum/history/oxchanute.htm> 30 June 2003)

Chattanooga Choo Choo, The. [on line] <http://www.choochoo.com/hist_song.shtml> (13 March 2002)

Church, R. J. *Those Daylight 4-8-4's*. Omaha, NE: Kratville Publications, 1966

Civil Engineers and Architect's Journal, The. London

Clarke, Thomas C. et al. *The American Railway*. New York: Arno Press, 1976

Classic Trains, Waukesha, WI

Clemens, Samuel. *The Complete Short Stories of Mark Twain*. New York: Bantam Books, 1990

Colburn, Zerah. *Locomotive Engineering and the Mechanism of Railways*. London: William Collins, Sons, and Company, 1871

Colby, C. B. *Railroads U.S.A.* New York: Coward, McCann and Geoghegan, 1970

Collier's Encyclopedia. New York

Comstock, Henry B. *The Iron Horse.* New York: Galahad Books, 1971

Contributions of the Lowell (MA) *Historical Society*

Contributions from the Museum of History and Technology. Washington

Cook, Richard J. *The Beauty of Railroad Bridges.* San Marino, Calif.: Golden West Books, 1987
———. *The Twentieth Century Limited, 1938-1967.* Lynchburg, VA: TLC Publishing, Inc., 1993

Coolidge, Calvin. *The Autobiography of Calvin Coolidge.* New York: Cosmopolitan Book Company, 1929

Couper, William. *Claudius Crozet.* Charlottesville, Va.: The Historical Publishing Company, Inc., 1936

Covici, Pascal, Ed. *The Portable Steinbeck.* New York: The Viking Press, 1966

Cudahy, Brian J. *How We Got to Coney Island.* New York: Fordham University Press, 2002
———*Under the Sidewalks of New York.* Brattleboro, VT: The Stephen Greene Press, 1979

Cunningham, John T. *Railroads in New Jersey.* Andover, N.J.: Afton Publishing Company, Inc., 1997

Cunningham, William A. *The Railroad Lantern.* Plano, TX: Privately printed by the author, 1997

Curtis, James C. *The Fox at Bay.* Lexington, KY: The University Press of Kentucky, 1970

Curtis, Susan. *Dancing to a Black Man's Tune.* Columbia, MO: University of Missouri Press, 1994

Dahl, John C. *Great Railroad Stations - Cincinnati Union Terminal.* RSHS Depot Email List. [on line]
<http://www.trainweb.org/rshs/GRS%20-%20Cincinnati.htm>. [30 June 2003]

Dalzell, Robert F., Jr. *Daniel Webster and the Trial of American Nationalism, 1843-1852*. Boston: Houghton Mifflin Company, 1973

Daniels, Winthrop M. *American Railroads, Four Phases of Their History*. Princeton: Princeton University Press, 1932

Darrah, William C., *Pithole, The Vanished City*. Published privately, 1972

Davidson, Charles and Lincoln Diamant. *Stamping Our History*. New York: Carol Publishing Group, 1990

Davidson, Sue. *Getting the Real Story, Nellie Bly and Ida B. Wells*. Seattle: The Seal Press, 1992

Davis, Colin J. *Power at Odds, The 1922 National Railroad Shopmen's Strike*. Urbana, IL: University of Illinois Press, 1997

Derrick, Peter. *Tunneling to the Future*. New York: New York University Press, 2001

Deschner, Donald. *The Complete Films of Cary Grant*. Secaucus, NJ: The Citadel Press, 1973

Details of the Wreck. Casey Jones Railroad Museum State Park. [on line]. <http://www.trainweb.org/caseyjones/wreck.htm> (14 February 2003)

Dickinson, Emily. *The Complete Poems of Emily Dickinson*. Little Brown and Company, Boston, 1960

Dillon, Richard. *High Steel*. Millbrae, CA: Celestial Arts, 1979

Dilts, James D. *The Great Road*. Palo Alto: Stanford University Press, 1993

Dispatcher, The. San Francisco

DiRenzo, Anthony, Ed. *If I Were Boss, The Early Business Stories of Sinclair Lewis*. Carbondale, IL: The Southern Illinois University Press, 1997

"Dorothy Parker." *Dictionary of Literary Biography*, V. 86, *American Short Story Writers, 1910-1945, First Series*, 1989. Literarature Resource Center. [on line] Gale Group Databases. Mary Jacobs Library, NJ. <http://www.infotrac.galegroup.com> (16 July 2003)

Douglas, George H., *All Aboard*. Paragon House, New York, 1992.

Dow, George. *World Locomotive Models*. New York: Arco Publishing Company, Inc., 1973

Dreimiller, David. *Signal Lights*. Solon, Ohio: Published by the author, 1990.

Drinker, Henry S. *Tunneling, Explosive Compounds, and Rock Drills*. New York: John Wiley and Sons, 1878

Drury, George H. *The Historical Guide to North American Railroads*. Waukesha, Wisc.: Kalmbach Books, 1985

DuBois, W. E. B. Biography in the ThinkQuest Internet Challenge Library. [on line]
<http://www.thinkquest.org/library/10320/dubois.htm> (3 February 2003)

Dunbar, Seymour. *A History of Travel in America*. New York: Tudor Publishing Company, 1937

Dunn, Steve. *The Iron Horse in Schenectady* (video). Schenectady, NY: WMHT Educational Telecommunications. [on line]
<http://www.wmht.org/ironhorse/pro_desc_ih.htm> (7 June 2003)

Dwyer, Jim. *Subway Lives*. New York: Crown Publishers, 1991

Ebony Magazine, March 1975; *Contemporary Black Biographies*, The Instructor Publications, Inc.

"Edna Ferber." *Twentieth Century Romance & Historical Writers*, 3rd ed. St James Press, 1994.
Reproduced in *Biography Resource Center*. Farmington Hills, MI: The Gale Group, 2002
<http://www.galenet.com/servlet/BioRC> Document Number: K2404000154

Edson, William D. *Railroad Names*. Potomac, Md.: Privately published by the author, 1984

Edwards, Llewellyn N. *A Record of History and Evolution of Early American Bridges*. Orono, Maine: University Press, 1959

Eliot, T. S. *The Complete Poems and Plays, 1909-1950*. New York: Harcourt Brace and World, Inc., 1952

Ellet, Charles, Jr., *Report and Plan for a Suspension Bridge Proposed to be Constructed Across the Mississippi River at Saint Louis*. Printer: William Stavely and Company, Philadelphia, 1840

Ellicott City (MD) *Bicentennial Journal*

Ellis, C. Hamilton. *The Lore of the Train*. New York: Crescent Books, 1973

Emerson, Ralph Waldo. *The Collected Works of Ralph Waldo Emerson, Volume I.* Cambridge, Massachusetts: Harvard University Press, 1971

Encyclopedia Americana

Encyclopedia Britannica

Encyclopedia Brittanica, The [on line] Biography of Scott Joplin. <http://blackhistory.eb.com/micro/306/45.html> (17 March 2002)

Engineering. London

Ehrlich, Elizabeth. *Nellie Bly*. New York: Chelsea House, Publishers, 1989

European Scientific Notes. London: U. S. Office of Naval Research, N.d.

Evans, Rowland and Robert Novak. *Lyndon B. Johnson: The Exercise of Power.* New York: The New American Library, 1966

Eyles, Allen. *John Wayne and the Movies*. New York: Grossett and Dunlap, 1976

Farwell, Byron. *Stonewall*. New York: W. W. Norton & Company, 1993

Faulkner, William. *Collected Stories*. New York: Random House, N.d.
———-. *The Faulkner Reader*. New York: Random House, 1954

Ferber, Edna. *Saratoga Trunk*. New York: Doubleday, Doran and Company, 1941

Ferrell, Robert H. *The Presidency of Calvin Coolidge*. Lawrence, KS: University Press of Kansas, 1998

Finch, James K. *The Story of Engineering*. Garden City, New York: Doubleday and Company, 1960

First Semi-Annual Report to the President and Directors of the South-Carolina Canal and Rail-Road Company by Their Committee of Inquiry. Charleston: A. E. Miller, 1828

Fischler, Stan. *Uptown, Downtown*. New York: Hawthorn Books, Inc., 1976

Fitzgerald, F. Scott. *Taps at Reveille*. New York: Charles Scribner's Sons, 1935

Folsom, Burton W. *The Myth of the Robber Barons*. Herndon, Va.: Young America's Foundation, 1991

Forney, Matthias N. *The Car-Builder's Dictionary*. New York: The Railroad Gazette, 1879

Foster-Harris, William. *The Look of the Old West*. New York: The Viking Press, 1955

Frank Leslie's Popular Monthly. New York

Freedland, Michael. *Irving Berlin*. New York: Stein and Day, 1974

Freedom Train Timeline [on line].
<http://www.freedomtrain.org/ft_timeline.html> (29 June 2003)
<http://www.freedomtrain.org/research_ft.html> (29 June 2003)

Frost, Robert. *Complete Poems of Robert Frost*, New York: Holt, Rinehart and Winston, 1968

Fuller, Wayne E. *The American Mail*. Chicago: The University of Chicago Press, 1972

Furia, Phillip. *Irving Berlin*. New York: Schirmer Books, 1998

Gadsden, James. Biography in the The Columbia Electronic Encyclopedia. [on line]
<http://www.kids.infoplease.lycos.com/ce6/people/A0819974.html> (17 November 2002)

Gallo, Rose Adrienne. *F. Scott Fitzgerald*. New York: Frederick Ungar Publishing Co., 1978

Galloway, John D. *The First Transcontinental Railroad*. New York: Simmons-Boardman Publishing Company, 1950

Gies, Joseph. *Bridges and Men*. Garden City, New York: Doubleday and Company, 1963

Gladstein, Mimi Reisel. *Atlas Shrugged, Manifesto of the Mind*. New York: Twayne Publishers, 2000

Golden Spike, The, James Douglas, "Historical and Geographical Features of the

Rocky Mountain Railroads," New York: American Geographical Society, 1969

Goldstone, Richard H. *Thornton Wilder, An Intimate Portrait*. New York: Saturday Review Press / E. P. Dutton & Co., Inc., 1975

Gordon, John S. *The Scarlet Woman of Wall Street*. New York: Weidenfeld & Nicolson, 1988

Gould, Levi S. *Ancient Middlesex*. Somerville, MA: Somerville Journal Print, 1905

Gould, Lewis L. *The Presidency of Theodore Roosevelt*. Lawrence, KS: University Press of Kansas, 1991

Grafton, John. *New York in the Nineteenth Century*. New York: Dover Publications, Inc., 1977

Graham, Otis. L., Jr. *Franklin D. Roosevelt, His Life and Times*. Boston: G. K. Hall and Company, 1985

Grant, H. Roger. *We Took the Train* Dekalb, Ill.: Northern Illinois University Press, 1990

Grant, H. Roger and Charles W. Bohi. *The Country Railroad Station in America*. Sioux Falls, SD: The Center for Western Studies, 1988

Grant, Ulysses S., III. *Ulysses S. Grant, Warrier and Statesman*. New York: William Morrow and Company, 1969

Gray, Carl R., "The Significance of the Pacific Railroads," A lecture delivered at Princeton University on April 9, 1935

Gross, Ruth Belov. *True Stories About Abraham Lincoln*. New York: Scholastic, Inc, 1973

Growing With Schenectady - American Locomotive Company. Brochure in the Collection of the Schenectady County (NY) Public Library. [on line] <http://www.schenectadyhistory.org/railroads/alcohistory/> (7 June 2003)

Gunnarsson, Robert L., *The Story of the Northern Central Railway*. Greenberg Publishing Company, Sykesville, Maryland, 1991

Haine, Edgar A. *Railroad Wrecks*. New York: Cornwall Books, 1993

Hamm, Charles. *Irving Berlin*. New York: Oxford University Press, 1997

Hardeman, D. B. and Donald C. Bacon. *Rayburn*. Austin, Texas: Texas Monthly Press, 1987

Hare, Jay V. *History of the Reading*. Philadelphia: John H. Strock, 1966

Harlow, Alvin F. *Steelways of New England*. New York: Creative Age Press, Inc., 1946

Harper's Monthly Magazine, New York.

Hart, Moss. *Act One*. New York: Random House, 1959

Harte, Bret. *What the Engines Said*. Roth Publishing Editorial Board. Poem Finder [on line]. Mary Jacobs Library, NJ.
<http://www.litfinder.com/poemfinder> (26 December 2001)

Harte, Francis Bret. *The Engineer's Signal*. Roth Publishing Editorial Board. Poem Finder [on line]. Mary Jacobs Library, NJ.
<http://www.litfinder.com/poemfinder> (26 December 2001)

Harwood, Herbert H., Jr. *Impossible Challenge*. Baltimore: Barnard, Roberts, and Company, Inc., 1979

Haskins, James. *Scott Joplin*. Garden City, NY: Doubleday & Company, Inc., 1978
———. *Thurgood Marshall*. New York: Henry Holt and Company, 1992

Hawthorne, Nathaniel. *The Complete Novels and Selected Tales of Nathaniel Hawthorne*. New York: The Modern Library, 1937

Heilbroner, Robert L., "Epitaph for the Steel Master," *American Heritage*, August 1960

Heller, F. J., "Evolution of Tank Car Design Through Engineering," a paper presented at the American Society of Mechanical Engineers Conference on Petroleum Mechanical Engineering and Pressure Vessels and Piping, Denver, Colorado on September 13-17, 1970

Hemingway, Ernest. *The Complete Short Stories of Ernest Hemingway*. Charles Scribner's Sons: New York, 1987.

Henderson, G. F. R. *Stonewall Jackson and The American Civil War*. New York: DeCapo Press, Inc., 1988

Henry, Robert S. *This Fascinating Railroad Business*. Indianapolis: The Bobbs-

Merrill Company, 1942

———. *Trains*, Indianapolis: The Bobbs-Merrill Company, 1938

Hilton, George W. *American Narrow Gauge Railroads*. Palo Alto: Stanford University Press,1990.

———. *The Great Lakes Car Ferries*, Berkeley, Calif.: Howell-North Books, 1962

Historical Review of Berks County (PA)

History of the Baldwin Locomotive Works, 1831-1923. Published by the Baldwin Locomotive Works, Philadelphia, 1923

History of the Delaware and Hudson Company, 1823-1923. Albany: The Delaware and Hudson Company, 1925

Hogg, Garry, *Union Pacific*. Walker and Company, New York, 1967

Holbrook, Stewart H. *The Story of American Railroads*. New York: Crown Publishers, 1947

Hollingsworth, Brian, *The Illustrated Encyclopedia of North American Locomotives*. Salamander Books, Ltd., London, 1984

Hollister, Will C. *Dinner in the Diner*. Corona del Mar, CA.: Trans-Anglo Books, 1977

Holman, C. Hugh., Ed. *The Thomas Wolfe Reader*. New York: Charles Scribner's Sons, 1962

Holmes, Charles S. *The Clocks of Columbus*. New York: Atheneum, 1972

Holmes, Oliver Wendell. *The Complete Poetical Works of Oliver Wendell Holmes*. Boston: Houghton Mifflin Company, 1908

Hood, Clifton. *722 Miles*. Baltimore: The Johns Hopkins University Press, 1993

Howard, Robert W., *The Great Iron Trail*. G. P. Putnam's Sons, New York, 1962

Hubbard, Freeman: *Encyclopedia of North American Railroading*. McGraw-Hill Book Company, New York, 1981

Hungerford, Edward. *The Story of the Baltimore and Ohio Railroad, 1827-1927*.

V. 1 and 2, New York: G. P. Putnam's Sons, 1928

Husband, Joseph. *The Story of the Pullman Car.* Chicago: A. C. McClurg & Company, 1917

Hynes, Gerald C. *A Biographical Sketch of W. E. B. DuBois.* W. E. B. DuBois Learning Center. [on line]
<http://www.duboislc.org/man.html> (3 July 2003)

Illinois Central Magazine. Chicago

Interborough Rapid Transit. Arno Press, New York, 1971

International Herald Tribune. New York

Interstate Commerce Commission, *Annual Reports.* Washington

Irving Berlin Press Release. United States Postal Service. [on line]
<http//www.usps.com/news/2002/philatelic/sr02_061.htm> (12 July 2003)

Isely, Jeter Allen. *Horace Greeley and the Republican Party.* New York: Octagon Books, 1965

ISO 690-2, *Information and documentation — Bibliographic references — Part 2: Electronic documents or parts thereof.* Ottawa, Canada: ISO/TC 46/SC 9 Secretariat, National Library of Canada [on line]
<http://www.nlc-bnc.ca/iso/tc46sc9/standard/690-2e.htm> (17 June 2003)

Jacob, Kathryn Allamong. *Testament to Union: Civil War Monuments in Washington, D.C.* Baltimore: The Johns Hopkins University Press, 1998

Jacobs, David and Anthony E. Neville. *Bridges, Canals and Tunnels.* Eau Claire, Wisc.: E. M. Hale and Company, 1968

Jensen, Oliver. *The American Heritage History of Railroads in America.* New York: Bonanza Books, 1981

Jersey Central Lines. Clark, NJ

Jervis, John B. *Railway Property.* Philadelphia: Henry Carey Baird, 1872

Johns Hopkins Magazine, The. Baltimore

Josephson, Matthew. *Edison.* New York: McGraw-Hill Book Company, Inc., 1959

Journal of the Association of Engineering Societies. New York

Journal of the Franklin Institute:. New York

Kaempffert. Waldemar. *A Popular History of American Invention*. New York: Charles Scribner's Sons, 1924

Katcher, Leo. *Earl Warren, A Political Biography*. New York: McGraw-Hill Book Company, 1967

Kay, F. George. *Steam Locomotives*. New York: Galahad Books, 1974

Kendrick, Alexander. *Prime Time, The Life of Edward R. Murrow*.Boston: Little, Brown and Company, 1969

Kent, Zachary. *Andrew Carnegie*. Springfield, NJ: Enslow Publishers, Inc., 1999
———-. *Encyclopedia of Presidents, Ulysses S. Grant*. Chicago: Children's Press, 1989.
———-. *Encyclopedia of Presidents, Theodore Roosevelt*. Chicago: Children's Press, 1988.

Ketchum, Richard M. *Will Rogers, The Man and His Times*. New York: American Heritage Publishing Company, Inc., 1973

Kimbel, Bobby Ellen, Ed. *Dictionary of Literary Biography, V. 86: American Short Story Writers, 1910-1945, First Series*. State College, PA: Pennsylvania State University, The Gale Group, 1989

Kinert, Reed. *Early American Steam Locomotives*. New York: Bonanza Books, 1962

Kinney, Harrison. *James Thurber, His Life and Times*. New York: Henry Holt and Company, 1995

Kirkland, Edward C. *Men, Cities, and Transportation*. Cambridge: Harvard University Press, Massachusetts, 1948

Kirkman, Marshall M. The *Science of Railways, V.1*. "Railway Equipment," Chicago: World Railway Publishing Company, 1899

Kisor, Henry. *Zephyr*. New York: Times Books, 1994

Klein, Aaron. *Encyclopedia of North American Railroading*. New York: Exeter Books, 1986

Klein, Maury. *Union Pacific*. Garden City, New York: Doubleday and Company, 1987

Knapke, William F. with Freeman Hubbard. *The Railroad Caboose*. San Marino, Calif.: Golden West Books, 1968

Knickerbocker, The. New York

Korman, Joseph D. *The Union Stations*. Brochure published by the Cincinnati Union Terminal. [on line]
<http://www.quuxuum.org/~jorkor/unionstations/cinut-04.gif> [30 June 2003]
<http://www.quuxuum.org/~jorkor/unionstations/cinut-05.gif> [30 June 2003]

Kouwenhoven, John A. *The Columbia Historical Portrait of New York*. Garden City, N.Y.: Doubleday and Company, 1953

Kroeger, Brooke. *Nelly Bly*. New York: Random House, 1994

Landmarker, The. Winter 1979-80, James G. Bogle, "The Locomotive Texas." Published by the Cobb County Landmarks Society, Inc., Marietta, GA

Lane, Wheaton J. *From Indian Trail to Iron Horse*. Princeton: Princeton University Press, 1939

Learned, Walter, Ed. *Treasury of American Verse*. Books for Libraries Press: Freeport, NY, 1969

Leslie's Weekly (see *Frank Leslie's Popular Monthly*)

Letters from:

>   Anne Calhoun, Librarian/Archivist, B&O Railroad Museum, to the author, dated June 22, 2001 and December 11, 2001.
>
>   E. Milby Burton, Director of the Charleston Museum, to William W. Humphreys of the Charleston Development Board, dated October 25, 1960
>
>   Moses Kimball to Dr. Leroy M. Yale, dated December 21, 1830
>
>   Jean D. Schlademan, USPS, to the author, dated August 23, 2001
>
>   Thomas Taber, III, Muncie, PA, to the author, dated March 13, 2001
>
>   Jane Thacker, ISO/TC 46/SC 9 Secretariat, International Standards

Organization, to the author, dated 17 June 2003.

LeVot, André. *F. Scott Fitzgerald.* Garden City, NY: Doubleday & Company, 1983

Lewis, Oscar. The *Big Four.* New York: Alfred A. Knopf, 1941

Lewis, Sinclair. *Main Street.* New York: New American Library, 1961

Leyendecker, Liston E. *Palace Car Prince.* Niwot, Colo.: University Press of Colorado, 1992

Lienhard, John. *The Engines of Our Ingenuity,* No. 288: Octave Chanute. Radio program produced by KUHF-FM Houston. [on line] <http://www.uh.edu/engines/epi288.htm> (30 June 2003)

Linn's Stamp Yearbook. Sidney, OH

Livesay, Harold C. *Andrew Carnegie and the Rise of Big Business.* Boston: Little Brown and Company, 1975
———. *Samuel Gompers and Organized Labor in America.* Boston: Little, Brown and Company, 1978

Lonedale Operator, The. EMC: Abstracts, Educational Media Collection at the Univesity of Washington. [on line] <http://www.css.washington.edu/emc/titles.php?abstracts=1&mid=1718> (7 June 2003)

Long, S. H. *The Rail Road Manual or a Brief Exposition of Principles and Deductions Applicable in Tracing the Route of a Rail Road.* Boston: William Wooddy, 1829

Longfellow, Henry W. *The Complete Poetical Works of Henry Wadsworth Longfellow.* New York: Houghton, Mifflin and Company, 1902

Lopata, James A. *Talk of the Town,* Review in *The Off-Off Broadway Review,* 2000. [on line] <http://www.oobr.com/top/volSix/twentysix/0311parker.html> (25 March 2002)

Lounsbury, Thomas R. *The Yale Book of American Verse.* New Haven, CT: Yale University Press, 1912

Lovell, Joseph D. *Pennsylvania Railroad Altoona Machine Shops Construction Number List, 1866-1904.* Philadelphia: Library of American Transportation,

1984

Lucas, Walter A. 100 *Years of Railroad Cars*. New York: Simmons-Boardman
Publishing Corporation, 1958

Luff, John N. *The Postage Stamps of the United States*. Np: The Scott Stamp and
Coin Company, Ltd., 1902

MacGill, Caroline E., *History of Transportation in the United States before 1860*.
Pub: Peter Smith, Printer: The Murray Printing Company, Forge Village,
Massachusetts, 1948

Marre, Louis A. *Diesel Locomotives: The First 50 Years*. Waukesha, WI:
Kalmbach Publishing Company, 1995
———-. *The Contemporary Diesel Spotter's Guide*. Waukesha, WI: Kalmbach
Publishing Company, 1995

Marshall, David, *Model Railroad Engineering*. Harper and Brothers, New York,
1942

Marshall, John. *Rail, The Records*. Enfield, England: Guinness Superlatives,
Ltd., 1985

Martin, M. W. *Topical Stamp Collecting*. New York: Arco Publishing Company,
1975

Martinez, Orlando. *Panama Canal*. New York: Gordon & Cremonesi, 1978

Maryland. Annapolis, MD

Marzulla, Elena, Editor. *Pictorial Treasury of U. S. Stamps*. Omaha, NE:
Collector's Institute, Ltd., 1974

Mason, Alpheus Thomas. *Harlan Fiske Stone, Pillar of the Law*. New York: The
Viking Press, 1956

Maw, William H. and James Dredge. *Modern Examples of Road and Railway
Bridges*. London: Engineering, 1872

May, Earl Chapin. *Model Railroads in the Home*. New York: Funk & Wagnalls
Company, 1939

McAfee, Ward. *California's Railroad Era*. San Marino, Calif.: Golden West
Books, 1973

McCabe, John. *George M. Cohan, The Man Who Owned Broadway.* Garden City, NY: Doubleday & Company, Inc., 1973

McCann, Graham. *Cary Grant, A Class Apart.* New York: Columbia University Press, 1996

MCCSC Learning Network. Monroe County Community School Corporation, Bloomington, IN. [on line] <http://www.mccsc.edu/~jcmslib/mlk/marshall/biography.htm> (13 January 2003)

McClure, Alexander K. *"Abe" Lincoln's Yarns and Stories.* Philadelphia: International Publishing Company, 1901

McCormac, Eugene Irving. James Polk, To the End of a Career. Newtown, CT: American Political Biography Press, 1995. A reprint of the 1922 edition published by the University of California Press.

McCormick, Michael J, Ed. *Subway Series, The.* N.p.: The Sporting News, 2000

McCoy, Donald R. *Calvin Coolidge, The Quiet President.* New York: The Macmillan Company, 1967

McCullough, David. *The Great Bridge.* New York: Simon and Schuster, 1972
———-. *The Path Between the Seas.* New York: Simon and Schuster, 1977
———-. *Truman.* New York: Simon and Schuster, 1992

McFeeley, William S. *Grant.* New York: W. W. Norton and Company, 1981

McGee, Dorothy Horton. *Herbert Hoover, Engineer, Humanitarian, Statesman.* New York: Dodd, Mead and Company, 1967

Meitche, W. *Our Town.* Barron's Booknotes. [on line] <http://www.pinkmonkey.com/booknotes/barrons/ourtown3.asp>

Meltzer, Milton. *The Many Lives of Andrew Carnegie.* Danbury, CT: Franklin Watts, 1997

Mercer, Lloyd J. *Railroads and Land Grant Policy.* New York: Academic Press, 1982

Merchants Magazine and Commercial Review, The. New York

Metcalf, George R. *Black Profiles.* New York: McGraw-Hill Books, 1968

Middleton, William D. *The Time of the Trolley*. Milwaukee: Kalmbach Publishing Co., 1967

———. *When the Steam Railroads Electrified*. Milwaukee: Kalmbach Books, 1974

Miers, Earl Schenck. *Abraham Lincoln in Peace and War*. New York: American Heritage Publishing Company, Inc., 1964

Millay, Edna St. Vincent. *Collected Poems*. Harper & Brothers Publishers, New York, 1956

Miller, John A. *Fares, Please*. New York: Dover Publications, Inc., 1960

Miller, Nathan. *Theodore Roosevelt, A Life*. New York: William Morrow and Company, 1992

Model Railroader. Waukesha, WI

Modelski, Andrew M. *Railroad Maps of North America*. Washington: Library of Congress, 1984

Monorails of... The Monorail Society. [on line]
<http://www.monorails.org/tMspages/NAmer.html> (30 June 2003)
<http://www.monorails.org/tMspages/Europe.html> (30 June 2003)

Montgomery County Public Schools, Rockville, MD. [on line]
<http://www.mcps.k12.md.us/schools/thurgoodmarshalles/supremecourt.html>
(13 January 2003)

Moody, John. *The Railroad Builders*. New Haven: Yale University Press, 1919

Moore, Donna and Kathy Fox. Review of *The Toast of New York*. The Ultimate Cary Grant Pages. [on line]
<http://www.carygrant.net/reviews/toast.html> (10 January 2003)

Morris, Juddi. *The Harvey Girls*. New York: Walker and Company, 1994

Mott, Edward H. *Between the Ocean and the Lakes, The Story of Erie*. New York: Ticker Publishing Company, 1908

Murray, Robert K. *The Harding Era*. Minneapolis: University of Minnesota Press, 1969

Myerson, Joel, Ed. *Dictionary of Literary Biography, Volume 1*. Chicago, The Gale Group, 1978

Mystic's 2001 U. S. Stamp Catalog. Camden, NY: Mystic Stamp Company, 2001

Nash, Ogden. *The Selected Verse of Ogden Nash*, NY: The Modern Library, 1945

National Car and Locomotive Builder (see *American Railroad Journal:*)

National Geographic Magazine. Washington

National Railway Historical Society Bulletin. Philadelphia

New York Times. New York

New Yorker, The. New York

Nock, O. S.: *Dawn of World Railways,The, 1800-1850*. The Macmillan Company, New York, 1972

O'Connell, John. *Popular Mechanics Railroad Album*. Chicago: Popular Mechanics Press, 1954

"Octave Chanute." *Dictionary of American Biography Base Set*t. Biography Research Center. [on line] Gale Group Databases. Mary Jacobs Library, NJ. <http://www.galenet.com>(21 August 2001)

O'Dell, Andrew C. and Peter S. Richards. *Railways and Geography*. London: Hutchinson University Library, 1971

Ogburn, Charlton. *Railroads: The Great American Adventure*. Washington: National Geographic Society, 1977

Oliver, Smith Hempstone., *The First Quarter Century of Steam Locos in North America*. Smithsonian Institution, Washington, DC, 1956

Oran Z Pan African Black Facts and Museum. Thurgood Marshall Wax Figure. [on line] <http://www.oransblackmuseum.com/wax_figures/thurgood_marshall.htm> (13 January 2003)

Overbey, Daniel L., *Railroads, The Free Enterprise Alternative*. Quorum Books, Westport, Connecticut, 1982

Oxford English Dictionary. New York

Pangborn, J. G. *The World's Railway*. New York: Bramhall House, 1974 (Reprint of 1894 Edition)

Papers and Practical Illustrations of Public Works. John Roebling, "Memoir of the Niagara Falls and International Suspension Bridge." London: John Weale, 1856

Parker, Dorothy. *Dorothy Parker*.New York: The Viking Press, 1944

Parsons, William B. *Track*. New York: Engineering News Publishing Company, 1886

Passenger, Freight and Work Equipment on the Delaware and Hudson. Albany: The Delaware and Hudson Company, 1927

Patterson, James T. *Mr. Republican*. Boston: Houghton Mifflin Company, 1972

Peach, Todd and Sharon. *The Freedom Train*. [on line] <http://www.thepeaches.com/music/composers/berlin/1947.html> (27 January 2003)

People Mover. Detroit Department of Transportation [on line] <http://www.thepeoplemover.com/> (7 June 2003)

Perkins, Dexter. *Charles Evans Hughes and American Democratic Statesmanship*. Boston: Little, Brown and Company, 1956
———. *The New Age of Franklin Roosevelt*. Chicago: The University of Chicago Press, 1957

Perret, Geoffrey. *Eisenhower*, New York: Random House, 1999
———. *Ulysses S. Grant, Soldier and President*. New York: Random House, 1997.

Petroski, Henry. *To Engineer is Human*. New York: St. Martin's Press, 1985

Pfeffer, Paula F. *A. Philip Randolph,Pioneer of the Civil Rights Movement*. Baton Rouge, LA.: Louisiana State University Press, 1990

Phillips, Lance. *Yonder Comes the Train*. New York: A. S. Barnes and Company, 1965 (72)

Phillips, Ulrich B. *A History of Transportation in the Eastern Cotton Belt*. New York: The Columbia University Press, 1908

Photographs from:

Toledo-Lucas County Public Library

Union Pacific Railroad Museum

Pittenger, William, *Capturing a Locomotive*. J. B. Lippincott and Company,

Philadelphia, 1882

Posner, Richard A., Ed. *The Essential Holmes*. Chicago: The University of Chicago Press, 1992

Postcard sold by the Baltimore and Ohio Railroad at the New York World's Fair, 1939

Postage Stamps of the United States, 1847-1961. Washington: United States Post Office Department, 1962

Proceedings and Addresses, Celebration of the Beginning of the Second Century of the American Patent System. Washington: Published by the Executive Committee, 1891

Proceedings of the United States District Court - Massachusetts District. October Term 1853, "Ross Winans vs. The Eastern Railroad, Evidence for Respondents", Moore and Crosby, Printers, Boston, 1854.

Quiett, Glenn C. *They Built the West*. New York: D. Appleton-Century Company, 1934

Rae, William F. *Westward by Rail*. New York: Indian Head Books, 1993

Railfan and Railroad Magazine. Newton, NJ

Railroad and Engineering Journal, The (see *American Railroad Journal*)

Railroad Magazine (see *Railfan and Railroad Magazine*)

Railroaders, The. New York: TIME-LIFE Books, 1973

Railroad Car Journal, The. New York

Railroad Gazette, The. New York

Railroad History (formerly *Bulletin of the Railway and Locomotive Historical Society*). Urbana, IL

Railroad Men. New York

Railroad Network, The. Review and comments regarding *Baltimore Sun* editorial. [on line] <http://www.railroad.net/forums/messages.asp?TopicID=1865> (10 January 2003)

Railway and Locomotive Historical Society Newsletter. Manassas, VA

Railway Age. New York

Railway History Monograph. Crete, NE

Rand, Ayn. *Atlas Shrugged*. New York: Penguin Books USA Inc., 1992

Ransome-Wallis, P. *World Railway Locomotives*. New York: Hawthorn Books, Inc., 1959

Reck, Franklin M. *The Romance of American Transportation*. New York: Thomas Y. Crowell Company, 1962

Reed, Robert C., *The New York Elevated*. New York: A. S. Barnes and Company, 1978
———. *Train Wrecks*. Seattle: Superior Publishing Company, 1968

Reference Book of The Westinghouse Air Brake Company. Pittsburgh: The Westinghouse Air Brake Company, 1876

Reinfeld, Fred. *Commemorative Stamps of the U. S. A*. New York: Bramhall House, 1956

Reinhardt, Richard. *Workin' on the Railroad*. Palo Alto, California: American West Publishing Company, 1970

Remini, Robert V. *Martin Van Buren and the Making of the Democratic Party*. New York : Columbia University Press, 1959

Report of Board Convened to Determine a Standard for Construction of the Pacific Railroad. February 24, 1866, Washington: Government Printing Office, 1866

Report on Session 1851 - Reports and Minutes of the Evidence taken before the Select Committee of the House of Lords appointed to Consider the Bill intitled (sic) AN ACT further to Amend the Law touching Letters Patents for Inventions. Published by the House of Commons, July 4, 1851. Irish University Press Series of British Parliamentary Papers, V.1, Shannon, Ireland: Irish University Press, 1968

Ricci, Mark, Boris Zmijewsky and Steve Zmijewsky. *The Films of John Wayne*. New York: The Citadel Press, 1970

Riegel, Robert E. *The Story of the Western Railroads*. New York: The Macmillan Company, 1926

Riley, James Whitcomb. *The Complete Poetical Works of James Whitcomb Riley.* New York: Grosset & Dunlap, 1937

Robertson, Donald B. *Encyclopedia of Western Railroad History.* Caldwell, Idaho: The Caxton Printers, Ltd., 1986

Robertson, James I., Jr. *Stonewall Jackson, The Man, The Soldier. The Legend,* New York: Macmillan Publishing Company, 1997

Robinson, Archie. *George Meany and His Times.* New York: Simon and Schuster, 1981

Rodgers, Carrie C. *My Husband Jimmie Rodgers.* Nashville, TN: Country Music Foundation Press, 1995

Roebling, John A. *Final Report to the Presidents and Directors of the Niagara Falls Suspension and Niagara Falls International Bridge Companies, May 1, 1855.* Rochester, New York: Lee, Mann and Company, 1855

Roper, Peter. *The Medal of Honor.* Newspaper article in *The Pueblo Chieftain,* June 25, 1995. [on line] http://www.homeofheroes.com/moh/history/history.html> (30 June 2003)

Rotary Snow Plow. Pamphlet No. 10015 of the American Locomotive Company, Ocean: N.J.: Specialty Press, Inc. 1973

Rowsome, Frank, Jr. *Trolley Car Treasury.* New York: Bonanza Books, 1956

Rozwenc, Edwin C. *Roosevelt, Wilson and the Trusts.* Boston: D. C. Heath and Company, 1950

Russell, Don, Ed. *Trails of the Iron Horse.* Garden City, New York: Doubleday and Company, 1975, Nellie Snyder Yost, "The Wedding of the Rails"

Sam DeVincent Collection of Illustrated American Sheet Music, Subseries 4.2, Irving Berlin. National Museum of American History. [on line] <http://americanhistory.si.edu/archives/d5300jb.htm> (25 January 2003)

San Francisco-Oakland Bay Bridge, The. Caltrans District 4. [on line] <http://www.dot.ca.gov/dist4/calbrdgs.htm> (3 July 2003)

Sandhurst, P. T. *The Great Centennial Exhibition, 1876.* Publisher not identified, N.d.

Sandström, Gösta E. *Tunnels.* New York: Holt, Rinehart and Winston, 1963

Saratoga Trunk. Review of the motion picture. [on line]
<http://www.amazon.com> Books: *Saratoga Trunk* (9 October 2002)

Saroyan, William. *The Human Comedy*. New York: Harcourt, Brace & World,
Inc., 1943

Saxton, Martha. *Louisa May*. Boston: Houghton Mifflin Company, 1977

Seidman, Joel. *The Brotherhood of Railroad Trainmen: The Internal Political Life
of a National Union*. New York: John Wiley and Sons, Inc., 1962

Sellers, Charles. *James K. Polk, Jacksonian*. Princeton, NJ: Princeton University
Press, 1957

Seymour, Charles. *Woodrow Wilson and the World War*. New Haven: Yale
University Press, 1921

Shafer, Mike and Brian Solomon. *Pennsylvania Railroad*. Osceola, WI: MBI
Publishing Company, 1997

Schafer, Mike and Joe Welsh. *Classic American Streamliners*. Osceola, WI: MBI
Publishing Company, 1997

Schreiber, Sr., Les, *Encyclopedia of Designs, Designers, Engravers, Artists of United
States Postage Stamps, 1847-1900*. Np: The American Philatelic Society

Science Record. New York

Scientific American. New York

Scientific American Supplement. New York

Scribner's. New York

Scudder, Horace E. *The Complete Poetical Works of James Russell Lowell*.
Cambridge, Massachusetts: The Riverside Press, 1925

Scull, Theodore W. *Hoboken's Lackawanna Terminal*. New York: Quadrant
Press, Inc., 1987

Seibel, George A. and Olive M. Seibel. *Bridges Over the Niagara Gorge*. Niagara
Falls: Niagara Falls Bridge Commission, 1991

Shaughnessy, Jim. *Delaware & Hudson*. Berkeley, Calif.: Howell-North Books,
1967

Shepard, Irving. *Jack London's Tales of Adventure*. Garden City, New York: Hanover House, 1956

Shepherd, Donald and Robert Slatzer with Dave Grayson. *Duke, The Life and Times of John Wayne*. New York: Doubleday and Company, 1985

Sinclair, Angus. *The Development of the Locomotive Engine*. Cambridge: The MIT Press, 1970

Smith, Stephen, Ed. *Romance and Humor of the Rail*. New York: G. W. Carleton and Company, 1873

Smithsonian Institution, National Museum of American History, Washington

Snell, J. B., *Early Railways*. Octopus Books, Ltd., London, 1972

Snyder, Robert W. *Transit Talk*. Brooklyn, NY and New Brunswick, NJ: The New York Transit Museum and Rutgers University Press, 1997

Sobczak, A. J., Ed. *Cyclopedia of Literary Characters, V. 1*. Pasadena, CA: Salem press, Inc., 1998

Sokolofsky, Homer E. and Allan B. Spetter. *The Presidency of Benjamin Harrison*. Lawrence, KS: University Press of Kansas, 1987

Solomon, Brian. *The American Diesel Locomotive*. Osceola, WI: MBI Publishing Company, 2000

South Carolina Historical Magazine, The. Charleston

South Carolina Resources and Population. 1883, N.p.

Southern Confederacy. Atlanta, GA

Stackman, Will. Review of *STOP! LOOK! LISTEN!* Aisle Say (Boston). [on line]
<http://www.aoslesay.com/MA-STOP.html> (11 January 2003)

Stamps and Stories. Washington, DC: United States Postal Service, 1981

Starr, John W., Jr. *One Hundred Years of American Railroading*. New York: Dodd, Mead & Company, 1928

Stein, Jean and George Plimpton. *American Journey, The Times of Robert Kennedy*. New York: Harcourt Brace Jovanovich, 1970

Stein, Jess, Editor-in-Chief *The Random House Dictionary of the English Language*. New York: Random House, 1966

Steinman, David B. *The Builders of the Bridge*. New York: Harcourt, Brace and Company, 1945

Steinman, David B and Sara R. Watson, *Bridges and Their Builders*. New York: G. P. Putnam's Sons, 1941

Stevens, Frank W. *The Beginnings of the New York Central Railroad*. New York: G.P. Putnam's Sons, 1926

Stevers, Martin D. *Steel Trails*. New York: Grosset and Dunlap, 1933

Stevenson, David. *Sketch of the Civil Engineering of North* America. London: John Weale, 1859

Stover, John F. *American Railroads*. Chicago: The University of Chicago Press, 1997
———-.*History of the Baltimore and Ohio Railroad*. West Lafayette: Purdue University Press, 1987
———. *Iron Road to the West*. New York: Columbia University Press, 1978
———. *Life and Decline of the American Railroad. The*, New York: Oxford University Press, 1970
———. *The Routledge Historical Atlas of the American Railroads*. New York: Routledge, 1999

Stresau, Hermann. *Thornton Wilder*. New York: Frederick Ungar Publishing Co., 1971

Sullivan, A. S. *Accident Report: Collision of trains 1 and 83, Vaughn, 4-30-1900*. [on line] <http:///www.taco.com/roots/caseywreck.html> (14 February 2003)

Summers, Mark W. *Railroads, Reconstruction, and the Gospel of Prosperity*. Princeton: Princeton University Press, 1984

Sunderland, Edwin S. S. *Abraham Lincoln and the Illinois Central Railroad*. New York: Privately printed, 1955

Supreme Court Historical Society, The. Glencoe Online. The McGraw-Hill Companies. [on line] <http://www.landmarkcases.org/brown/background3.html> (13 January 2003)

Sutton, David. *The Complete Book of Model Railroading*. Englewood Cliffs, New

Jersey: Prentice-Hall, Inc., 1964

Taber, Thomas T. *The Delaware, Lackawanna & Western Railroad in the Nineteenth Century, 1828-1899*. Muncy, Pa.: Thomas T. Taber, III, 1977

Talbot, Fred A., *Cassell's Railways of the World, Volumes 1 and 2*. Simmons-Boardman Publishing Company, New York, N.d.

Technology and Culture. Baltimore

Thom, Helen Hopkins. *Johns Hopkins, A Silhouette*. Baltimore: The Johns Hopkins Press, 1929

Thomas, Emory M. *Robert E. Lee*. New York: W. W. Norton & Company, 1995

Thomas, Richard Louis. *Linn's Who's Who on U. S. Stamps*. Sidney, Ohio: Amos Press, 1991

Thompson, Dennis L. *Taxation of American Railroads*. Westport, Conn.: Greenwood Press, 1981

Thoreau, Henry D. *Walden*. New York: Thomas Y. Crowell & Co., 1910

"Thornton Wilder." *Dictionary of Literary Biography, V. 7, Twentieth-Century American Dramatists*. Literature Resource Center [on line] Gale Group Databases. Mary Jacobs Library, NJ. <http://www.infotrac.galegroup.com> (28 March 2002)

Thurgood Marshall Press Release. United States Postal Service. [on line] <http//www.usps.com/news/2002/philatelic/sr03_004.pdf> (12 July 2003)

Toast of New York, The. Review in *Photoplay* Magazine. [on line] <http://www.geocities.com/~themistyone/tony.htm> (10 January 2003)

Train Shed Cyclopedia. Number 54, "Bridges and Trestles", Publisher: Newton K. Gregg, Novato, California, 1977

Train Sheet. Roselle, NJ

Trains. Waukesha, WI

Transactions of the Newcomen Society. London

Transport Heritage. Trenton, NJ

Trefousse, Hans L. *Andrew Johnson*. New York: W. W. Norton & Company, 1989

Trenton (NJ) *Times*

True Story of Casey Jones, The. Erie Railroad Magazine, V. 24, April 1928. [on line]
<http://www.taco.com/roots/caseyjones.html> (14 February 2003)

Turnbull, Archibald D. *John Stevens, An American Record*. New York: The American Society of Mechanical Engineers, 1928

Underground Railroad, The. Public Broadcasting System (PBS). [on line]
<http://www.pbs.org/wgbh/aia/part4/4p2944.html> (3 February 2003)

United States Postal Service. (various stamps)

U. S. Army, Center of Military History. Listings of Medal of Honor Citations. [on line]
<http:///www.army.mil/cmh-pg/moh1.htm> (30 June 2003)

von Gerstner, Franz A. Ritter. *Die Innern Communicationen der Vereinigten Staaten von Nordamerica*. Vienna: L. Forster's artistsche Anstalt, 1842

Vose, George L. *Manual for Railroad Engineers*. Boston: Lee and Shepard, 1873.

Voss, William. *Railway Car Construction*. New York: R. M. Van Arsdale, 1892

Wager, Jennifer. *W. E. B. DuBois: Freedom Fighter*. The W. E. B. DuBois Virtual University. [on line]
<http://www.members.tripod.com/dubois/jenn.html> (3 July 2003)

Wait, John C. *The Car-Builder's Dictionary*. New York: The Railroad Gazette, 1895

Waitley, Douglas. *The Age of the Mad Dragons*. New York: Beaufort Books, 1981

Wall, Joseph Frazier. *Andrew Carnegie. Pittsburgh: Pittsburgh University Press, 1989*

Wardwell, W. Emory. Unpublished MS, "Random Thoughts on Early Train Operation in New England," Worcester, Mass.: 1953

Watkins, J. Elfreth. *The Camden and Amboy Railroad, Origins and Early History.* Washington: Gedney and Roberts, 1892

Webb, Robert N. *The Illustrated True Book of American Railroads.* New York: Grosset & Dunlap, 1957

Weber, Thomas. *The Northern Railroads in the Civil War.* New York: King's Crown Press (Columbia University), 1952

Weightman, W. J. *Report on Mountain Railways.* Indian Government Technical Paper No. 150, Bombay: 1903

Wellington, Arthur M. *The Economic Theory of the Location of Railways.* New York: John Wiley and Sons, 1887

Westing, Fred. *Pennsy Steam and Semaphores.* Seattle: Superior Publishing Company, 1974
———. *The Locomotives That Baldwin Built.* New York: Bonanza Books, 1966

When That Midnight Choo Choo Leaves for Alabam'. Parlor Songs MIDI collection. [on line] <http://parlorsongs.com/issues/2001-2/thismonth/feature.asp> (29 June 2003)

White, G. Edward. *Earl Warren, A Public Life.* New York: Oxford University Press, 1982

White, John H., Jr. *American Locomotive Builders.* Washington: Bass, Inc., 1982
———. *The American Railroad Freight Car.* Baltimore: The Johns Hopkins University Press, 1993
———. *The American Railroad Passenger Car, The.* Baltimore: Johns Hopkins University Press, 1978
———. *The John Bull.* Washington: Smithsonian Institution Press, 1981
———. *Early American Locomotives.* New York: Dover Publications, Inc., 1972
———. *A History of the American Locomotive.* New York: Dover Publications, Inc., 1979

Whitman, Walt, *Complete Poetry and Collected Prose.* Np: The Library of America, 1982

Withuhn, William L, Ed. *Rails Across America.* London: Salamander Books, Ltd., 1993

Whittier, James Greenleaf. *The Complete Poetical Works of Whittier.* Boston: Houghton Mifflin Company, 1894

Williams, John H., *A Great & Shining Road*. Times Books, New York, 1988.

Williams, Tennessee. *A Streetcar Named Desire*. New York: New Directions Publishing Company, 1947

Wilson, Mitchell. *American Science and Invention*. New York: Simon and Schuster, Inc., 1954

Wilson, Neill C. and Frank J. Taylor. *Southern Pacific*. New York: McGraw-Hill Book Company, 1952

Withuhn, William L, Ed. *Rails Across America*. London: Salamander Books, Ltd., 1993

Wood, James Playsted. *Sunnyside, A Life of Washington Irving*. New York: Pantheon Books, 1967

Wood, Nicholas. *A Practical Treatise on Railroads*. Philadelphia: Carey and Lea, 1832. (1825 edition printed by Knight and Lacey, London.)

Woodward Heritage: Attractions [on line] Woodward Heritage, c.2000-2002 [cited 7 June 2003]. People Mover. Available from: <http://www.woodwardheritage.com/attractions/people.mover.html>.

World Book 2000. Chicago: World Book, Inc., 2001

World of Hibernia, The. HoHoKus, NJ

Wright, Norman E., Sr. *World Railways Philatelic*. Albuquerque, NM: American Topical Association, 2000

Wright, Richard K. *Southern Pacific Daylight Train 98-99*. Thousand Oaks, CA: Wright Enterprises, 1970

Wright, William. *Pictorial History of the Locomotive*. Chicago: Chicago Pneumatic Tool Company, 1899

Yenne, Bill, Ed. *The Golden Age of American Rail Travel*. Greenwich, CT: Dorset Press, 1990

Young, Andrew D. and Eugene F. Provenzo, Jr. *The History of the St. Louis Car Company*. San Diego: Howell-North Books, 1981.

Younger, William Lee. *Old Brooklyn in Early Photographs*. New York: Dover Publications, Inc., 1978.

Zucker, Norman L. *George W. Norris, Gentle Knight of American Democracy.* Urbana, IL: University of Illinois Press, 1966

INDEX BY SCOTT NUMBER

GENERAL INDEX

Gadsden Purchase, 35, 41, 42, 76
Garfield, James (U. S. President), 83, 177
Garrett, John (railroad official), 47, 54
geared locomotives, 132, 186, 187
General Electric Company, 110, 111, 130, 131
General Motors Corporation. *See* Electro-Motive Division
Goethals, George (Army engineer), 112
Gompers, Samuel (labor leader), 140, 150
gondola cars, 4
Gould, Jay (railroad official), 83, 84, 139, 171, 177
Grange, Grangers, 71-73, 147
Grant, Cary (actor), 177, 178
Grant, Ulysses S. (U. S. President), 82-84, 177, 178
"grasshopper" locomotive, 14, 181
"Gravity Road", 3, 6
Greeley, Horace (newspaper editor), 178
Griffith, D. W. (motion picture director), 178
Hallidie, Andrew (inventor), 160
handcar, railroad, 93, 94
Harding, Warren G. (U. S. President), 145, 146
Harnden, William (express service operator), 64
Harriman, Edward (railroad official), 141
Harrison, Benjamin (U. S. President), 178, 179
Harrison, Joseph, Jr. (locomotive builder), 24
Hart, Moss (playright), 179
Harte, Bret (author), 75, 179, 180
Harvey Girls, 70
Haupt, Herman (engineer, Army general), 195
Hawthorne, Nathaniel (author), 180
Hayes, Rutherford B. (U. S. President), 138, 139
Hemingway, Ernest (author), 180
Henry, John (railroad laborer), 86-88
Hill, Jim (railroad official), 141
Holmes, Oliver W. (Sr.) (poet), 154
Holmes, Oliver W., Jr. (jurist), 142
Homestead Act, 58
Hoover, Herbert (U. S. President), 145, 146
Hopkins, Johns (merchant, philanthropist), 46
hopper cars, 4. *See also*: "jimmy" and "pot hopper"
horse car, 152, 154, 157-60, 161. *See also* treadmill car
hospital car, 170
Howard, William (railroad surveyor), 10
Hughes, Charles E. (jurist), 143
Huntington, Collis (railroad official), 84
inclined planes, 11, 14

Pioneer horse-drawn car, 12, 13, 157
Polk, James (U. S. President), 187
Pony Express, 63
"pot hopper" coal cars, 4, 52, 53
Pullman (Standard) Company, 41, 48-50, 71, 117, 124, 128, 139, 140, 141, 172
Pullman, George (car builder), 40, 49, 50, 195
rack railway. *See* cog railway
rail, standard, 17
railroad, first in America, 1
railroads (by name): Amtrak, 196; Atchison, Topeka & Santa Fe, 122, 123;
    Atlantic & Great Western, 68; Atlantic Coast Line, 129; Auburn &
    Syracuse, 60; Baltimore & Ohio,3, 4, 10-14, 27, 46-48, 50, 52-54, 56, 62,
    70, 71, 93, 116, 118, 120, 139, 157, 181, 195; Blue Ridge, 87; Boston &
    Albany, 91, 92; Boston & Lowell, 91, 93; Boston & Worcester, 64;
    Brooklyn Elevated Railway Company, 194; Brooklyn-Manhattan Transit
    Corporation, 183; Camden & Amboy, 10-12, 18, 19, 62, 67, 84, 99;
    Canadian Pacific (Canada), 100; Central Pacific, 35, 59, 67, 74-77, 99;
    Central (Railroad) of Georgia, 129; Central Railroad of New Jersey, 130,
    172; Charleston & Hamburg (*see* South Carolina Canal & RR Co.);
    Chesapeake & Ohio, 14, 19, 67, 87, 135, 195; Chicago & Alton, 49, 71, 78;
    Chicago & Northwestern, 61, 63, 72; Chicago, Burlington & Quincy, 72,
    117, 118, 129, 141, 172, 176; Chicago, Milwaukee & St. Paul (& Pacific),
    72, 118, 119; Chicago, Rock Island (& Pacific), 72, 109, 129; Cincinnati,
    Hamilton & Dayton, 30; Cincinnati Traction Company, 31; Clay Street
    Hill RR Company, 161; Con Rail, 196; Cumberland Valley, 48; Delaware
    & Hudson Canal Company (and Railroad), 3, 5, 6, 8, 13, 61; Delaware,
    Lackawanna & Western, 74, 97, 129; Denver, Rio Grande & Western, 129;
    East Tennessee and Virginia, 181, 182; (New York &) Erie, 28, 61, 82, 171,
    177; Erie & Kalamazoo, 165; Fitchburg, 169; Flint & Pere Marquette, 67;
    Frankfort & Lexington, 5; Grand Trunk, 45, 95; Granite, 1, 2; Great
    Northern, 129; Great Western, 71; Hannibal & St. Joseph, 62; Illinois
    Central, Introduction, 34, 35, 37, 107, 109, 150; Independent Subway
    System, 183; Indianapolis Union, 32; Interborough Rapid Transit, 163;
    Ithica & Owego, 73; Kansas Pacific, 70, 93; Key System, 194; Lake Shore
    & Michigan Central, 138; Lexington & Ohio, 100; Liverpool &
    Manchester (England), 9; Long Island, 67, 163; Louisa, 86; Louisville &
    Nashville, 57; Louisville, Cincinnati & Charleston, 42; Madison &
    Indianapolis, 80; Manassas Gap, 52-54; Manitou & Pike's Peak, 81; Mauch
    Chunk & Summit Hill, 2, 3; Mexican Central (Mexico), 84; Michigan
    Central, 94, 165; Missouri-Kansas-Texas, 174, 182; (Gulf) Mobile & Ohio,
    107, 118; Mohawk & Hudson, 20, 84; Mount Washington Cog Railway,
    81; New Castle & Frenchtown, 84; New Jersey Railroad & Transportation
    Company, 11; New Orleans & Carrollton, 167; New York & Harlem, 157-
    59; New York & Putnam, 163; New York Central (and Hudson River), 40,
    74, 78, 92, 98, 101-4, 120, 125-28, 138, 159, 193; New York, New Haven

stamp groups: Celebrate the Century series, 109; Columbian Exposition commemoratives, 1893, Introduction, 101; Pan-American Exposition issue,
101; pictorial stamps of 1869, Introduction, 21; trans-Mississippi series of
1898, Introduction, 88, 89, 91; transportation series, 1981-1995, 93
station, railroad, 32, 33, 47, 55, 57, 92, 105, 106, 196
steelmaking, 41
Steinbeck, John (author), 189
Stephenson, George (British locomotive builder), 9, 18, 20
Stephenson, John (car builder), 158
Stevens, John (railroad and locomotive pioneer), 5, 17, 80
Stevens, Robert (railroad and locomotive pioneer), 17, 19, 20
Stevenson, Robert Lewis (author), 59, 78
stock car, 50-52
Stone, Harlan F. (jurist), 149
streamlining and streamlined trains, 116-129
strikes, railway, 138-41, 146, 148-50, 172
subways, 155, 156, 162-65
surveys, railroad, 10, 11, 42, 43, 185
Taft, Robert A. (U. S. Senator), 31
Taft, William Howard (U. S. President), 31
tank car, 69,70
telegraph, 26-28, 39
tender, locomotive, 18, 127, 128
Thoreau, Henry (author), 189, 190
Thorpe, Jim (athlete), 189
Thurber, James (author, cartoonist), 190
Toonerville Trolley, 165, 166
toy trains, Introduction, 112-15
track pans, 127, 128
trains (by name): *Acela*, 135, 196; *Aristocrat*, 118; *Blue Comet*, 172; *Broadway
Limited*, 120, 128; *Burlington Zephyr*, 117, 118; *California Zephyr*, 129;
Cannonball Express, 107; *Champion*, 129; *Chief*, 122; *Choctaw Rocket*, 109;
City of Los Angeles, 122; *City of Miami*, 109; *City of New Orleans*, 109; *City
of Salina*, 117; *Coast Daylight*, 125; *Comet*, 118; *Congressional Limited*, 120,
121; *Crusader*, 129; *Daylight*, 123-25; *Denver Rocket*, 109; *Des Moines
Rocket*, 109; *Empire Builder*, 129; *Empire State Express*, 101-4; *Golden Rocket*,
109; *Green Diamond*, 109; *Hiawatha*, 118-20; *Jeffersonian*, 120; *Kansas City
Rocket*, 109; *Lightning Express*, 30, 31; *M10000*, 117, 118, 120; *Mercury*,
120, 125; *Morning Daylight*, 125; *Nancy Hanks II*, 129; *Nellie Bly*, 172; *Noon
Daylight*, 125; *Olympian*, 119; *Panama Limited*, 109; *Peoria Rocket*, 109;
Phoebe Snow, 129; *Rebel*, 118; *Rocky Mountain Rocket*, 109; *Royal Blue*, 118;
Silver Comet, 129; *Silver Slipper*, 117; *Southerner*, 129; *Spirit of St. Louis*,
120; *Sunset Limited*, 129; *Super Chief*, 122; *Texas Rocket*, 109; *Trail Blazer*,
120; *Twentieth Century Limited*, 31, 103, 120, 125-28, 176, 177, 188;
Windsplitter, 116; *Zephyr Rocket*, 109

Notes

Notes

Notes

Notes

Notes

Notes

Notes